System Documentation: The In-Line Approach

David F. Chinell

JOHN WILEY & SONS

New York • Chichester • Brisbane • Toronto • Singapore

This publication is designed to provide accurate and authoritative information in regard to the subject matter covered. It is sold with the understanding that the publisher is not engaged in rendering legal, accounting, or other professional service. If legal advice or other expert assistance is required, the services of a competent professional person should be sought. FROM A DECLARATION OF PRINCIPLES JOINTLY ADOPTED BY A COMMITTEE OF THE AMERICAN BAR ASSOCIATION AND A COMMITTEE OF PUBLISHERS.

Copyright © 1990 by John Wiley & Sons, Inc.

All rights reserved. Published simultaneously in Canada.

Reproduction or translation of any part of this work beyond that permitted by section 107 or 108 of the 1976 United States Copyright Act without the permission of the copyright owner is unlawful. Requests for permission or further information should be addressed to the Permission Department, John Wiley & Sons, Inc.

Library of Congress Cataloging-in-Publication Data

Chinell, David F.
   System documentation: the in-line approach/by David F. Chinell.
     p. cm.
   Includes bibliographical references.
   ISBN 0-471-50492-0
   1. Electronic digital computers—Documentation.   I. Title.
QA76.9.D6C45   1989
005.1'5—dc20   89-37351
                                                                            CIP

Printed in the United States of America

90 91 10 9 8 7 6 5 4 3 2 1

For Donna,
who knew I was an author

Contents

Acknowledgments	xi

Introduction   1

Purpose of This Book	1
Intended Audience	2
Subjects Covered	3
Lesson One	4

1   *Old Problems, New Perspectives*   7

What Is System Documentation?	8
Theory of System Documentation	9
The System Players	11
Documentation Problems	12
Reasons Documentation Fails	14
Engineering versus Crafting	16
Logical versus Physical	16
The User Interface	17
Problem: What Is versus What Should Be	18

v

Add-On versus In-Line Documentation	20
The Engineering Approach	23
Documentation as a System	24
Benefits of In-Line Documentation	25

2 Documentation as a Process and a System — 28

System Development Process	29
Documentation Process	36
Integrating the Processes	42
Documentation System	57
Integrating the Documentation System with Shop Operation	60

3 The System Model — 63

Developing a System Model	64
Selecting and Defining System Elements	66
Common Groups of Elements	68
Batch Function Group	69
Online Function Group	72
Information Group	74
Exchange Group	75
Assembling the Groups	76
Customizing the Models	78

4 Filling the System File with Specifications — 82

How to Determine Attributes	83
Logical and Physical Attributes	84
Hard and Soft Attributes	85
Common Attributes	88
Document Control	93
Designing Specifications	94
Storage and Retrieval	97

Contents   vii

5 Specifying the Batch Function Group   99

Batch System	99
System Chart	103
Subsystem	105
Subsystem Chart	108
Transaction	109
Job	112
Run	116
Run Chart	119
Program	123
Module	131

6 Specifying the Online Function Group   135

Online System	135
Menu	139
Function	142
Program and Module	146

7 Specifying the Information Group   148

File	148
Record	154
Data Item	158

8 Specifying the Exchange Group   166

Form	167
Screen	172
Report	177
Message	184

9 The Basics of Technical Writing — 189

The Importance of Effective Communication — 190
The Purpose of Technical Writing — 190
Rules of Grammar — 191
Techniques of Technical Writing — 191
Writing Better — 197
Working Methods — 198

10 Creating Text — 202

Words — 202
Sentences — 205
Paragraphs — 210

11 Creating Graphics — 214

Purposes and Types of Graphics — 214
Tables — 215
Graphs — 216
Charts — 218
Diagrams — 222
Pictures — 225
Samples — 226

12 Organization — 228

Instruction versus Description — 228
Structure — 229
Outline — 241
Sequence — 244
Document Structure — 248

13 Extracting Manuals — 249

- Plan — 250
- Draft — 273
- Edit — 276
- Review — 277
- Release — 278
- Maintain — 278
- Four Model Libraries — 281

14 Reference Aids — 292

- Manual Table of Contents — 293
- List of Figures and Tables — 294
- Introductory Text — 294
- Tabs — 295
- Chapter Table of Contents — 296
- Headers and Footers — 296
- Pagination — 297
- Headings — 298
- Figure Captions — 300
- Cross-References — 300
- Appendix — 301
- Glossary — 302
- Index — 303
- Reference Card — 305

15 Online Documentation — 307

- Problems with the Online Medium — 310
- General Techniques for Online Documentation — 312
- Specific Techniques for Online Documentation — 320
- The Development of Technical Writing — 327

Index — 329

Acknowledgments

I developed my techniques for system documentation in an eclectic fashion. That is, I shamelessly appropriated whatever ideas were useful from whoever had them. I have been helped by dozens of technical writers and system engineers whom I have never met, but whose published works have inspired and encouraged me greatly.

I am particularly indebted to these authors: R. John Brockmann, Chris Gane, Doann Houghton-Alico, John M. Lannon, Sandra Pakin, Diana Patterson, Jonathan Price, and Trish Sarsen.

Several corporations not only supported me but also contributed to my development as a technical writer and documentation specialist. They were progressive enough to let me try out new ideas and methods, and patient enough to let me keep trying until I got them right.

To these corporations I offer my sincere thanks: Digital Components Ltd., Michelin Tires (Canada) Ltd., Georgia Power Corporation, Florida Data Services, North American Financial Services, Ltd., Software Development Corporation, and Soflex Corporation.

Corporations did not share ideas and experiences with me, but people did. The users and computer professionals of these corporations created the environment and provided the stimulus for my ideas to grow and develop. Without these people I could never have written this book.

Of these thousands of people, I would like to acknowledge two system engineers, Brian Morell and Barry D. Woodberry. They were there at the very beginning of my career in information systems. They helped me establish a solid foundation, but more, they got me into the habit of discussing, challenging, and improving all facets of system engineering and documentation.

I must also thank Dr. Althea Jenkins and Alan Lebish, dedicated and experienced librarians, who provided great assistance in researching this material. They helped me trace the thoughts I'd absorbed back to their sources, to make sure I had the ideas right.

For me, the journey from thought to print is long and difficult. My editorial guides at John Wiley & Sons were Teri Zak, Ellen Greenberg, and Jeffrey Brown. Their encouragement was essential. Nicole Bianco reviewed the manuscript as I prepared it. Her suggestions improved the book substantially.

Finally, thanks go to my partner, Donna M. Pinkston, who funded me with the energy of loving support and kept my fingers at the keyboard through thick and thin.

D.F.C.

Introduction

PURPOSE OF THIS BOOK

System designers, builders, and users acknowledge that poor system documentation is a widespread problem. But the real problem is deeper than the documents. EDP (Electronic Data Processing) professionals have placed too little emphasis on their documentation skills. They rely heavily on technical writers, specialists from another field, to complete the job of documentation. This imbalance of skills is the basic problem from which other documentation problems develop.

This book is designed to help EDP professionals improve their documentation skills. It contains theories and techniques that enable you to create or improve on any form of system documentation, from system specifications to user manuals.

Two kinds of information are presented here, theoretical and practical. The theory is the most powerful means of improving system documentation. The practical information in this book consists of tools, methods, and techniques that have proven themselves in the field.

This book shows you how to create and install a documentation system. It also presents documentation as a process and shows you how to integrate documentation activities into your system development process.

Add-on documentation is created after a system has been developed. Its creation is a separate process. By integrating the documentation and system development processes, you create in-line documentation.

Migrating from add-on to in-line documentation is neither quick nor easy, but it is worthwhile. In-line documentation requires that system designers and builders change their work methods and habits. However, the improvement in system documentation justifies the effort. This book helps you shift from the add-on approach to the in-line approach to system documentation.

INTENDED AUDIENCE

This book is written for EDP professionals with little or no formal training in technical writing or system documentation. Members of various data processing organizations can benefit from this material.

In small EDP departments the manager is usually responsible for preparing and enforcing documentation standards. Department managers can benefit from the theories and overviews presented in this book. System analysts and programmers, who routinely generate and use system documentation, can benefit from the practical information.

In small software firms, responsibility for documentation is more difficult to place. The owners and top management of such companies can recognize their documentation problems and will find appropriate solutions in this book. Analysts and customer service representatives are often responsible for creating documentation and will benefit from the practical ideas presented here.

In medium to large EDP departments and software firms, improvements must start with top managers. Larger data processing organizations usually have a documentation or publications manager. These are the readers who can benefit most from this book.

EDP consultants will also find this book valuable. It contains the information they need in order to design or improve system documentation for their clients.

Since this book treats all facets of system documentation, independent programmers can use it to complete their education. This book will help them bring their documentation skills up to the quality level of their programming skills.

This book will also help technical writers who are new to the field of system documentation. It explains each kind of document and shows how documentation and writing activities fit into the overall development of a system. This combination of overview and detail can ease the writer's entry into the field.

SUBJECTS COVERED

This book treats all aspects of application system documentation, from product designs to technical specifications to reference and user manuals. The ideas and techniques presented here can be applied to any size system, from freestanding utilities to corporate management information systems.

Since it is very broad in scope, there is a danger that the material could be too shallow to be practical. However, I have taken pains to present a level of theory that will allow you to design your own detailed tools and methods. In addition, I show a few effective and practical ways to accomplish each step.

Chapter 1 contains the highest level of theory. It presents several basic philosophies that put system documentation in the right perspective. Chapter 2 develops models of the documentation process and the system development process. The key to the in-line approach is integrating these two processes. Documentation can also be viewed as an information system, though it seldom is. This chapter encourages you to use the system tools you already have to solve documentation problems.

One of the hardest things about documenting a system is determining just what a system is. In Chapter 3 you learn how to solve this problem by creating a model of an information system. Once you know the elements that compose a system, it is easy to determine which attributes of each element need to be specified.

Chapter 4 defines an important data base, called the System File. This contains the information that comprises the system documentation. In this chapter you learn how to specify the elements in the system model.

Chapters 5 through 8 focus on specifications for four groups of system elements: the batch function group, the online function group, the information group, and the exchange group.

While you can accumulate a vast amount of data about an information system, you can't simply ship data bases to your end users. The data must be extracted and massaged into useful manuals. Chapters 9 through 11 are devoted to the basics of technical writing. These show you how to create text, how to create graphics, and how to organize text and graphics into documents.

After learning the basics of technical writing, you are ready to design and produce manuals. Chapter 13 covers this aspect of system documentation. In this chapter you learn which kinds of manual are needed and what each kind should contain.

Chapter 14 is devoted to reference aids that enhance system documentation. Few people read manuals sequentially. More often, they access the information in manuals in a random use fashion. Reference aids make random access possible.

Chapter 15 explores online documentation. Before you rush ahead on this latest wave of technology, be sure you are not simply repeating old mistakes in a new medium. Online documentation imposes its own requirements and limitations. This chapter presents useful ideas for online help systems and online manuals.

LESSON ONE

Having read this introduction, you may be ready to learn one of the most valuable techniques for system documentation and technical writing. Notice that the Introduction contains three essential parts: the purpose, the audience, and the subject of the book. These form the rough blueprint or plan of any piece of technical writing.

Before you write the first word of any document, write the purpose, subject, and audience plan. The plan for this book was written first. During the course of writing the book, I made a few minor changes to the plan, but I referred to it constantly to keep myself on track.

Even a brief statement of the document plan keeps you to your subject. It helps you visualize and address your intended audience with the right tone and level of detail. Knowing the purpose of your document increases your effectiveness as a writer.

Unless the plan will be included in the document it defines, it need not be your best writing. Don't worry about redundancy: the plan is really three different perspectives of the same document. To create a document plan, answer these questions as simply and clearly as you can:

- What is the purpose of this document?

- What audience will read this document?
- What subject matter does this document contain?

Take a few minutes to think about this. Try it on your next writing project. Then congratulate yourself for learning the first and biggest lesson about system documentation.

1
Old Problems, New Perspectives

When I began working with information systems, I threw away my training and experience as an engineer. I was prepared to treat information systems, software, and documentation as totally new things. Looking back, I consider this a mistake.

Evidently I was not alone in making this mistake. Many EDP (Electronic Data Processing) professionals have the same attitude. They think of computer science as a young discipline, one for which methods and techniques have not been perfected. Despite the battle cry of harried project managers—"Don't reinvent the wheel!"—most EDP professionals insist on treating their work efforts, products, and documentation as something brand new.

Software and computer-based information systems *are* relatively new products. However, the methods used to create, operate, and maintain them need not be new. System design and construction efforts can be improved by using long-established and proven methods.

I was able to reclaim some old perspectives, and to gain some new ones, as I worked at system development and documentation. The concepts and perspectives presented in this chapter were developed in discussions with other system engineers. Each idea was also tested and proven in practical application.

Some of the ideas in this chapter will be familiar to technical writers, or to those with engineering education or experience. However, the *application* of these ideas to the field of system documentation is new.

Before we explore new perspectives and ideas, let's make sure we're talking about the same thing when we say "system documentation."

WHAT IS SYSTEM DOCUMENTATION?

In this text, *system* means a computer-based information system. This excludes purely manual information systems and computer operating systems but includes what are commonly termed *application systems*. The software for an application system is designed and built by system analysts and programmers.

The theories and techniques presented here apply to application systems of any size, from freestanding, single-program utilities to corporate management information systems with hundreds of programs.

Within this scope there are many, many different kinds of system document. Some examples:

- Product design
- System specification
- Test plan
- Installation guide
- User manual
- Reference manual

It also helps to know what kinds of information are excluded from system documentation. The information needed by any EDP shop can be divided into three categories, or files. These are shown in Figure 1-1.

Historical or project information is excluded from system documentation. A project is a planned and controlled expenditure of resources, intended to create or revise an information system in a finite period of time. The system is the end result, or product, of the project.

The Project File is more or less a historical record of the effort undertaken to create or revise a system. It includes estimates and plans, letters and memos, and tentative designs. The Project File contains any and all information needed to execute and manage the project.

Information about users or clients is also excluded from system documentation. The Client File holds information about the user

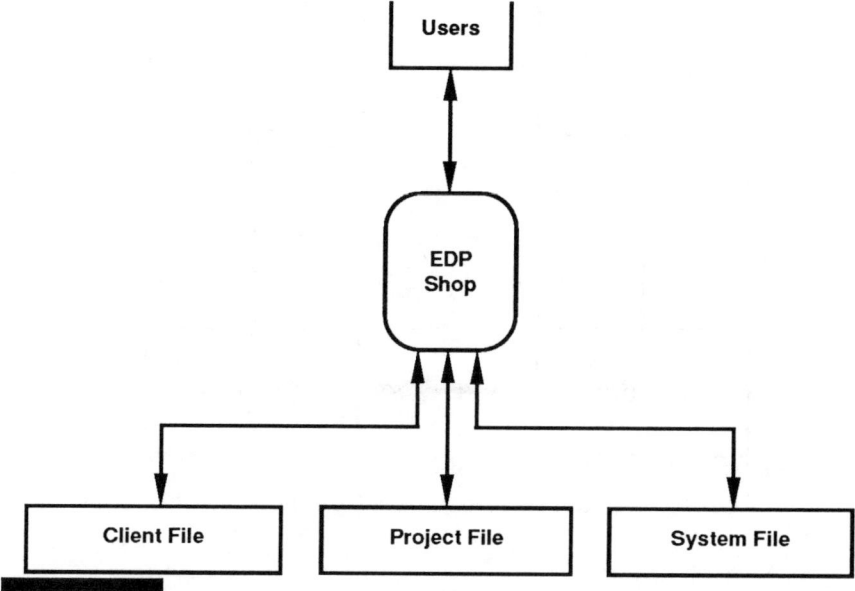

Figure 1-1: EDP Shop Information

community. Users may be individual retail purchasers of software products, the members of an entire corporation, or the staff of a single department within a company.

The Client File usually records communications and interactions with the user. It may describe the user's business operation and information needs. It may also contain the details of the user's hardware and software.

The System File contains information about your products, information systems. System documentation is a reflection of the system itself. As such, it is never historical, but always current and active. System documentation reflects the "latest and greatest" version of your product.

THEORY OF SYSTEM DOCUMENTATION

In the Introduction to this book, you discovered that all documents have a purpose, a subject, and an audience. We can find an answer to the question What is system documentation? by studying system documents from the three perspectives of purpose, subject, and audience. We'll start with purpose.

Above all other purposes, system documentation serves as a

10 • System Documentation

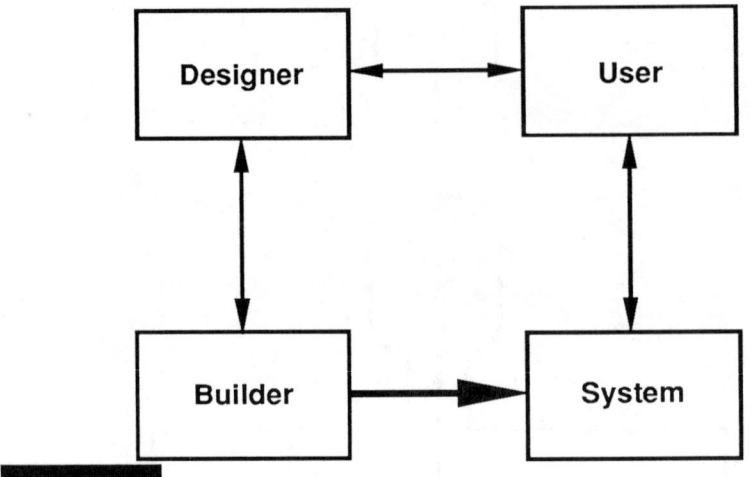

FIGURE 1-2: System Document Communication Bridges

communication bridge between the user, the designer, and the builder of a system. These communication bridges are shown in Figure 1-2.

System documents let the user and the designer communicate about the design of the product. Designers and builders communicate the details of system development in another series of system documents. Documentation is also a bridge between the user and the system itself.

System documents can also bridge the time gap between those who build and those who maintain systems. This is true whether the maintenance programmer is a new employee, working years after the original system was installed, or you yourself, planning a revision only weeks after the first version of a system was completed.

System documentation can serve other purposes. It can be a sales tool, a training technique, or a reference guide. Again, in satisfying each of these purposes, system documentation acts as a communication bridge between two or more people.

Now let's look at system documentation from the perspective of its subject. What kind of information is found in system documentation?

System documentation is a description of what the system is, what it does, and how it does it. Thus, we find overview and detail information about the structure, functions, and operation of a system in the system documentation.

System documentation also contains information needed to operate the system. Both users and operators need to know how to make the system perform its functions.

System documentation includes information needed to enhance or revise the system. This kind of information can be implicit or explicit. Where expansion and updating are planned into the design of a system, the system documentation includes this information explicitly. Even when no formal plans for revision or expansion exist, system designers and builders need the information implicit in system documentation to plan and execute their changes.

Finally, let's look at system documentation from the perspective of the audience it addresses. As we have seen, system documentation can be addressed to users, designers, builders, and operators of a system. System documentation is also used by those who provide user support and by those who revise or maintain the system.

From each perspective, you can see that system documentation is communication. Documentation communicates useful information between two or more people involved with the creation or use of a system.

Notice that this definition does not specify the medium for communicating information. System documentation is not restricted to the printed page. Marketing and training information has long been communicated in audio and video tape. Online help systems and online user manuals are an exciting new medium for system documentation.

While the medium of system documentation is not limited, useful documentation still needs a form. The form or order of information is as important as the information itself. This book presents several useful forms for system documentation.

THE SYSTEM PLAYERS

Since system documentation is communication between people, it is important to form a clear picture of who the people are. Some of the "players" involved in the system game are users, designers, builders, installers, operators, and supporters.

Users are the people who use the system to help them do their jobs. The user can be a single individual who buys a packaged accounting system or the entire staff of a consulting firm who use a computer-assisted design (CAD) system.

System designers are commonly called system analysts or senior programmers. The term *analyst* is a poor choice, because these individuals not only analyze information needs but also design information systems intended to meet these needs.

System builders may be called programmer/analysts, programmers, or coders. Their job title depends on how much experience or design ability they contribute to the process of developing a system.

Installers are the people who place an information system into its environment and ensure that the system initially functions correctly. Users of software packages often perform this function themselves.

System operators are needed for systems that run on large, centralized computers. Operators run the mechanical or machine parts of the system. For systems that run on minicomputers or personal computers, the user acts as the operator.

Supporters include those who train users and those who provide ongoing support to users. While trainers need face-to-face interaction with the users, ongoing support staff commonly provide their services via telephone.

Notice that maintenance people are not included in this list of system players. Each maintenance project can be seen as a miniature system development effort that requires the efforts of designers and builders.

The list of system players needs not describe separate individuals. The user will often act as his own installer, operator, and supporter. The designer, builder, installer, and supporter of a system can be an individual programmer. The names of the system players represent the roles or functions that must be performed to create and use an information system. Some of these names differ from commonly used EDP terminology; however, I have chosen them because they more accurately describe the functions being performed.

DOCUMENTATION PROBLEMS

Inadequate system documentation is a widely acknowledged problem in EDP. What exactly is wrong with system documentation? Over the years I have heard quite a variety of complaints, but these can be reduced to a few basic problems.

Both users and EDP professionals complain that system documentation is either too technical or too simplistic, either too specific or too general to be of any real use. These complaints stem from the same basic problem: the audience has not been defined, evaluated, and addressed. Too often, one all-encompassing system document is created, intended to meet all the information needs of all the system players. As a result, diverse audiences find the single "system manual" contains the wrong kinds and levels of information.

Another common complaint is that system documentation is inaccurate because it quickly becomes out-of-date. Most system documentation is created by a process that is separate from the system development process. As such, it is passive documentation. There is no motivation for revising such documentation, other than the gradually increasing complaints of those who try to use the documentation.

When these complaints come from clients or users, there is strong financial motivation to revise the system documents. However, when complaints come from inside the EDP shop, from programmers or operators, there is little motivation for revision. When nobody uses a particular system document, there is no motivation to keep it up-to-date.

From EDP professionals, the most frequent complaint is that system documentation is too expensive to create and maintain. They also insist that documentation is a needless encumbrance that compromises their ability to respond quickly to the needs of their users.

Indeed, the way most EDP professionals approach system documentation is cumbersome and expensive. Many system builders rely on technical writers to create their system documentation after the system has been built. Because documentation is thought of as the last step in the system development process, it is often thrown together at the last minute, with little planning or forethought.

One solution is to abandon all phases of system documentation, and to rely on technical writers to produce only user documentation. This is a dangerous and expensive solution. Without system documentation, several important communication bridges are missing from the process of developing a system. Figure 1-3 shows some of these important bridges.

For example, the product design is the only way the user can participate in designing and specifying the performance of a system before it is actually built. Without system specifications, the designer and builder have no reliable framework for communicating design details and construction variations. When user manuals or reference manuals are needed, technical writers face a tedious process of

14 • System Documentation

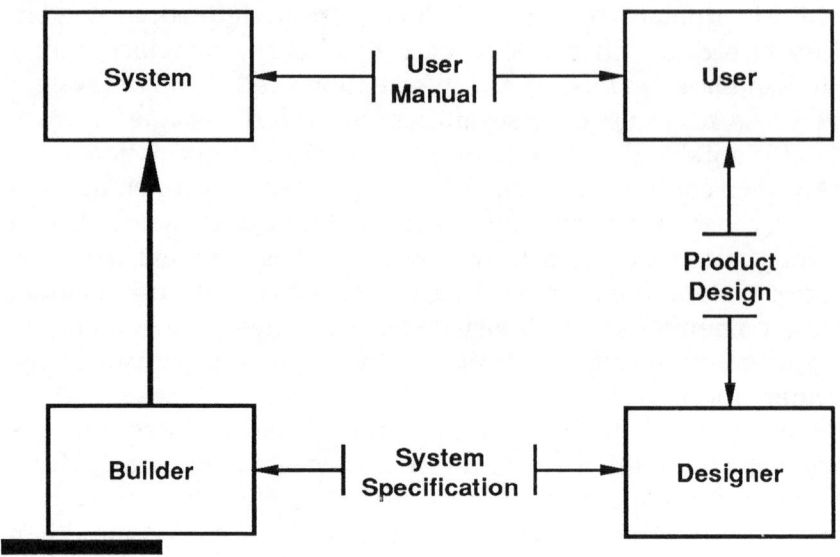

FIGURE 1-3: Communication Bridges

research if there is no system documentation. The information contained in such manuals must be retrieved or reconstructed. Creating manuals by interviewing system designers and builders, or by evaluating program listings, is indeed a very expensive way to create system documentation.

REASONS DOCUMENTATION FAILS

This book is not a new documentation methodology. It does not present any new documentation tools or techniques. None are needed. Our system documentation efforts do not fail because of problems with our tools or techniques. They fail because of problems in the work methods we use as system designers and builders. The problem is not *what* we're doing, but *how* we're doing it.

System documentation fails to improve because EDP professionals fail to improve their work methods. Documentation efforts fail when documentation is produced as a separate process. System documentation works only when it is an effortless by-product of the system development process.

Textbooks often stress the need for high level management support for documentation. In practice, such support is rarely effective. Asking managers if they support system documentation is like asking them if they believe in "goodness." Of course, everyone will agree that their systems need and should have "good documentation."

System designers and builders or their managers may work through the painful process of creating documentation standards or standard procedures for documenting systems. Managers or owners of EDP shops may even try to enforce the standards. This seldom has the desired effect. As long as system designers and builders view documentation as a superfluous chore, they will avoid it. System builders always have the ultimate excuse: "I can finish the coding by the deadline, but only if I leave the documentation until later."

The motivation to create system documentation cannot be imposed from above. It must start with your efforts at desk or keyboard. System documentation works when it is a necessary ingredient of your work as a system designer or builder.

In addition to basic methods and motivations, system documentation efforts can fail due to a host of subtle psychological factors. Here are some case histories.

PROBLEM: The programmers attended all the meetings about system documentation, but they still didn't use the system binders.

SOLUTION: A large set of bookshelves was purchased. The shelves were clearly labeled System File, and the system binders were put in the bookshelves. When the programmers saw that there was a centralized location to store and access the information they were assembling in the system binders, the System File concept became real and tangible. "System File" became a working phrase in the shop.

PROBLEM: The users just weren't using the manual, even though all the information they needed was there. Each function was explained in an appropriate level of detail.

SOLUTION: The pages of the user manual were reformatted so that the width of the text column was reduced from six inches (sixty characters) to four inches (forty characters, or about one and a half alphabets). This format change increased the number of pages by only 5 percent. However, the readability of the text was so improved that user inquiries dropped by 35 percent over the next three months.

ENGINEERING VERSUS CRAFTING

There are solutions to all of the problems associated with system documentation. One solution lies in the difference in perspective between engineered and crafted products.

To understand the system documentation problem, compare the software industry to the automobile building industry. The first cars were built piece by piece, one at a time, with no plans or specifications. Each part was custom fitted to the next.

This approach called on the craftsmanship of the builders. They created rugged, reliable automobiles. Yet their products were a maintenance nightmare for their customers. When a part broke, an entire machine shop was needed to rebuild the replacement part and have it fitted to the automobile.

The situation improved when engineering practices were applied to the car building process. With designs and specifications organized and recorded, parts became standardized and interchangeable. Inexpensive maintenance was possible since spare parts could be manufactured and fitted reliably.

In the software industry, we're still building our products as if we were craftspeople, not engineers. To make system documentation work, we must follow the same steps as the automobile builders did. We must introduce design and specification procedures, integrating them with the software development process. The more integrated they are, the broader and less expensive the beneficial results can be.

LOGICAL VERSUS PHYSICAL

System documentation includes an expression of the design of the system. This allows the users to test the design, rather than build and test the system itself. Testing is done on paper, at a nonphysical or *logical* level. Testing a system that has already been built is a *physical* way of testing a design to see if it solves the problem. It is also a tremendously expensive way.

Not just any product design document will serve the purpose of testing the system at a logical level. The product design must be created with this specific purpose and audience in mind. It must contain the right subject matter, presented in the right format.

PROBLEM: The inventory manager received the General System Design Specification (all four hundred pages of it) three months ago. He was repeatedly asked for a sign-off, but finally coding had to start in order to stay on schedule. Now the system is nearly finished. The parallel test is being run, and the manager says the reports are all wrong.

SOLUTION: Take away the General System Design Specification. This document bears no relation to what the users will actually experience when the system is built and installed. Provide the department manager with a product design that represents or simulates the proposed system.

Confronted with a poorly organized, highly abstract product design, a user might say, "You go ahead and program it; then I'll tell you what's wrong with it." This approach results in the construction of prototype systems and throwaway code.

Without an effective product design, the system designer cannot tell the user how the finished system will look or act. Thus the user cannot participate in the design or logical testing of the system.

THE USER INTERFACE

Is light a wave or a particle? You may recall from high-school physics that it is neither and both. The behavior of light depends on what kind of experiment, or context, you are using. Sometimes light exhibits the behavior of a wave, sometimes that of a particle.

Is system documentation a part of the system, or something separate from it? Like the nature of light, the nature of system documentation depends on which context you choose to use.

When software is crafted, the process of creating system documentation is a separate activity. Documentation is a separate thing, a body of information that describes something else, the system. However, with engineered software and systems, system documentation is an integral part of the system development process. The system documentation is a part of the system, created during the same process that creates the system.

I used to refer to system documentation, particularly user manuals, as "features" of a system. This created clashes of terminology with marketing people, who tend to think of features as special functions. What I meant by features was those things that users actually experience with their five senses.

Perhaps it would be better to use a relatively new term, "user interface." At the risk of terminology clashes with system designers, I want to make the term "user interface" stretch to cover what I used to call "features."

The user interface is more than just the screen and menu design of an online system. It is the part of a system that the user sees, touches, or hears. So far, information systems don't interact with the users' sense of smell or taste. But who knows?

Consider these examples of system elements that the users experience with their senses: they see screens of data, prompts or messages, printed reports, and flashing lights; they handle data storage media, such as tapes or diskettes; and they hear sounds that signal unusual situations.

Clearly, the user documentation is part of the user interface of a system. It is something the user sees and touches. Perhaps it is something the user hears, as in the case of an audio cassette tutorial program.

System documentation is also an integral part of the finished software product. One should no more buy a system built without documentation than a house built without blueprints. EDP professionals have long enjoyed users' tolerance for crafted software and systems, but this tolerance is rapidly vanishing.

More and more software is being engineered rather than crafted. The quality of such systems and system documentation is becoming a standard for comparison. Integrating documentation with the development process results in engineered software that is easier to sell, use, and maintain.

The idea of the user interface can be extended to encompass system players other than the users. Thus, the "human interface" might be defined as any part of the system experienced by the senses of the system players. This definition encompasses all parts of the system documentation.

PROBLEM: WHAT IS VERSUS WHAT SHOULD BE

One of the most valuable engineering perspectives I know is that a problem can always be seen as a discrepancy between what is and what should be.

This perspective immediately suggests alternative ways to resolve the discrepancy, to solve the problem. In addition to changing what is, you can also change what should be, or change both what is and what should be to bring them into agreement.

For example, I lived in a large city with an encircling beltway. This is heavily traveled, as people use it to get from one end of the city to the other. There was a problem though. The speed limit on the beltway was 55 miles per hour, but people habitually drove in excess of this limit, driving 60, 65, or even 70 miles per hour.

To add the radar equipment, patrol cars, and police officers needed to enforce this speed limit would have cost the city hundreds of thousands of dollars each year. The city solved the problem not by changing the speed of the drivers on the beltway (what is), but the speed limit (what should be).

By spending only a few thousand dollars for new signs, the city raised the speed limit on the beltway to 70 miles per hour. They solved the problem by changing what should be, making it match what is.

This perspective has value when applied to information systems and system documentation. Here is a common problem faced by managers of EDP departments.

PROBLEM: It was working fine for the old accounting manager, but the new manager says the system is disbursing all wrong.

SOLUTION: The system specifications showed that an unusual disbursement method was used, due to the particular nature of some direct labor costs. When he read the design specifications the new manager easily grasped the reasons for this nonstandard accounting practice and agreed that the system was performing correctly.

System documentation adds another dimension to a system. The system itself is the "what is" of most problems. The system documentation, in particular the detailed design specification, is the "what should be" of the system. If there are no system documents, then there is no statement of what should be, other than the opinions or expectations of the users.

Aside from answering the question of who should bear development or revision costs, system documentation is invaluable in testing a new system. It allows you to ensure that "what is" matches "what should be." System documentation lets you find and resolve problems before a system is released for distribution or put into production.

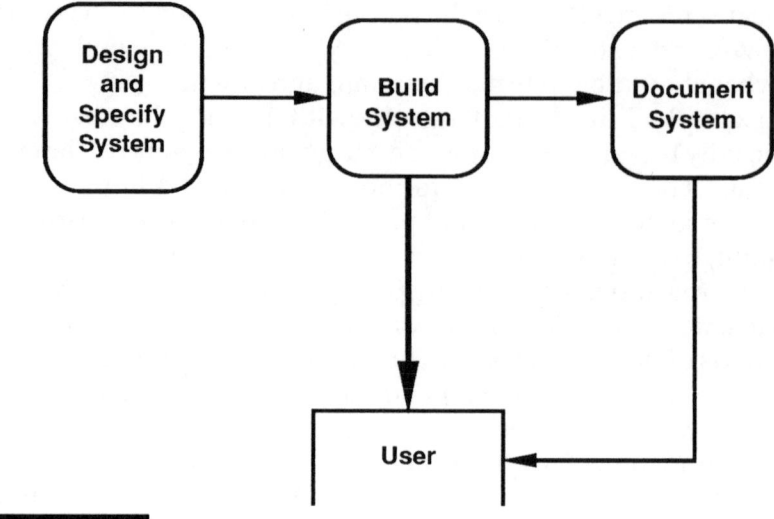

FIGURE 1-4: Add-On Documentation

ADD-ON VERSUS IN-LINE DOCUMENTATION

There is always danger in introducing new jargon, but I need to define two new terms here, terms that are central to the benefits you can gain from this text. These are add-on and in-line documentation. Figure 1-4 illustrates how add-on documentation is created.

As its name implies, add-on documentation is created in a separate process from the system development process. It is added onto the system. Often, this second process, the process of creating system documentation, happens after the system has been created.

Since there is no recorded body of information about crafted systems, the writers of add-on documentation face a terrible task. They must uncover or recover information about the system that is often hidden in program listings or tucked away in the back of a programmer's mind. The research cost of add-on documentation is tremendous.

The writers of add-on documentation face other problems in addition to the burden of research. I have "added on" user manuals for many crafted systems. Despite my efforts to make each manual complete and effective, I often hear complaints that a manual is too complicated or difficult to use.

In fact, such a user manual is an accurate reflection of the system it describes. The real problem is that the system itself is complicated and difficult to use. Good manuals can help a user to use a poor software product to the best effect, but there are limits to the problems that can be corrected by system documentation. This is particularly true when the documentation is created after the system has been built.

For example, a user manual can list and describe all the system reports in one chapter, but it cannot place the report functions on one convenient menu if they have been scattered throughout the system. System documentation can define preferred names for data items and explain aliases, but it cannot save the user from the chore of puzzling through inconsistent terms on data screens.

System documentation can reveal design flaws and inconsistencies. However, when the documentation effort takes place after the system has been built, there is little opportunity to correct such problems.

Add-on documentation cannot capture the "what should be" of the system. At best, it can only reflect "what is" for the finished system.

The answer is in-line documentation, that is, documentation created as an integral part of the system development process. See Figure 1-5 for an overview of the in-line documentation process.

In this diagram, the processes of documenting and building the system are joined together as two parts of one box. The documentation effort is integrated into the building effort. Both the documentation and the construction of the system happen at the same time, often in the same work steps.

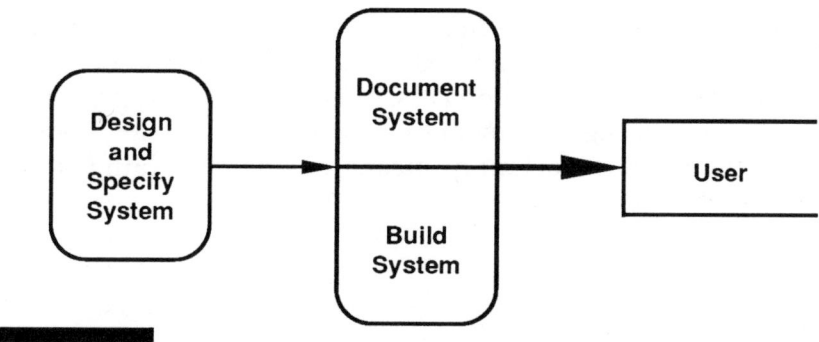

FIGURE 1-5: In-Line Documentation

In-line documentation is a natural by-product of the engineering approach to system development. When the system development process is complete, so is the system documentation.

Another distinction between add-on and in-line documentation is their active and passive natures.

Since in-line documentation is created as an integral part of the system development process, any revision or expansion to the system will automatically result in revisions or additions to the system documentation. In-line documentation is active documentation, by its very nature.

Add-on documentation is passive. It is not linked in any way to the system development process. Once written, add-on documentation is dead. It will only be revised if additional, subsequent add-on writing projects are undertaken.

Consider program specifications that are added-on to meet contractual obligations but are not used by the actual system builders. Once the system is sold or installed, there is no motivation to update the program specifications. They become obsolete when the first revision is made to the system.

Say you found a system function that was coded wrongly but about which no one ever complained. You'd wonder why. Perhaps you would find that the users habitually combined two faster and simpler functions to accomplish the task. Your reaction would probably be to remove the erroneous and superfluous function.

The same is true of system documentation. Recall that the purpose of system documentation is to communicate needed information among the system players. If the system document is not used, it should be deleted. There is simply no point to creating passive documentation. Unfortunately, the majority of system documents created today are passive and add-on.

To ensure that system documentation is active, you must use an in-line process. This means integrating the documentation process with the system development process. Integration of these processes does not mean adding documentation steps to an existing system development process. It simply means engineering rather than crafting software and systems.

THE ENGINEERING APPROACH

The steps in any engineering process are as follows.

1. Study
2. Design
3. Specify
4. Build
5. Test
6. Apply

First, the problem or need is studied. Then a product or solution can be designed in general terms. When the consumer, client, or user agrees with the design, the engineer then specifies the solution in enough detail to build it. The resulting product is then tested to ensure both that the product meets the specifications and that the solution does indeed solve the original problem. The final step is to apply the solution.

The product design, specifications, test plan, and reference manuals of the engineering process correspond to the system documents, which play an active and essential role in creating an engineered system.

The crafting approach to software design uses a kind of reverse engineering to create system documentation. Reverse-engineered system documentation starts after the system has been tested and installed. It begins with a detailed examination of the program code, in order to formulate the specifications to which the program could have been built. When enough specifications have been formulated in this way, one or more possible system designs begin to emerge. Often the only way to verify the overall design of a system is to interview the system designers, or even the original users.

There are other important differences between the engineering and crafting approach to system development. In engineering, the product design is formalized and expressed. This simply means that the design is worked out in some detail and converted to information that can be recorded and communicated and that it is, in fact, recorded and communicated.

On the other hand, the crafting approach to system development never formalizes or records the product design. The craftsman resolves the design details as production proceeds. The product design resides only in the craftsman's mind. It is seldom refined enough to be expressed, and is never actually expressed or communicated to anyone.

Crafting systems is the work of individuals. Granted, with enough management and administrative support, teams of craftsmen can build and eventually integrate separate pieces of a system. The additional management, testing, and debugging needed for such efforts are expensive ways of communicating the system design and specifications.

The engineering approach to system development is better suited to team efforts. Since the system design is communicated through the system documentation, it can be shared by any number of builders. The expense of coordinating and managing a team of system engineers is much lower than for a team of craftsmen.

The engineering approach to system development will be outlined in some detail in the next chapter. Meanwhile, here is a brief description of how the system engineering process works.

The software designer creates product designs or specifications that show both the user and the builder what the finished product will look and act like. These design documents are not intended as final versions. Rather, the user, designer, and builder use them as negotiating tools, balancing "what should be" against "what is," until the designs and the finished product agree.

The information in the designs and specifications forms a data base called the System File. From this data base, information can be extracted and developed into user and reference manuals as needed.

With this approach, no add-on documentation is needed, because the specifications *are* the documentation. System documentation is created as an integral part of the building process, and accurately reflects the finished product.

DOCUMENTATION AS A SYSTEM

There is one perspective that usually comes as something of a revelation to EDP professionals. It came to me in the midst of an understaffed and past-due project. The documentation was left until the end. As I stared at the pile of reference material I was struggling to organize, I thought: There is such a massive amount of information about even the smallest system. If only there were some systematic way to handle this information....

Suddenly it occurred to me that documentation *is* information. Surely system documentation could be treated as an information system. This perspective has proven very valuable.

System documentation is information about information systems. It can be handled very effectively with all the system approaches, tools, and concepts in which EDP professionals are expert.

It's a funny quirk, but system and programming people forget to apply their own expertise to this area of their work. Just because we, as system builders, are the users of an information system does not mean that we are allowed to build a low-quality or ineffective information system. We can and should use the same techniques for designing, building, and maintaining documentation systems as we do for other application systems.

> **PROBLEM:** He's stuck in loop on the Administrative Functions Menu. You want to fix it, but you can't find out which program generates the screen.
>
> **SOLUTION:** Design a documentation system that shows the source of every report and screen in the application system.

Support engineers and maintenance programmers need information to do their jobs. System documentation should be treated as an information system that provides the needed information to the right users.

System documentation can be a valuable development and maintenance tool, but only if it provides information to the people who need it.

BENEFITS OF IN-LINE DOCUMENTATION

With the right perspectives, you are in a position to understand some of the benefits of in-line system documentation. To begin with, you realize that system documentation should not be created by an add-on process but by an in-line process that is integrated with the system development process. You realize that effective system documentation is an effortless by-product of the engineering approach to system development. Finally, you realize that system documentation is just another form of information. It can be organized and maintained in a consciously designed documentation system.

Creating and maintaining product designs and specifications

has a definite cost. It may mean adjusting your work methods. It seems that there is twice as much to maintain, for not only does a system or program have to be revised, but so too does the system documentation. However, there are advantages that offset the apparent costs.

For the independent programmer or small software building firm, the advantage is that the system documentation is already done when the project is done. The documentation that must be added on to system designs and specifications is greatly reduced. Because system information is readily available, such documentation is also less expensive to create.

Middle-sized EDP shops or departments benefit from the engineering approach to system development by creating products that are uniform in quality and performance. System documentation provides a vehicle for communicating designs and specifications, and thus for standardizing them. This kind of communication is also essential in the transition from small, informal shops to larger, formally organized shops.

Large EDP concerns benefit most from the engineering approach by reducing development and maintenance labor costs. A standard documentation system makes staff members interchangeable, permitting a flexible match of resources to projects.

Regardless of the size of your shop, the time and money you spend to develop in-line system documentation has leverage. For minimal investments, maximal returns are realized.

These returns appear in several ways. One is increased project control. Because system documents are tangible products, they can be measured and can indicate the progress of system development. Further, the design process recorded in product designs and system specifications gives an increasingly accurate indication of the work required to develop a system.

The quality of the finished products will also increase. Engineered systems are better because the desired features can be stated, worked toward, tested, and realized. Since system documentation is a highly visible part of any system you create, any conscious effort to improve it also improves your product.

This is especially true of user manuals. Often the decision to purchase a software product is made on the basis of the user manual. This is not only because users realize that they need the kind of training and support that good user manuals provide. It is also because the user manual is part of the user interface, part of the system the user actually touches, sees, and experiences. While users may not be able to experience the system in operation before buying it, they can experience the user manual.

Another advantage is reduction of development and maintenance costs. When the design of a product has been formally expressed, it becomes available to anyone who can read and understand the design document. Thus, several programmers can work on the same product simultaneously.

The staff of your software company or EDP department can become familiar with a single, consistent way of documenting systems. They can use that skill to understand and work on any of your software products. This means that a programmer is not tied to a specific job because he or she is the only one who understands a particular system. A good documentation system makes for staff flexibility. This in turn makes resource allocation more flexible, and reduces development and maintenance costs.

Savings can also be realized in training new employees. Rather than learning six different software products, new employees need only learn one documentation system. The time spent in training new employees, the learning curve costs, are minimized.

Maintenance costs can also be reduced by effective system documentation. One of the most time-consuming jobs for maintenance programmers is gaining familiarity with the software being revised. This is true whether the maintenance programmer is a new or experienced employee.

Maintenance programming is almost a process of mind reading. You have to understand the thinking of the original programmer to understand and appropriately revise the program. If this thinking has been formalized and recorded in the system documentation, you can save hours of research into program listings. One of the most useful things to know, the purpose of a program, is often lost when the original designer and builder have left the shop. It is difficult for an add-on documentation effort to recover such information.

2

Documentation as a Process and a System

In this chapter I present models of the three things you need in order to improve your system documentation. First, we'll examine a general model of the system development process. This process is used to create an entire information system, no matter what its size.

Next, we'll look at a model documentation process. This process results in the creation of a single system document. By applying the documentation process at each step of the system development process, you can integrate system development and system documentation. We'll explore the integration of these two processes in detail.

Finally, we'll look at the documentation system that results from integrating system development with documentation.

Developing a model is similar to creating a document. The usefulness of the model can only be measured against its intended purpose. This is true whether you are modeling a program with a flowchart or modeling a suspension bridge with a blueprint.

The models presented here—the system development process, the documentation process, and the documentation system—share a common purpose. They are intended to show you the in-line approach to system documentation.

Many of the detailed steps actually needed to create a system have been summarized as a single, generalized step in the system development process. Similarly, the model of the documentation process has been generalized so that it applies to all system documents.

In practice, you will need to expand upon these simple models to create your own processes and systems. You can start by comparing the models to your own situation to spot deficiencies and areas for improvement. This allows you to develop processes that are tailored to the client environment, system products, and size and staffing of your shop.

In this chapter we'll focus on *what* must be done, not *how* it is done. The following chapters are devoted to the details of how you can create effective in-line system documentation.

SYSTEM DEVELOPMENT PROCESS

PROBLEM: It will cost thousands to make all the revisions.

SOLUTION: Create and use a system development process that reflects the engineering approach.

PROBLEM: We'll never make the software revision deadline. We need more people on the project, but they'll have to be trained.

SOLUTION: Create and use a uniform system development process. An outline of your process is easy for new staff to grasp. Keep the process simply defined to curtail learning curves.

Lower development and revision costs are possible with a clearly defined system development process. A common work method increases the flexibility of your staff and makes resource allocation more cost-effective.

A carefully designed system development process shows you where you are, where you are going, and how to get there. In other words, it provides you with the information you need to do your job. This knowledge improves your attitude and that of your staff, and thus increases your productivity.

Even independent programmers and small EDP shops can benefit from a consciously designed system development process. The system development process breaks the development effort into a series of manageable steps. It is your general plan for all software and system development. A system development process emphasizes the natural division of development tasks and thus improves project estimating and control. Dividing system development into separate steps also helps you focus on each step, and on improving and balancing your skills.

Medium-sized EDP shops or departments benefit from the uniform work methods of a standard system development process. Uniform work methods facilitate teamwork. The system development process helps you keep track of multiple projects, each of which can be started, interrupted, or interleaved more smoothly.

A standard system development process allows communication among project team members, and between different projects. It adds uniformity to your work efforts, and to the resulting products.

Most large shops will already have created a standard system development process. This is an essential tool for planning, estimating, and controlling multiple projects. If you use a system development process, you are already familiar with its benefits. However, you may want to review your current process, revising it to improve your system documentation.

In reality everyone already uses some form of system development process. These range from the intuitive steps taken by individual system builders to corporate standards that run to hundreds of pages. Your task is not to create a system development process, but to consciously design one that is useful.

Recall the steps in the engineering approach: study, design, specify, build, test, apply. Figure 2-1 shows how these steps can be incorporated into a general system development process. Bear in mind that this is the process used to create or revise an entire system. Let's look at each step in the process.

DESIGN

The first step of the system development process encompasses the first two steps of the engineering approach, study and design. In commonly used EDP terms, this step is often called "analysis and design." It includes a study of the problems or needs in the user community and the production of a general design for a solution or product.

In the design step, the user and the designer work together to develop the product design. The designer may also call on the technical expertise of the builder, to help create or select alternative designs.

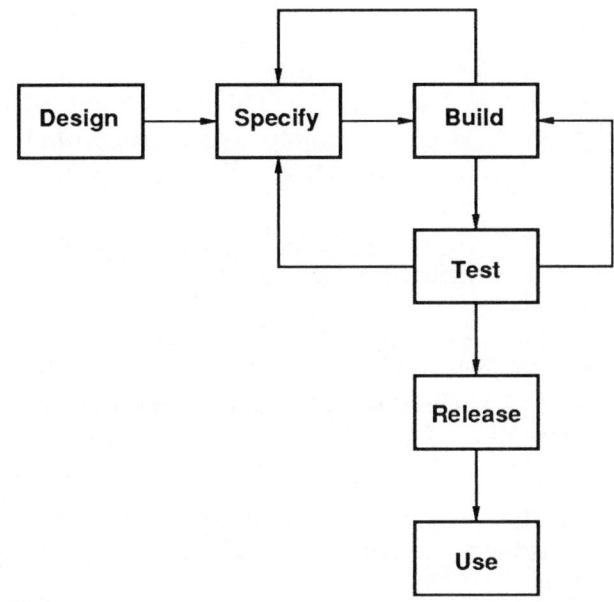

FIGURE 2-1: System Development Process

While design often focuses on the system itself, it is equally important to design the system's environment. The most important part of a system's environment is not the hardware it runs on but the users who use it.

> **PROBLEM:** Sure, he saw the warning message, but he didn't know what it meant or what to do about it. Now the master file is corrupted. It will take three days to re-enter the transactions.
>
> **SOLUTION:** Designate three audiences for the error messages produced by this (mainframe) system: the clerical user, the system administrator, and the operator. Make sure that each error message is directed to the correct audience. Include reference sections in the user and operator manuals that explain the error messages and define what steps to take.

Prompts and error messages appear in a variety of formats and in different media. Defining the users of a system helps the system designers and builders create effective error messages, get them to the right person, and suggest appropriate actions.

SPECIFY

The next step in the system development process is to specify the details of the proposed system. This is often referred to as the detailed design or physical design step. In order to build the system, the builders will need more detail than a general product design can contain.

In this step, the designer specifies each and every element of the system, from data items to subsystems or menu structures.

> **PROBLEM:** The integration test went fine for the first three subsystems. But the rest—eight subsystems and 31 programs—use four different record layouts for the master file. You can't recompile the programs until you figure out which layout is correct. What do you do?
>
> **SOLUTION:** Rather than refer the builders to layouts shown in other program listings, provide them with specifications for critical record layouts.

The system specifications are the "what should be" of the system. When system builders must rely on "what is," on parts of the system that have already been built, discrepancies can propagate through the system. This is especially true of systems built in sections by separate teams.

Sooner or later in the development process, detailed design decisions must be made. It is less expensive to make these decisions before building begins.

BUILD

When enough details about the system have been specified, the next step of the system development process begins. Using the details of the system specification, the builders build the system. The purpose of this step is to create the system product.

Though I present the system development process as a linear series of steps, in practice it is often iterative. During the build step, problems will emerge. There may be inconsistencies in the design or specification of the system. The builders may encounter technical problems or discover more efficient ways of implementing the design. These problems may require repetition of the specification step or even the design step.

Remember that system documentation is part of the system it

describes. This step in the system development process includes construction of both software and system documents. It includes the creation of reference manuals of many kinds, from installation guides to user manuals.

TEST

The next step in the system development process is testing. The purpose of the test step is to find and resolve problems in the finished system. The designer, builder, and user may all participate in this step. The designer is responsible for creating a test plan and for recording and resolving problems.

Like the build step, the test step is iterative. Problems may need to be resolved by repeating the specify step, the build step, or both.

Engineered systems can be tested more thoroughly than can crafted systems. The differences between the two are illustrated in Figure 2-2.

In the crafting approach to system development, the system design is never formally expressed. This restricts you to two types of testing.

First, a system can be tested for its own integrity. Do the separate parts fit together to create a consistent whole? Even though "integration testing" sounds sophisticated, it actually refers to a crude form of testing. It is analogous to constructing a motor, then running the motor to see whether or not it will shake itself apart.

Second, the crafted system can be tested by installing it in the user environment and allowing the user to operate it. This form of testing makes undue demands of the user. He or she must ensure that the finished system meets needs that were defined weeks, months, or even years before.

By contrast, the engineering approach starts with the creation of design and specification documents. From these, both the software and the manuals can be built. This provides a third type of test—a test of the software against the documentation. The "what is" of the software can be compared with the "what should be" of the documentation, to find and resolve problems.

For example, the product design, system specifications, and user manuals are all statements of "what should be" for the system. All aspects of the system's construction and function can be tested against these system documents.

Since system documentation is part of the system, it too must be

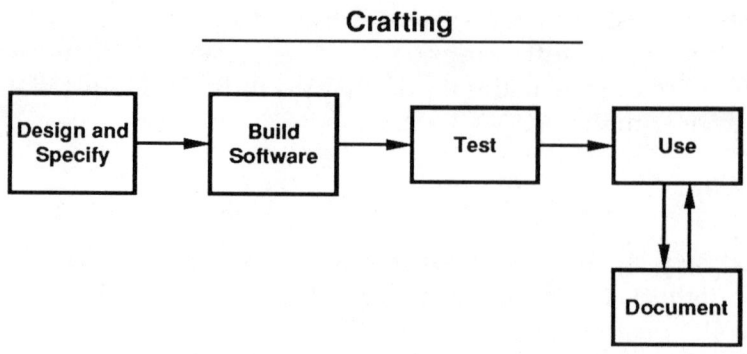

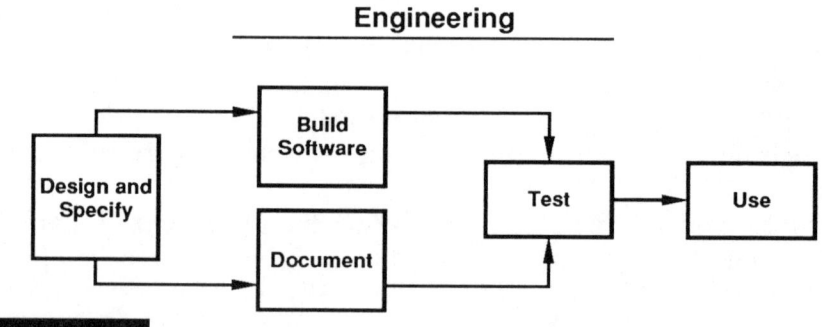

FIGURE 2-2: Testing Systems

tested. This step includes testing all system documents, from training programs to user manuals.

When testing is completed, the system documentation and software agree. The result is a system that is ready for release and use.

RELEASE

"Release" is a general term that covers production, packaging, distribution, and installation of the system. These activities occur whether the system is installed in a department of your company or offered for retail sale to the general public.

The designer and builder are responsible for producing and packaging the system. How the system is distributed and installed, and by whom, depends on the nature of the product. Whatever distribution method is used, it is essential that the release be controlled.

As time passes, the system will evolve. Problems will emerge as the system is thoroughly exercised by the users. Revisions and additions are a predictable feature of information systems. In a controlled release, each recipient of the system is recorded. Thus, when revisions occur they can be distributed to the installers, supporters, operators, and users of the system.

USE

The ultimate step in the system development process is, of course, the application of the solution to the problem, the application of the system to the user environment. This is also the ultimate test, answering the question, Does the product meet the need?

In this step the user interacts with the system, using it to do his or her job. The user interacts at the human interface, which includes the system documentation. Depending on the nature of the product, operators and supporters may participate in the use step.

Figure 2-1 does not include a box labeled "Maintenance," but you should consider maintenance as a repetition of the entire system development process, on a smaller scale. Each change to the system must be designed, specified, built, tested, and released before it can be put into use.

DESIGNING YOUR OWN PROCESS

When you try to create your own system development process, you will be in grave danger of getting tangled up in your own efforts. After all, the system development process touches all aspects and parts of your work as a system engineer.

Rather than perfect your process all at once, I suggest that you tackle one step at a time. Start with the design step. Determine your objectives and products. Try several different methods of creating the product design.

Apply this step to several different projects. By discovering and accommodating specific variations, you can develop a global process

You can record your system development process in the form of a simple block diagram accompanied by a checklist of tasks and activities. Also make note of the software and documentation products that result from each activity and step.

Follow the same procedure for creating the next step, the specification step. Having two steps will reveal inadequacies or problems in both, since you must now also consider their interaction.

Let your system development process evolve gradually within the context of your ongoing work. Remember to keep initial versions simple and flexible, for you will make changes with each new project.

DOCUMENTATION PROCESS

By consciously designing a system development process, you can improve your work methods and your products. Similarly, your documentation efforts and the system documents you create can be improved by consciously designing a documentation process.

There are any number of complex models for the documentation process. Some of them call for creating alpha, beta, and eventually gamma drafts of each document. Some deal with edited versions, approved versions, typeset versions, and printed versions of a system document.

The documentation process shown in Figure 2-3 is a simple model. It shows in a general fashion what must happen to create any system document. Note that this process results in the creation of a *single* document. Each system document is created by repeating the documentation process, or a suitable variation of it.

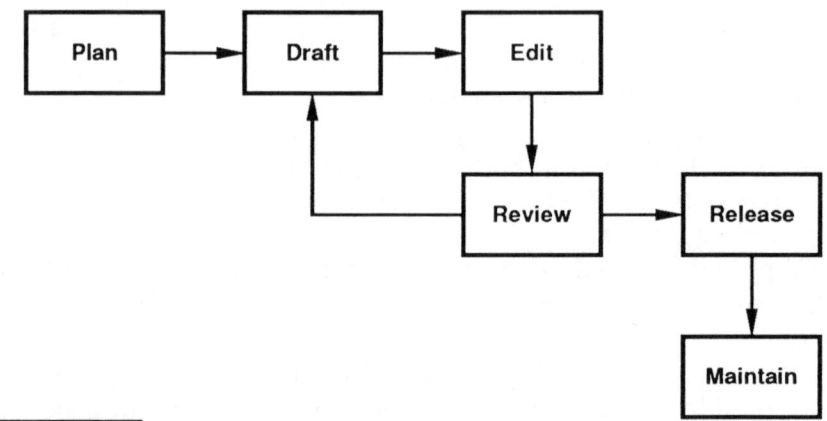

FIGURE 2-3: Documentation Process

As we examine the documentation process, I will often use terms that describe printed pages. Bear in mind that system documents are not restricted to this medium.

PLAN

The first step in the documentation process is planning the document. This is analogous to the design and specification steps of the system development process. The planning step answers questions at both the logical and physical level.

What is contained in a document plan? At the logical level, the plan contains definitions of the document's purpose, audience, and subject. At the physical level, the document plan includes a definition of the medium, format, and layout that will be used to present the information. The plan may also outline maintenance and revision provisions for the document.

The plan step itself can be divided into three main steps:

1. Define the audience, purpose, and subject.
2. Organize the material.
3. Design the format.

Despite the number of decisions required to plan a document, the document plan itself need not be lengthy or complex. For example, it is a good idea to restrict your definitions of the purpose, audience, and subject matter to single three-by-five index cards, or to a single paragraph each.

Define the Audience, Purpose, and Subject

Defining the audience makes it possible for you to match the document to the audience. You can define an audience by its attributes; for example, its background training, education, experience, and attitudes. Knowing your audience, you can match the tone, style, language, and emphasis of your document to your readers.

I find it helpful to break the audience for system documents into at least three categories: expert, informed, and novice.

Experts have a good grasp of the technical knowledge in their area. In writing for experts, you need not simplify or interpret information.

Informed readers know more than novices, but less than experts.

As you can imagine, this is a gray area. The needs of the informed reader are often hardest to identify. The informed reader will need some explanations and interpretations of the information presented in the document.

The novice has no exposure to the subject of the document. Care must be taken to introduce and define each term or concept that is new to the reader. You will need to translate the essential message into everyday English.

Defining the purpose of a document is a simpler process than you might suspect. Answer the question, "What should result when the reader uses this document?"

All system documents serve to communicate information among the system players. Within this general purpose, system documents serve a variety of specific purposes. They can be used to capture or exchange technical information, as training instruments, or as general reference material.

Defining the subject of a document is made easier by first defining the purpose and audience. When these are known, the appropriate subject material suggests itself. You can decide which material to include or exclude by testing it to see if it will serve the purpose of the document, for the given audience.

The subject can be defined by listing the information and material to be included in the document. Do not expend any effort on ordering or organizing the list. This happens in the next step.

Organize the Material

The second step in planning the document is to organize the content. Bear in mind that the organization should be obvious to and expected by the reader.

Readers bring their own clear expectations about how information will be organized. If you follow the organization your reader expects, the only new material you will be presenting is the factual content of the document. The reader only has to learn one new thing. If you impose an unexpected or unfamiliar form of organization, the reader must learn the organization as well as the facts.

You must also clearly show your reader the organization you have used. You can do this by making good use of headings, graphics, and spatial layouts. Several types of organization are useful in system documentation. Here are some examples:

- Chronological
- Cyclic
- Most to least important
- Order of reader need
- Increasing level of difficulty
- Alphabetic

Design the Format

The format of a system document is defined by its medium, overall appearance, and the layout of each element. These are important decisions in the design of a document. An appropriate format is essential for efficient communication of system information to the reader.

Designing a page format involves a series of decisions about the physical appearance of all pages in the document. For example, you might select the typeface used, define margin sizes, decide how many columns of text to use, and so on.

DRAFT

The second step in the documentation process is to create a draft, or working version, of the document you have planned. In this step, the reader's needs are matched to an appropriate style. Useful styles include the following:

- Text
- Specification sheet
- Data flow diagram
- Structured list
- Table, chart, or matrix
- Playscript

During this step, you also develop various techniques to help meet the needs of the readers. These include examples, metaphors, cases, and scenarios.

When creating the draft, you may encounter what writers refer to as a "block." Blocks can be internal, as when you face the blank screen or page. The blockage is between your thoughts and the text you are struggling to create. Blocks can also occur between you and the information you need. Perhaps design or specification decisions have not been made yet. Perhaps the information you need has not been recorded, and you must conduct interviews to get it.

EDIT

Once the draft is finished, the next step is to edit it. The purpose of editing is to refine the draft into a usable system document.

The editing process occurs on many levels and is often done in a series of separate passes. Here is a list of the different kinds of edit that are possible, though not always necessary:

- Clarification of text
- Adherence to company policy
- Integrity of style
- Format
- Mechanical style
- Technical accuracy
- Language

In the ideal situation, editing is done by someone other than the person who created the draft. This is matter of perspective. Only an objective opinion, a second eye, will do.

In less than ideal situations, you must act as your own editor. In this case, it helps to put as much time between the drafting and editing steps as possible. The object is to adopt the perspective of the reader, and this is difficult when you are still close to the effort of the writer.

REVIEW

When a useful version of the document has been drafted and edited, it is time to review. This is analogous to the testing step in the system development process. All system documents need to be tested against their document plan to make sure they meet the criteria defined there.

Some kinds of system document, such as operator or user manuals, require a technical review. This ensures that the information in the manuals is technically correct. Such manuals can be tested against the system designs and specifications or against the system itself.

When others review your documentation, be prepared to show them *how* to review. That is, you must tell them what contribution you expect them to make and show them how to make it. During and after the review, be prepared to provide feedback about the value the reviewer adds to the document.

Like system testing, the review step introduces an iterative loop to the documentation process. As a result of the review step, you may need to repeat the draft and edit steps.

RELEASE

Once the document has been tested and perfected, it can be produced in a form that is suitable for distribution to the intended audience. This is the release step in the documentation process.

Production of the document depends on the medium used. For example, printed material can be prepared on your own desktop publishing equipment or produced by an outside printing firm. Most EDP shops use outside help to produce audio or video material.

The release step includes packaging, distribution, and control of the document.

> **PROBLEM:** Okay, I revised the user manual. Who should get the updates?
>
> **SOLUTION:** Find a document release method that links the manual and the user.

A document control list should be created for each system document before it is first released. This list records the names of document holders. It may also contain a historical record of revisions sent to the holders.

MAINTAIN

Information systems are more susceptible to change than most other products. Consequently, revision and updating of system documents are important parts of the documentation process.

When system documents are updated, revisions must be distributed to all holders. These people need to know to which manual the revised pages belong and where to insert the pages to revise their copy. You can provide this information by printing the manual title and a page number on each page. Revision dates and marks help system document holders determine which version of a page is current and what changes have been made.

Maintenance considerations can also dictate the method of paginating and binding system documents. Documents that are frequently updated should be bound in loose-leaf binders. Stable documents may have their pages numbered sequentially from front to back, while changing documents may need page numbering within chapters.

One way to control the maintenance of a system document is to keep a master copy and a working copy. The master copy matches the distributed copies. It shows you what is in the hands of the readers. The working copy is marked to show pending revisions.

Each document should have a document control page that shows the system and version to which the document applies, the overall version or revision of the document itself, perhaps a manual serial number, and information about the registered holder of the document.

INTEGRATING THE PROCESSES

You now have models for the system development process and the documentation process. By applying the documentation process to each step of the system development process, you can integrate the two. This integration is part of the engineering approach that guarantees active, in-line system documentation.

Let's examine the integration of the system development process and the documentation process, considering one step at a time.

DESIGN STEP AND PRODUCT DESIGN DOCUMENT

Figure 2-4 is an expanded view of the first step in the system development process, the design step. The user, the designer, and sometimes the builder contribute to the creation of the first system document, the product design. The master copy of the product design is kept in the System File.

The process starts with a need in the user community. The designer studies the problem and creates a solution. The solution is expressed in the product design document. The user and the designer use this document to communicate about the design of the proposed system.

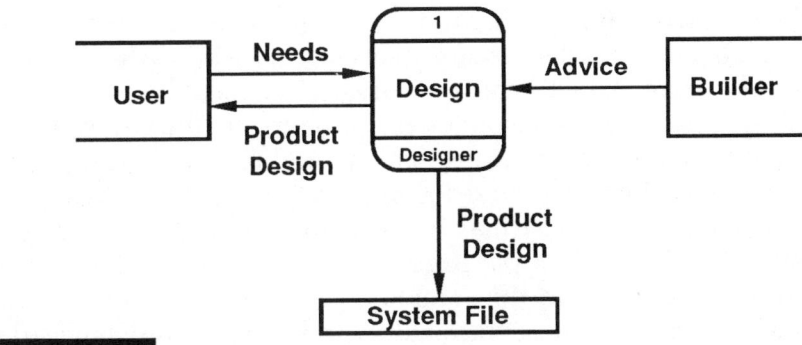

FIGURE 2-4: Design

The sources of user needs and requests are varied. The needs can be expressed directly by the users or communicated through marketing staff. They can originate with individual users, the managers of user departments, or the representatives of user groups.

The needs can be defined with various degrees of formality, ranging from simple memos to marketing reports or feasibility studies. These are not really system documents, since they reflect the problem, not the product. Of course these documents are important and should be cataloged in the Project File. However, the first definition of user needs to appear in the System File is contained in the product design document. This document may also be called the system architecture, general design, or logical design. I prefer the term *product design* because it reminds me that I am developing a product for my client, the user, and that the document contains a general level of design information, but no specific or technical details.

Plan the Product Design

As we've seen, planning a document begins with a definition of the audience. The audience of the product design is the users, who are expert in their business fields and range from novice to expert in information systems.

The purpose of the product design is to communicate the design of the system to the users. It must give them an experience of the system that is immediate and representative. To engage the users in the design process, the product design must show them what they will experience when the system is built. The users shouldn't have to deduce how the system will perform from an abstract document.

The subject matter of the product design document includes an overview of how the entire system works. It also shows the information structure and functional structure of the system.

The product design also contains layouts or samples of every item in the user interface: forms, screens, and reports. The user will also need to see the plan for the documentation package and samples of the user manuals. These may be as simple as page layouts, a table of content, and a few sample pages.

Product designs are the foremost candidates for multimedia treatment. System documentation is not restricted to any particular medium. Effective product designs often include mock-ups and demonstrations. Demonstrations provide the user with an experience of screen layouts, control techniques, or menu structures, and present the key functions of the system.

Draft the Product Design

To draft the product design, you create the text, samples, diagrams, demonstration software—in short, you create every element called for in the document plan. At the very least, you will want to define each input, function, and output of the system.

Edit and Review the Product Design

Before presenting a working draft to the user, you will want to edit the product design to ensure that the text is clear, that the style and format are matched to the reader, and that the design is complete and coherently expressed.

However, editing the product design need not be a critical operation. It is important to secure the user's participation in the design process. Letting the user correct a few obvious errors is a good way to show how his or her input is reflected in the product design.

You may wish to review the product design document before first presenting it to the user. Comparing the document plan with the finished document is a good way to ensure that your product design will communicate effectively. A technical review of the product design document will ensure that the system you've designed meets all the defined needs of the user.

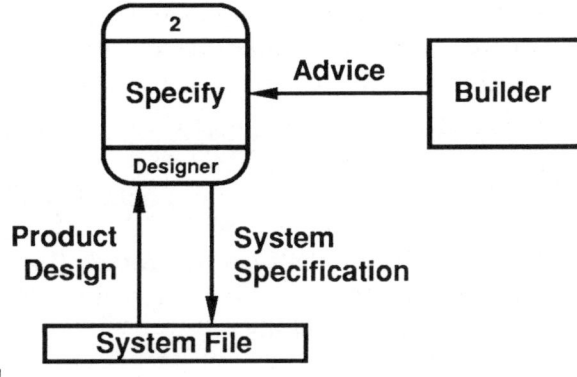

FIGURE 2-5: Specify

Release the Product Design

When you are satisfied with the product design document, you are ready to produce and distribute copies to the user. If there is more than one user, or if copies of the product design are distributed to other system players, you must record this information and ensure that all holders receive the revisions and updates.

The product design is a two-way communication bridge, linking the user and designer. It is reasonable to expect, even to desire, frequent revisions to this document during the design step.

SPECIFY STEP AND SYSTEM SPECIFICATION DOCUMENT

Figure 2-5 shows the details of the second step in the system development process, the specify step.

In this step, the designer converts the product design into system specifications. The designer may rely on the builder to provide technical advice. The resulting document is the system specification, which may also be called the functional specification or detail specification. It resides in the System File.

While the designer and builder may work together to generate detailed specifications, the designer is responsible for creating the system specification document.

PROBLEM: Sure, I could code the program according to this flowchart, but it would take four hours to pass the master file each night.

SOLUTION: Do not use detailed flowcharts to specify the programs. Create a program specification that shows the input and output, control structure, and calculations for the program. Let the builders use their expertise to implement the specification effectively.

Be wary of overspecifying the system. Provide the builders with specifications detailed enough to give them direction, but allow them room to apply their own skills.

Plan the System Specifications

In this case, the audience is the system builder, an expert who will use the system specifications to construct the software portion of the system. Like the product design, the system specification is a two-way communication bridge. Its purpose is to communicate construction details of the system between the designer and builder.

In Chapter 3, you will learn how to break down a system into its component elements and how to decide which attributes of each element need to be specified. This information is the subject of the system specification.

System specifications can be effective in two different media: printed pages and online data files. Although having the specifications available in an online system can be a great help, overall I favor the use of printed pages. The software is volatile during the building step, and the stability of printed specifications can be a valuable control feature.

System builders can often suggest improvements in the specification or design of a software system. Thus, the development of the system specification is often concurrent with and of the same duration as the building step.

Draft and Edit the System Specification

Drafting and editing the system specifications are part of the work process of the specification and building steps in the system development process.

The designer creates the first draft of the specification with enough detail and accuracy to allow the builder to create the software of the system. During the building process, the builder and designer draft, edit, and revise the system specifications in the process of communicating design details or changes.

Often, the designer need only create part of the specification, leaving the resolution of some technical details to the builder. For example, the designer may specify the content, keys, and sequence of a file but allow the builder to determine the best record sizes and blocking factors.

Review the System Specifications

It is rare that system specifications are completed entirely before the building process begins. A formal review of system specifications is seldom needed. As the designer, you will check each set of specifications for completeness before giving them to the builder. In addition, you may need to review the system specification package as it is being created, to ensure that the finished package conforms to contractual or policy requirements.

Release and Maintain the System Specifications

For independent programmers and small shops, the production, distribution, and control of system specifications can be very informal indeed. For larger shops or for team efforts, more elaborate document release techniques are essential.

Releasing system specifications may involve the production and distribution of printed material. Alternately, it may mean transferring data files from the "draft" to "development" directories of an online System File.

As the size of the system product and project increase, control of the system specifications becomes more important. Control is an essential ingredient of the maintenance plan for system specifications.

Maintain the System Specifications

Like the product design, the system specification is a volatile document. Make sure you create simple, rapid revision techniques.

It is imperative that all members of development teams are apprised of any changes to the system specifications that may affect their work. This includes the builders who are creating the remaining system documentation and preparing various training or reference manuals.

48 • System Documentation

BUILD STEP AND SYSTEM MANUALS

In the build step of the system development process, both the software and the manuals for the system are built. This step is shown in Figure 2-6.

My diagram shows separate boxes for these two construction processes. I model the build step in this way for two reasons. First, it emphasizes that both the software and the manuals are built here. Second, it shows that the two processes are independent. They can happen at different times in the overall development process and can be performed by different people.

The software builders (programmers) use the system specifications to construct and assemble the software components of the system. The resulting product is the system software. The software can be stored in any number of ways, but I have generalized these into a single "software file."

In this process, the software builders use the system specifications to communicate with the designer. Both the specifications and

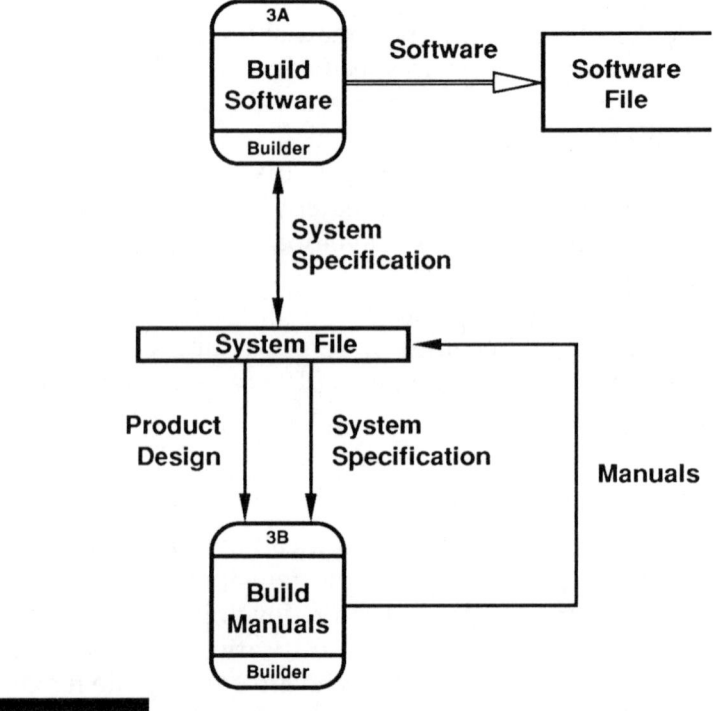

FIGURE 2-6: Build

the software are refined in a series of iterations, until both agree and are correct.

Other system builders (writers) create the system manuals. The writers use the product design and the system specifications to create the manuals defined in the product design. Examples are installation, operation, training, user, and support manuals. The manuals are stored in the System File.

Let's focus on the production of the system documents I refer to as manuals. These are the system documents most susceptible to an add-on treatment. Timing the creation of these documents to precede or coincide with construction of the software is one way to avoid add-on documentation.

Notice that with the in-line approach, system manuals can be built even in advance of the software. What creates this freedom is the existence of the product design and system specifications. When these documents are created in the design and specify steps of the system development process, you need not wait for the software to be finished. You need not study program listings or exercise the system to create the content of the manuals.

To simplify the application of the documentation process to this step in the system development process, I will consider only one type of manual, the user manual.

Plan the Manual

The first step in the documentation process is to plan the manuals. Fortunately, much of this planning will have been done in the design step, since the product design includes the general plan for each manual in the system. At this point in the system development process these plans must be reviewed, completed, and finalized.

Defining the audience of the user manual is relatively easy. When specific levels or types of user have been anticipated, when the characteristics, skills, experience, and education of these users are included in the product design, it is a simple matter to define the audience for any system manual.

You can create specific manuals tailored to each of the users defined in the product design or write a manual organized into sections that match the needs and abilities of each user.

Remember that even if you are writing for a single user, that user will evolve from a novice to an informed, even to an expert user of your system. Your manual must take this into account.

User manuals serve a variety of purposes. Of course the overall purpose is to communicate information about the system and its use. Specific purposes include providing detailed reference material, training sessions, or quick reference aids.

The specific purpose and specific audience of the user manual will determine its subject matter. In later chapters I'll suggest what each kind of user manual should include. We'll also take a close look at online user manuals, the newest medium for these system documents.

Draft, Edit, and Review the Manual

When the plan is complete, you can draft, edit, and review the user manual. Here you will focus on developing styles and techniques that communicate with the user effectively.

The iterative process of drafting and editing usually continues until you can produce a polished draft of the manual. The designer reviews this draft for conformity to the product design and document plan. The software builders may perform additional reviews to ensure technical accuracy.

I congratulate you if you are wondering why I do not include the user in the review process since only the user can determine whether or not the manual serves its intended purpose. Users cannot make this decision by simply reviewing the manual itself. Rather, they must *use* the manual to support their use of the system. Like the software, the manual must not only be reviewed but also tested.

Each manual created as a part of the system product must be tested in this fashion. For this reason, the user "reviews" the manual in the test step of the system development process.

Release and Maintain the Manual

Because a single system product may include several manuals and because several system players may contribute to the drafting, editing, and reviewing of the manuals, you will find it helpful to control the production and distribution not only of the final versions of manuals but also of the preliminary and intermediate versions. Manuals created in-line with the system development process are active. Changes to the product design or specifications trigger changes to the manuals as well as to the software. This approach makes it possible to guarantee that the manuals will be revised and maintained.

Regardless of when a manual is tested and completed, its final production, packaging, and distribution must be synchronized with that of the software. The final system product must be packaged and distributed in one step.

Once a system is released, the installers, users, operators, and supporters will detect problems. They will also suggest improvements or request enhancements to the product. Maintaining system manuals means repeating the draft, edit, and review steps. It also means producing and distributing revised pages and recording the distribution of revisions. The maintenance you anticipate will affect the design of the manual. Binding, pagination, revision marking, and control methods are influenced by maintenance activities.

TEST STEP AND TEST PLAN DOCUMENT

Figure 2-7 shows the test step of the system development process in detail. You will notice that I have divided the step into two parts.

Testing calls for a test plan. I have shown the creation of the test plan as the first part of the test step. However, creation of the test plan can, and usually does, occur earlier in the system development process. You may find it more convenient to create this document during the build step.

No matter when the test plan is created, it is the responsibility of the designer. The designer uses the product design and system specifications to create portions of the test plan. The plan is stored in the System File.

The user, designer, and builder all participate in the actual testing process. Both the software and the system documentation are tested according to the test plan. The diagram shows that all system documents are tested, or used to test the software. As a result, both the software and the system documents are revised.

While many problems can be detected and resolved internally, the system must also be tested by the user. External testing will reveal additional problems, which result in additional revisions.

We have already examined the various kinds of testing that are possible with engineered systems. I'll restrict my discussion of this step to the first process, creating the test plan.

Plan the Test Plan

The audience for the test plan includes the designer, builder, and user. Each of these system players has a different area and level of

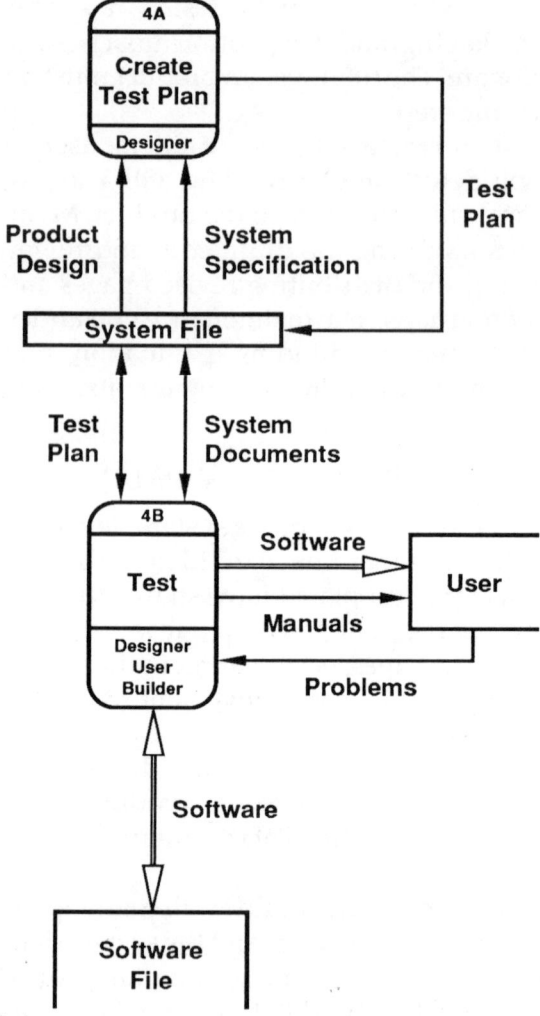

FIGURE 2-7: Test

expertise. Each section of the test plan must be written with its specific audience in mind.

The test plan serves several purposes. It helps the designer and builder test the system thoroughly against the product design and specifications. It shows the builder and the user exactly how to conduct each test. In addition, the test plan shows how to record and report the results of the testing process.

No doubt you begin to see similarities between the test plan and the product design. The designer does not create a final, inflexible version of the test plan but develops a working draft that will help the designer, builder, and user communicate during the test step.

The subject of the test plan includes a sequence of tests, instructions for performing the tests, the expected results, and eventually the actual results of each test. The test plan may include timetables and schedules for conducting the tests.

Draft, Edit, and Review the Test Plan

Drafting and editing the test plan is almost a mechanical process. You review each point in the product design and system specifications and determine whether it should be tested, and if so, how it will be tested.

Next, divide this comprehensive list of tests into groups, according to who will perform the tests. You can now draft and edit appropriate test procedures for each audience.

You will want to review the first working version of the entire test plan for completeness. Remember that the system documentation as well as the system software must be tested.

Release and Maintain the Test Plan

The test plan is produced and distributed to the system players who perform the tests. Since this document will undergo many revisions during the test step, editing and production may be informal. However, distribution and control of the plan are critical and should be carefully planned.

You will need to revise the test plan whenever the product design or system specifications are revised. Consequently, you will need to control the distribution of revisions to the test plan.

You could easily argue that the test plan is not a part of the system documentation. Complete system testing is usually a once-only process. The estimates and schedules needed to manage the test process clearly fall into the category of project documentation.

On the other hand, parts of the test plan are valuable throughout the life of the system, for example, the sequence of tests and the expected results. You can reduce testing time and effort during system maintenance projects by treating the test plan as an active system document.

You could separate the active and passive parts of the test plan

54 • System Documentation

and store each in the appropriate file. The system documentation portion of the test plan consists of information about what to test, how to test it, and what results to expect. The project documentation portion indicates who will perform each test, when it will be performed, and the actual results.

Including the test plan in the system documentation means that you must maintain it. Again, the in-line approach makes such maintenance simple. The test plan is derived from the product design and system specifications, so changes to these system documents trigger revisions of the test plan.

RELEASE STEP AND CONTROL LOGS

The penultimate step in the system development process is release. Figure 2-8 shows this step.

It is difficult to assign responsibility for the production, distribution, and control of the finished system product to a single system player. Depending on the nature of your shop and products, the release step may be performed by customer support staff, marketing

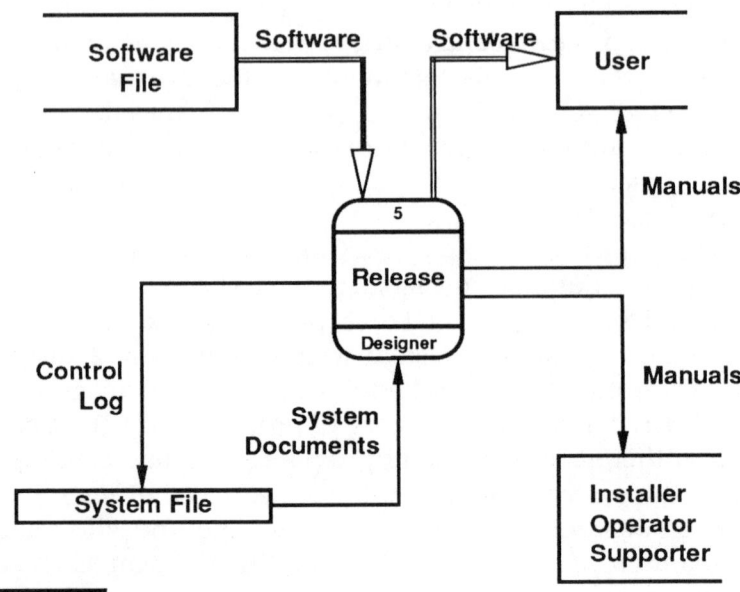

FIGURE 2-8: Release

staff, or even an independent software publisher. The diagram shows the designer in this role, since this engineer bears the ultimate responsibility for applying the solution to the problem.

In this step, final versions of the software and system documents are produced. The complete system product, composed of software and manuals, is distributed to the user or installed in the user environment. The designer creates or revises the control log.

Additional system manuals, such as installation guides, operator manuals, and support manuals may be distributed, depending on the nature of the product. The users of systems designed for personal computers act as their own installer, operator, and supporter. The information they need can be included in a single user manual or in a series of specialized manuals or booklets.

Complex systems may require installation by specially trained teams who need detailed instructions in the form of an installation guide or manual.

If your shop provides ongoing user support, your support staff will need access to the system documentation. This may be provided by an online support system or in the form of a support manual.

Mainframe systems and networks with remote user terminals require operators. These system players need instructions for operating the machine portions of the system. Operator manuals provide the needed information.

Releasing a system may also involve internal control procedures. For example, both the software file and the System File can be divided into development and production sections. The release step would include transferring software and documentation to the production areas of both files.

As you can see, this step in the system development process does not create any new system documents, with the possible exception of an overall or global control log.

Plan the Control Log

The general purpose of a control log is to record the distribution of the system and thereby control the distribution of revisions. It lists the holders of the software and the holders of each system manual and records which revisions have been sent to each holder. The audience of a control log includes all the system players in your shop.

Draft, Edit, and Review the Control Log

Surprisingly, it can be difficult to create control logs because of the diversity of the audience and the specific purposes the log must serve for each audience. The best approach is to keep the content and organization of the log simple. Rather than plan and create a series of unique control logs, you should develop a standard format to be used throughout your shop. Control logs drafted and edited according to your standard cannot meet the unique needs of a diverse audience. However, a standard format and content will ensure that each member of your organization knows what information is available and how to get it.

Release and Maintain the Control Log

If you feel dizzy, it is because you are standing at the edge of an endless spiral. Do control logs need control logs to record their distribution? And do those control logs need more control logs? The answer is an emphatic no.

To fulfill their purpose, control logs must be kept and maintained in one central location. They should not be copied and routinely distributed. To be sure, people will need and request copies of the latest version, but these should be treated as "dead" copies. It will help both you and the reader if you date the title page of each control log. This makes it easy to identify different versions of the document. It also helps to identify the control log as a dead copy. You could print a notice such as "This document will not be updated" on the title page.

This approach simplifies the maintenance of the control log. All that is required is that each release of software and documentation be added to the log.

USE STEP

The final and endless step in developing a system is using it. The user interacts with the system software, supported by the user manual, your support staff, and perhaps by operators. Refer to Figure 2-9 for a diagram of this step.

No documents are created in this step. The necessary system documents have already been created and stored in the System File.

Ideally, the user manual provides users with all the training and reference material they need in order to use the system effectively.

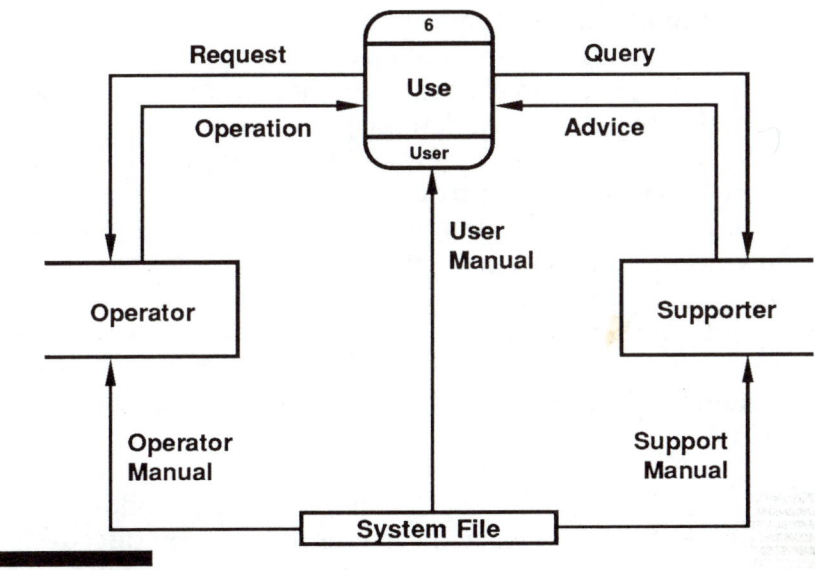

FIGURE 2-9: Use

When the user manual fails, the users query the supporter.

The supporter may have access to all of the system documents. Alternately, key information may be extracted and recorded in a support manual. This information allows the supporter to reply to user queries.

Operators respond to requests from the system and the users. The information they need to operate the system is contained in the operator manual.

To those of you familiar with the add-on approach to documentation, the final step in the software development process may seem anticlimactic. But remember, the whole purpose of the in-line approach is to remove last-minute scrambles to create add-on system documents. Not only is the final step in the process anticlimactic, it is also antitraumatic.

DOCUMENTATION SYSTEM

Thus far, I have shown you models for the system development process and the documentation process. I have also shown how these two processes can be integrated. All you need now is the model of a documentation system that will support both processes.

58 • System Documentation

At this point I must apologize for having played a trick on you. To show the integration of the system development and documentation processes, I used small portions of the documentation system model. All that remains is to link these pieces of the model together.

I'll describe this model by explaining the processes and data flows shown in Figure 2-10. No doubt you have already recognized the processes as the steps in the system development process and the data flows as various system documents.

In the design process, the designer converts the needs of the user into a rough product design. The user and designer use this document to communicate about the design of the proposed system, thereby refining it to a final product design. This is stored in the System File.

In the specify process, the designer converts the general product design into detailed system specifications. These are added to the System File, but are not finalized versions. Like the product design, the system specifications are a framework for communication. This time, however, the communication occurs between the designer and the builder during the next process.

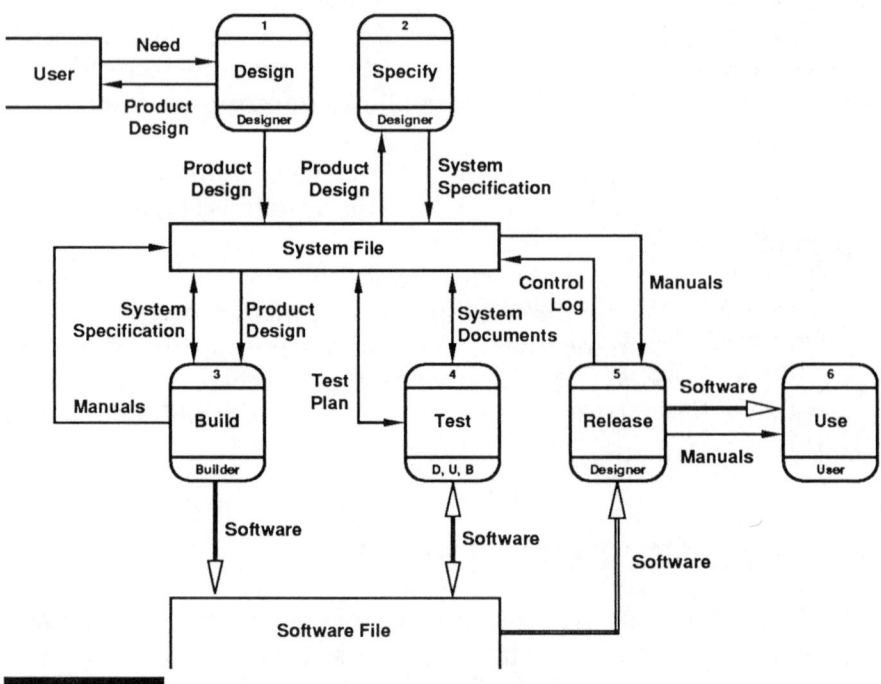

FIGURE 2-10: Documentation System

The build process includes two kinds of activity: building the software and building the system manuals. Programmers use the system specifications to create software, which is stored in the software file. Writers use the product design and the system specifications to build manuals, which are stored in the System File.

The designer, builder, and user all participate in the test process. Before testing begins, the designer uses the product design and system specifications to create a rough test plan. This document is revised as testing proceeds.

The test process includes several different types of test. Both the software and the manuals are tested against the product design and system specifications. The entire system is also tested in the user environment.

Testing reveals problems, which are resolved by revising the software, manuals, or specifications. At the end of the test process, all elements of the system agree and the tested versions are stored in the software file and System File.

In the release process, the software and manuals are produced and distributed. To ensure that the release is controlled, the designer creates a control log and adds it to the System File.

The finished package of software and manuals is put into use in the last step, the use process.

None of the information in the diagram or description of the documentation system should be new to you. What may be new is the perspective. We are examining your activities as a system engineer as if they were part of a documentation system, which in fact they are.

Whether you are a system analyst, a programmer, a technical writer, an operator, or a customer service representative, your job requires information about systems. Even if you are an independent software builder and play the designer, builder, and supporter roles by switching hats, you still need information about the systems you create.

As an EDP professional, you are expert in creating information systems. All you need do is apply your skills to solving your information needs. I encourage you to follow the steps of the system development process you have just learned. Unfortunately, not all of the system players will make their needs known as obviously your users will. You may need to study the work habits of those in your shop to uncover their information needs.

The documentation system model shown in Figure 2-10 is a

logical design only. To create your own documentation system you must convert this to a physical design and eventually to a set of system specifications.

> **PROBLEM:** We can make the enhancement the user wants if we change the Master File. But which other programs will be affected?
>
> **SOLUTION:** Create a documentation system that generates used-in lists. These show each program that uses a specific file.

Some of the needs you discover may suggest details of physical design. For example, automating the storage and retrieval of system specifications lets you generate a wide variety of cross-reference lists. Your support "manual" could even take the form of an online data base query system.

The System File plays a central role in the documentation system. Since system documentation comes in many media, you may need to implement this logical file as several physical files. You will need to make decisions about storing and retrieving information in the System File.

The documentation system is internal to your shop, but it is a system that is critical to your operation and success. Your development effort may be less formal than usual, but it should be your best effort.

I do not suggest that you stop all projects and focus on developing your documentation system. As in the system development process, you *already* have a documentation system. What you need to do is consciously improve the existing system over an extended period of time.

By all means, create an overall product design, but complete the development process one step at a time, in one area at a time. Rather than solve all your internal information problems at once, meet a few related needs with each new version of your documentation system. When you and your staff experience improvements in your work environment, support and motivation for the project will increase.

INTEGRATING THE DOCUMENTATION SYSTEM WITH SHOP OPERATION

Documentation processes and systems cannot be imposed from above. System documentation will only work when people want it to work. You must have their support. The best way to create this support is to show people that system documents make their jobs easier and make their products better. There are several key points to watch when integrating a documentation system into your operation.

The first integration point is between the user and the designer and involves the product design and its use. It is important to show the user how to use the product design document to participate in the design process. As a designer, you must learn to create product designs that serve this purpose.

Effective product design documents make the user's job easier. They allow the user to understand the proposed system, evaluate its suitability, and suggest improvements. Users who are responsible for approving or authorizing system development can do so confidently, once they have a clear understanding of the product design.

In addition, the product design document is an ideal focal point for planning enhancements and revisions. Using the product design in this way also encourages you to revise systems in a thorough, structured fashion.

The second key integration point is between the designer and the builder. Programmers must not see the system specifications as a curtailment of their creative abilities. As a designer, you must find a balance between specification and space. The ideal balance occurs when the specifications give the programmer enough direction to proceed and enough space to implement the specification creatively.

The first thing programmers should experience about system specifications is that they make their jobs easier by providing all the needed information in one convenient package. Often, programmers have been trained to reverse-engineer their software. First, they build the software. Then, if there is enough time or pressure, they create specifications for the software they have built. This order must be reversed so that the builders come to expect general specifications to initiate their work.

Ideally, the designer and the builder use the system specifications as a framework for discussing implementation details. The designer provides this framework in the form of general specifications. The builder adds detailed specifications during the construction of the software.

A third key integration point lies between the designer and the writer, or builder of system manuals. There is no problem of motivation here. Writers are overjoyed to lay aside their burden of research.

In addition, writers welcome the opportunity to contribute to the development process by supporting designers and programmers in the creation of product designs and system specifications.

The danger is that the writers may not be advised of changes to the product design or system specifications. When you implement an in-line approach to system documentation, be sure that the builders of system manuals are kept informed of design and specification revisions, just as the software builders are.

The best way to accomplish this is to organize your work on a project basis. Writers should be project team members, just as analysts and programmers are. This gives the interaction and cohesion needed.

The final key integration point is between the writers and readers of system manuals. Your documentation system must include feedback loops so that the readers and writers can work together to improve the manuals. Feedback loops are an inherent part of the testing step. Make sure you do not break these loops.

> **PROBLEM:** My programmers are paid to code. They're not novelists.
>
> **SOLUTION:** Distribute the writing tasks to those who have the needed skills. Designers create the specifications. Programmers provide the technical data. Writers create the manuals.

Who does all this writing? As you have seen, the system development process implies a natural division of writing tasks among the system players.

The designer and user write the product design. The designer and builder each contribute to the system specifications. In a similar process, the designer and builder create the system manuals. Manuals call for the special skills of a technical writer, but these skills are no more difficult to acquire than those of designers or programmers.

The remainder of this book is dedicated to improving your writing abilities.

3

The System Model

We have seen that the in-line approach to system documentation depends heavily on system specifications. Figure 2-10 showed that the product design and system specifications form the basis of the System File.

With the in-line approach, system elements are specified early in the system development process. This gives the software builders (programmers) the information they need; it also creates a general data base of technical information about the system. This data base funds the information needs of other system players. It gives the manual builders (writers) the information they need to create manuals.

Dividing information about systems into technical and user documentation reflects an add-on approach; technical and user documentation are seen as two separate and unrelated things. When you take the in-line approach, it is more helpful to think of system documentation as either primary or derived. The product design and system specifications are primary documentation. Installation, user, operator, and support manuals are derived documentation.

In this chapter and the next, I discuss system specification, a vital aspect of the in-line approach. We will examine system specification on a logical level by developing general models for information systems.

DEVELOPING A SYSTEM MODEL

In my first assignment as a system analyst, I was added at the last minute to a project team that was developing a large batch payroll system. My assignment was to assist in integration and parallel testing and to "tidy up" the documentation.

I was handed stacks of program listings, job control language decks, report layouts and samples, input forms, and notes on some backup procedures. There was no organization to this documentation. I couldn't even tell if it was complete or consistent. Where could I begin, and how was I to proceed with documenting this system?

Fortunately, at that time I was reading a textbook on technical writing. From it I learned three useful techniques that saved me from despair: classification, partitioning, and defining.

Both classification and partitioning are methods of division. Partitioning divides a single thing into its component parts. Classification divides a group of things into smaller, distinct classes.

You already use these techniques unconsciously. Suppose, for example, that you are shopping for a personal computer. To make sense of the different products available, you might start by partitioning PCs into their major parts: CPU, disk drive, monitor, and keyboard. Armed with this information, you would shop around and return with a list of ten possible computer systems.

To make sense of your list, you might classify the PCs into groups according to several characteristics, for example, price range, storage capacity, or processing speed.

These two ways of dividing information about PCs are shown in Figure 3-1. Partitioning divides your information into component parts. Classification divides your information into different types of system.

Once you grasp the basic concepts of partitioning and classification it is simple to apply them to system specification. Partitioning lets you break the system down into its component parts, such as programs, files, and screens. Classification lets you group information about these elements into meaningful classes, such as subsystems, functions, or even manuals.

There are several guidelines for using these techniques sensibly. The most important is that partitioning and classification must be consistent with your purpose. This guideline applies to so many documentation activities that it provides an ideal documentation motto: Know your purpose!

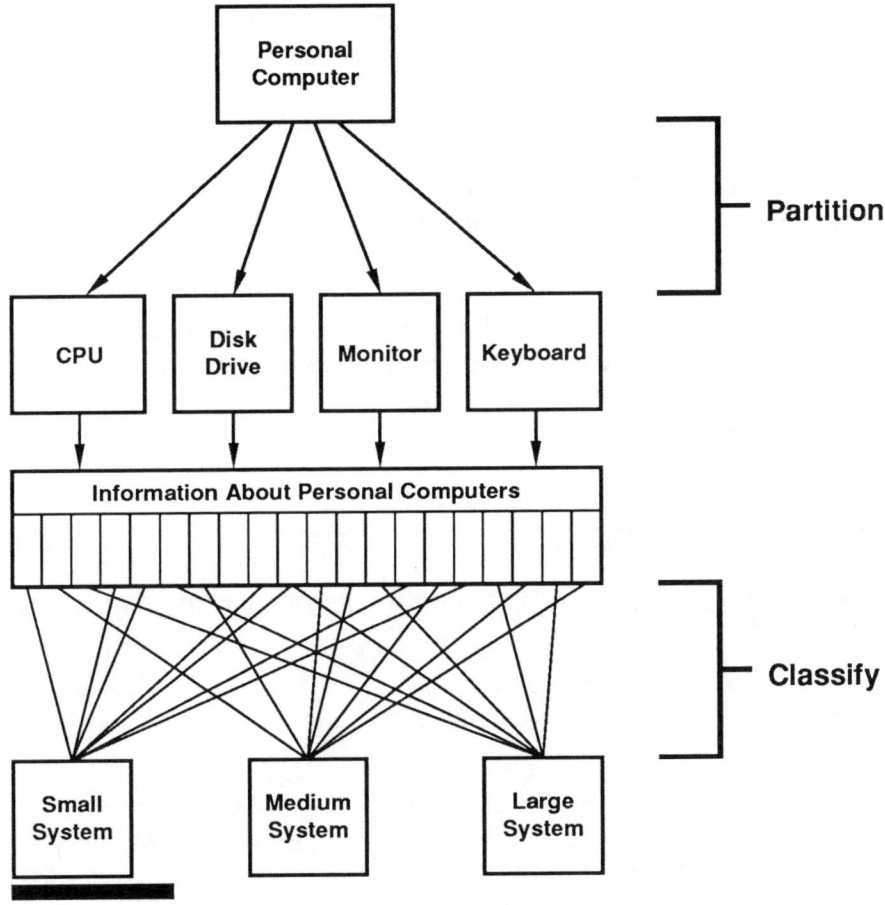

FIGURE 3-1: Partition and Classify

The purpose of partitioning and classifying systems is to create effective system documentation. I use partitioning, classification, and definition to create system models suitable for creating system specifications. Bear in mind that these models do not serve all purposes. They may not be ideal for training users or for marketing a software product.

Other useful guidelines for modeling systems are to subdivide the system as far as necessary to accomplish your purpose and to make sure there is no overlap of the parts.

Developing a system model is a core activity of the in-line approach. The system model answers questions about what to document and how to document it, and provides a framework of definition through which the information about a system can be screened.

Here are the steps to follow in modeling and specifying a system:

1. Define the elements that comprise the system.
2. Determine which attributes about each element need to be specified.

This chapter focuses on defining the elements and the structure of system models. Chapters 4 through 8 examine the attributes of system elements that need to be specified.

SELECTING AND DEFINING SYSTEM ELEMENTS

How do you go about selecting or defining system elements? There are several approaches:

- Experience and exposure
- Logical or physical existence
- Need

Experience and exposure are perhaps the easiest ways to determine what elements will comprise your system model. When you develop and use information systems, you are exposed to a wide variety of potential system elements. For example, builders of online mainframe systems can benefit by studying new approaches used in PC-based systems, where the distinction between menu, information, and dialog screens has been sharpened.

System elements may suggest themselves because they have a clear physical or logical existence. Few EDP professionals would question the existence of the system element called "program." Programs have a *physical* existence.

Functions, on the other hand, have no clear physical existence. They may represent a few lines of code in one program, an entire program with several screens or reports, or even a chain of programs. However, functions have a definite *logical* existence for the system users. The users perceive functions as the basic processing elements of the system. Thus, it makes sense to define and specify functions as system elements.

Documentation needs may suggest system elements. One of the

first system elements I created was the "job" or manual procedure. This element gives you a way to design, create, and record tasks that the system players must perform.

Myths and nursery tales make much of knowing a person's "true name." I chased the true name of this element for many years. "Routine" and "procedure" were ruled out, as they referred to portions of programs. "Job" seemed to be reserved for strings of programs run in batch and mainframe environments, complete with "job" control languages. I thought I had found an indisputable name in "task," but then came multitasking computers. Finally, I decided that the name of a system element should make sense to the system players who most often deal with the element. I discovered that the true name of manual procedures is "job."

In the batch environment in which I started my career as a system builder, dozens of manual procedures were required for using and operating systems. The users needed instructions for preparing and submitting input data; keypunch operators needed keypunching instructions; operators needed clearly defined procedures for operating each subsystem. These instructions were scattered and inconsistent; many were written by the users and operators themselves.

By defining "job" as a system element, I was able to incorporate all these instructions into the specification and documentation of a system. I needed a category, a slot into which the information could be placed. I needed a system element called "job."

No matter how you select system elements, it is essential that you define each element clearly. Clarity is the key to effective communication and documentation. Clear writing starts with clear thinking, and clear thinking depends on understanding what your terms mean. By defining elements, you describe and delimit them, preventing them from overlapping and giving them precise meaning. You ensure that the members of your shop communicate and work uniformly and consistently.

The simplest way to define something is to classify and then differentiate it. Consider the following definition of *modem*.

Modem: a communication device that converts data to a form that can be transmitted, as by telephone, to computer equipment, where a similar device reconverts it.

The first part of the definition, "a communication device" classifies modems. The remainder of the definition differentiates modems from other communication devices.

You are now prepared to study the system models I have developed. I will start by defining and explaining the biggest and most complex models. Later, I will show you how these can be simplified and adjusted according to your specific situation.

Before we start I want to reassure you. Do not be intimidated by the number of elements in these models. Realize that you are already specifying and building all of these elements. The system models do not add more elements than you need to specify, they simply present more numerous and more distinct categories in which you can place your specifications.

COMMON GROUPS OF ELEMENTS

All system models are composed of three groups of elements. These groups are shown in Figure 3-2, which might also be called the most general system model. As you can see, the three groups of elements are the function group, the information group, and the exchange group.

The function group contains those elements that transfer or transform information. It contains all the procedures of the system, whether they are manual or machine procedures. For example, the function group contains jobs and programs.

The information group contains system elements that are the data of the system. This group contains such elements as data items, records, and files.

The exchange group is composed of system elements that exchange information between the system and the system players.

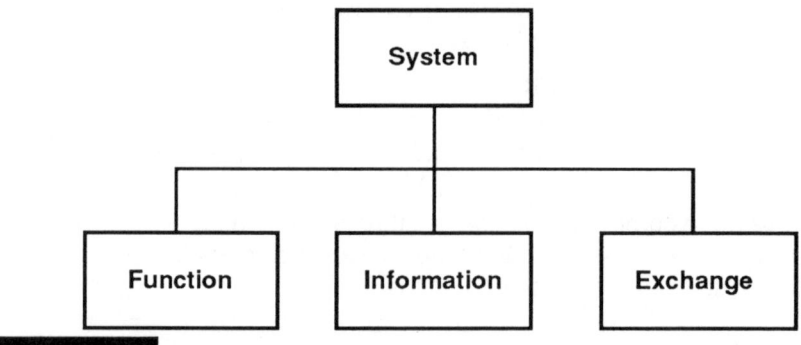

FIGURE 3-2: Common Element Groups

Elements such as forms, screens, and reports are of concern primarily to the system users. Elements such as messages may address the installer, operator, or supporter of a system.

No single system model will serve in all situations; however, the primary differences between models appear in the function group. For this reason, we'll study two different function groups: one for batch systems and one for online systems.

By combining these groups you can create a total model for either batch or online systems. The information and exchange groups are essentially the same for both online and batch systems.

I will not continue with the graphic technique of Figure 3-2, the organization chart. Rather, I will present the models in the form of structured lists. We'll explore this technique in a later chapter, but for now it is enough to point out that the information in a structure chart can be presented in an alternate form.

To demonstrate that structured lists and organization charts contain the same information, consider Figure 3-3. It is a partial organization chart of this book, translated from the table of contents. As you can see, structured lists are a condensed way of presenting content and hierarchy.

BATCH FUNCTION GROUP

Figure 3-4 shows the model for the batch system function group. It shows that a batch system is composed of one or more subsystems. Each subsystem is composed of one or more transactions, one or

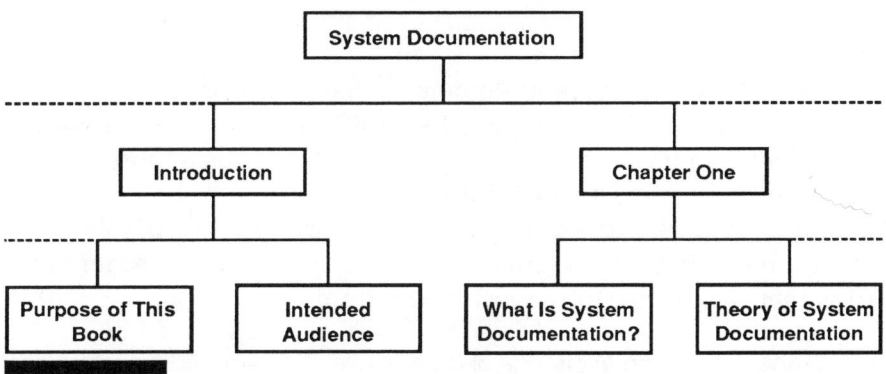

FIGURE 3-3: Structure Chart for This Book

```
Batch System
  Subsystem
    Transaction
    Job
    Run
      Program
        Module
```

FIGURE 3-4: Batch Function Group

more jobs, and one or more runs. Runs are composed of one or more programs, which in turn are composed of modules.

Don't worry if some of the terms are new to you. Here are definitions and explanations of each element in the group.

> **Batch System:** an information system that processes data in batches. It meets one or more information needs of the user. The software of a batch system does not communicate with the user during processing. Batch systems are composed of subsystems.

The batch system element is not a concrete entity. It is a classification tool that groups together all the elements that compose a batch system. It is the largest entity dealt with by those who develop and document systems.

> **Subsystem:** a specified sequence of manual and machine procedures operated on fixed or demand cycles, which meets one information need of the user. Subsystems are composed of transactions, jobs, and runs.

Like the batch system element, subsystems have no concrete existence. They are collections of subordinate elements. However, the subsystem has a strong logical existence. It has a more specific purpose, as it meets a single information need.

Subsystems are the daily, weekly, monthly, and yearly cycles of batch processing. They are also the predetermined "on demand" runs that the users can request at any time.

> **Transaction:** an exchange of data between a user and a system, that accomplishes a defined function for the user. A transaction can also be an exchange of data within a system, triggered by a specified event, that accomplishes a defined function.

Transactions are more than the physical forms or records used to handle transaction data. They include the manual and machine procedures needed to accomplish an exchange of information. Like the subsystem, transactions are more logical than physical. They are a tool for grouping physical elements.

Transactions are particularly useful for presenting system information to users, since users often think of system processing not in terms of subsystems or runs, but in terms of the transactions they wish to perform.

Job: a specified manual procedure, needed for the operation of a subsystem. Jobs are detailed instructions that a properly trained user or operator can perform.

Jobs are procedures such as preparing and submitting input forms, requesting demand runs, keypunching or converting written information to magnetic media, operating computer machinery, distributing output reports, and recording control totals.

Run: a specified machine procedure needed for the operation of a subsystem. Runs are the basic functional units of computer machinery, conducted by operators in batch processing. They are composed of programs.

Run is a generic name. The specific name depends on the hardware and operating system you use. Runs may be called jobs, control strings, library procedures, and so on.

A run is a collection of operating system instructions. These instructions handle peripheral devices, communicate with the operator, and trigger a sequence of programs.

Program: an executable set of machine instructions that will process data in a specified manner, given the correct machine setup and run time variables.

I classify sorts and utilities as programs. While you could create additional system elements for sorts, the result is not worth the extra effort.

Notice that the program is not responsible for peripheral setup or run time parameters. The run makes sure that the environment for a program is correct, instructing operators where to place the files the program will need. Run time variables can be supplied to the program by the run or by the operator.

Notice too that I do not define programs as being composed of modules. True, a program is generally made up of smaller sections of code. However, not all sections of code are specified separately from the program itself. Only certain special groups of code are defined as modules.

> **Module:** a nonexecutable set of machine instructions, needing a program to support its use. Modules handle small segments of common data processing problems for several programs.

Examples will clarify this definition. Almost every shop has a library that includes date verification, data formatting, and error message modules. Modules are chunks of code that need to be specified independently of programs because they are not unique to a single program.

ONLINE FUNCTION GROUP

Figure 3-5 shows the model for the online system function group. An online system is composed of one or more menus. Each menu contains a list of functions that the user can request. The functions are composed of one or more programs, which again may call upon one or more modules.

> **Online System:** an information system that processes data in real time. It meets one or more information needs of the user. The software of an online system communicates and interacts with the user during processing. Online systems are composed of groups of functions called menus.

Like the batch system element, the online system is a classification tool. It groups all the elements that compose an online system.

```
Online System
    Menu
      Function
        Program
          Module
```

FIGURE 3-5: Online Function Group

Menu: a screen image displayed on the user's monitor that lists system functions the user can select. Menus are composed of functions.

Menus are primarily logical. They may be created by a program or module but have no concrete existence of their own.

The menus of an online system define its functional structure. They can be organized into a menu map, an organization chart of all the system functions.

Function: a single, specific data processing task selected by the user and performed by one or more programs. Functions meet one information need of the user.

In some ways, the online function is similar to the batch subsystem. It meets a single information need; it consists of a sequence of manual and machine procedures.

Since online systems instruct users and operators, the functions can be seen as including jobs. Similarly, functions perform the same sequencing and initiating role as the batch run.

Like subsystems and menus, functions are logical elements. They exist in the perception of the user. The actual software that performs the function resides in programs.

Program: an executable set of machine instructions that will process data in a specified manner.

For online systems, the restrictions about machine setup and run time variables are removed from the definition of a program. This simply means that the program must assume responsibility for setting up data or display peripherals, and for acquiring run time parameters. This usually happens via dialog screens or prompt messages.

Module: a nonexecutable set of machine instructions needing a program to support its use. Modules handle small segments of common data processing problems for several programs.

The definition of *module* is the same for online systems as for batch systems. Modules are segments of code used by several programs in the system and are specified independently of the programs.

INFORMATION GROUP

We have examined the function group as it applies to batch and online systems. The remaining groups, information and exchange, apply to *both* batch and online systems.

Figure 3-6 shows the model of the information group. It shows that a file or data base contains one or more records. A record contains several data items. Here are definitions and explanations for each of the information elements.

> **File/Data Base:** an ordered collection of related records. A file is a physical collection of records, usually stored on a single physical device. A data base is a logical collection of records, stored on one or more devices as required.

Files and data bases are methods of classifying records. There are so many data base systems and schemes that it is impractical to suggest even a general model for a data base. Files, on the other hand, can be defined and specified in a general fashion.

Because a file is associated with a single physical storage medium, it assumes a different identity when transferred to another medium. The same collection of records on tape and on disk are different files.

The same reasoning applies to the sequence or order of the records in a file. When a group of records is sorted into a different sequence, it becomes a different file.

> **Record:** a specified collection of related data items, identified by one or more key data items.

This definition implies that slightly different collections of data items are completely different records. While this point may seem petty, it will save you hours of decision and headache when specifying your systems.

```
File / Data Base
Record
Data Item
```

FIGURE 3-6: Information Group

```
          Form
          Screen
          Report
          Message
```

FIGURE 3-7: Exchange Group

Data Item: the smallest meaningful piece of information in a system. A data item is a value in a context.

A data item is more than a field in a record. A field is merely a storage area. It becomes a data item only when the storage area has a context or meaning assigned to it and a value stored in it.

Data items are like chemical elements: They cannot be decomposed. Data items can be assembled into groups smaller than records, but these groups are not data items.

EXCHANGE GROUP

The exchange group, shown in Figure 3-7, contains system elements that exchange information between the system and the user. The group has no hierarchical structure. It is composed of four elements: form, screen, report, and message. Definitions and explanations of these elements follow.

Form: a source document prepared by the user which acts as input to a system. Forms are paper documents.

The term *form* is generally applied to a wide variety of items, including input forms, data screens, and report pages with pre-printed headings or columns. My definition of this system element restricts it to input prepared by a user on paper.

Screen: a display of information or text on a monitor, intended to gather input from or display output to a user. A screen is one complete visual unit, to be read as a whole. A screen usually occupies the entire display area of the monitor.

Compare this element with forms and reports, and you will

quickly spot the distinctions. Forms and reports are restricted to the medium of paper. A screen is restricted to the monitor. Forms are restricted to input and reports to output, but screens can function in either direction.

Screens can be further partitioned, according to their function and the kind of information they display, into menu screens, data screens, and dialog or talk screens. Menu screens present a list of functions to the user and solicit his or her selection. Data screens either display information or allow the user to enter or revise data. In this way, data screens are similar to forms and reports. Talk screens engage the user in dialogue, usually to gather parameters or run time variables for selected functions.

These distinctions are handy when describing a system in user manuals but are not necessary for the purpose of specifying a system.

> **Report:** an output document printed by the system. Reports convey information to the user. They are printed on paper.

This definition delimits the report element and distinguishes reports from forms and screens. The key attributes of reports are that they are output from the system and that they are restricted to the printed page.

> **Message:** a unit of text generated by a system, which advises a user or operator of unusual conditions encountered in operating any part of the system.

Messages are not restricted to any particular medium. They can appear on user screens, on the operator's console, or on reports, or they can be placed in files. They are used by the system to convey operating information to the reader or to solicit decisions and responses.

ASSEMBLING THE GROUPS

Before we continue, let's take a moment to summarize and survey what we've covered. Figures 3-8 and 3-9 show the complete batch and online system models. These models are created by assembling the appropriate function, information, and exchange groups.

```
Batch System
   Subsystem
      Transaction
      Job
      Run
         Program
            Module

File / Data Base
   Record
      Data Item

Form
Report
Message
```

FIGURE 3-8: Batch System Model

Each element in the system model can be specified. The element specifications give you a consistent, organized way of filling the System File. Information in the System File is used to build the software and manuals that make the system.

```
Online System
   Menu
      Function
         Program
            Module

File / Data Base
   Record
      Data Item

Screen
Report
Message
```

FIGURE 3-9: Online System Model

As I said at the outset, these are the most detailed models you will ever need to use. They result from partitioning the system as far as is practical and consistent with our purpose. Having seen the detailed models, you are ready to learn how to simplify them.

CUSTOMIZING THE MODELS

I have shown you not only the system models I use but also how I developed them. I did this so that you could create your own models or customize my models to match your particular shop and products. You may need to customize the system models to better meet the information needs of your system players. You may also want to scale the models up or down to suit the size of your systems or the size of your shop.

You have already learned how to select and define a new system element, so I will devote the rest of this chapter to showing you how to eliminate elements from the models. In most cases system elements are not simply discarded; rather, they are absorbed into superior elements. Let's look at the common element groups one by one.

BATCH FUNCTION GROUP

As we have seen, the batch system and subsystem specifications do not define physical elements. They show the relationships between subordinate elements—the transactions, jobs, runs, and programs. I want to discourage you from eliminating system and subsystem specifications, since they are vehicles for recording this valuable information.

The best way to reduce the functional elements in the batch model is to incorporate transactions, runs, and jobs into the subsystem element. When you do this, the subsystem specification not only *lists* but also *contains* these subordinate elements.

Job specifications can also be grouped into manuals that are global for your shop. Examples of such manuals are keypunch specification binders or operator manuals.

You may decide to eliminate the formal specification of modules and rely on your knowledge of available library routines. Alter-

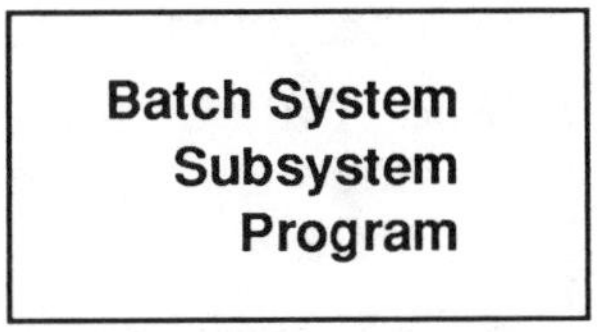

```
┌─────────────────┐
│  Batch System   │
│   Subsystem     │
│    Program      │
└─────────────────┘
```

FIGURE 3-10: Small Batch System Model

nately, module specifications can be incorporated into your program specifications.

For small batch systems, you could use a model such as the one shown in Figure 3-10. This model uses only three elements: the batch system, the subsystem, and the program.

In this case, the system specification shows how the subsystems are related. The subsystem element includes transactions, jobs, and runs. The job information tells the user how to request the subsystem. The run information tells the operator how to run the program or sequence of programs. The transaction information shows the user how to accomplish each subsystem function.

ONLINE FUNCTION GROUP

Similarly, you can use a simplified system model for small online systems. This model is shown in Figure 3-11.

This model has only two elements, the online system and the function. Reducing the system model to this extent is possible only when the system has a simple menu structure and when programs and functions are essentially identical. As with the batch system, online module specifications can be incorporated into the program or function.

The online system element shows the relationships between the

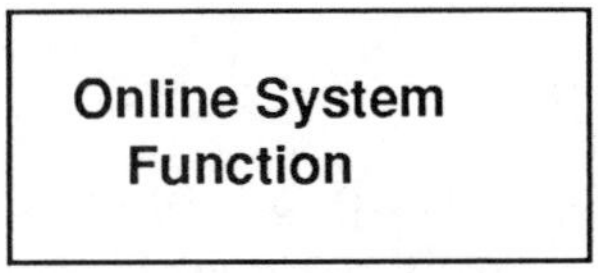

```
┌─────────────────┐
│  Online System  │
│    Function     │
└─────────────────┘
```

FIGURE 3-11: Small Online System Model

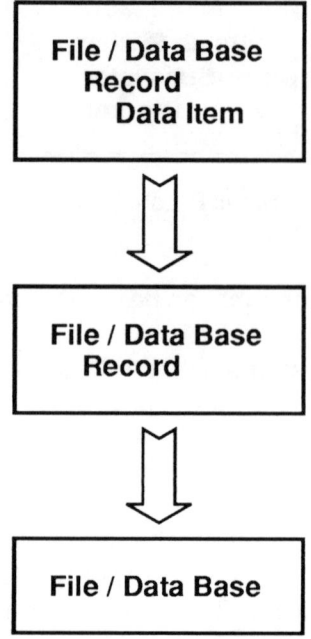

FIGURE 3-12: Collapsed Information Groups

functions. The function element combines both menu and program information.

INFORMATION GROUP

The information group is the easiest to collapse, as shown in Figure 3-12. As you can see, the data item can be incorporated into the record element. The record specification then includes brief definitions of the data items. The next step is to collapse the record into the file or data base item. Thus, file specifications would include record layouts, which in turn would include data item definitions.

EXCHANGE GROUP

Elements in the exchange group cannot be collapsed into each other. They must be deleted entirely from your system model or collapsed into elements in the function group.

Screens and reports can be collapsed into programs. The program specification would then include screen and report layouts and definitions of calculated data items.

For batch systems, information about input forms can be incorporated into a general keypunch manual. Similarly, information about preparing and distributing reports can be grouped into a global data control manual.

Messages need not be specified individually, provided they are included in program specifications.

4

Filling the System File with Specifications

PROBLEM: You got the project done on time, but only because you forgot about the documentation until later. But "later" never comes. Gradually, the existing system documentation becomes outdated and worthless.

SOLUTION: Do the documentation (in the form of specifications) *before* the coding. There is tremendous staff motivation to create this kind of in-line documentation as part of the project because it provides the system builders—in fact all the system players—with the information they need to do their jobs.

Specifications serve several purposes. Their primary role is to enable the system builders to build the various elements that compose the system. But the system specifications also meet the information needs of other system players.

Specifications are the primary documentation in the System File. From this primary information, secondary or derived documents can be created. This arrangement is illustrated in Figure 4-1.

In the last chapter, I suggested two steps to follow when you are deciding how to specify your system: define the elements that comprise the system, and determine which attributes about each element need to be specified. In the last chapter we tackled the first step. In this chapter we'll start the second step by establishing a general or theoretical framework for specifying system elements. A

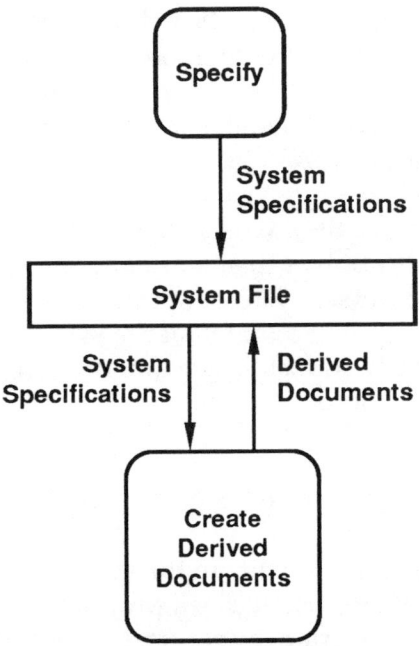

FIGURE 4-1: Primary and Derived Documentation

specification defines or lists the critical attributes of a system element. In Chapters 5 through 8, I will show you the critical attributes for each element in the system models.

HOW TO DETERMINE ATTRIBUTES

Of course, you need not choose the same attributes as those I present in this text. But if you want to determine which attributes to specify for yourself, be aware that selecting attributes differs from selecting system elements.

When you develop a system model, you partition and classify information about systems into various elements. Your purpose is to organize the information more effectively. However, when you select attributes for specification, your purpose is to design an effective *documentation system*. The process of selecting which attributes of an element you will specify is part of the analysis and design process for the documentation system. You are selecting the data items of your documentation system.

You will be attempting to satisfy all the information needs of all the system players. Thus, the methods and selection criteria are different.

As in selecting system elements, experience and exposure are useful in selecting attributes. You will be exposed to a wide variety of attributes in this text.

The acid test for deciding whether or not to include a particular attribute in a specification is this: Does anyone need to know this information? Or conversely: Have I specified everything about this element that needs to be known by all the system players?

Remember to apply your skill as a system engineer to the process of designing specifications.

LOGICAL AND PHYSICAL ATTRIBUTES

We have seen that some elements in the system model are physical and some are logical. For example, a program is physical; it has a concrete existence. A function, by contrast, is logical; it exists only in the perception of the user. Similarly, some attributes of system elements are physical, while others are logical.

When you specify the fields in a record, you are specifying the actual physical mapping of magnetic storage media. The language, operating system, and hardware determine which attributes you must specify about the field. However, when you specify a data item, you are specifying a logical system element. The data item has a certain size, regardless of how it is stored physically. The size of a data item is a logical attribute.

The nature and values of physical attributes are largely determined by the hardware and software environment of your shop. For logical attributes, you will need to devise your own schemes of defining and recording values. These need to be simple, clear, and consistent.

While physical attributes are designed to satisfy the environment of your shop, logical attributes are designed to satisfy the needs of the system players. I've defined the following system players:

- User
- Designer
- Builder
- Installer

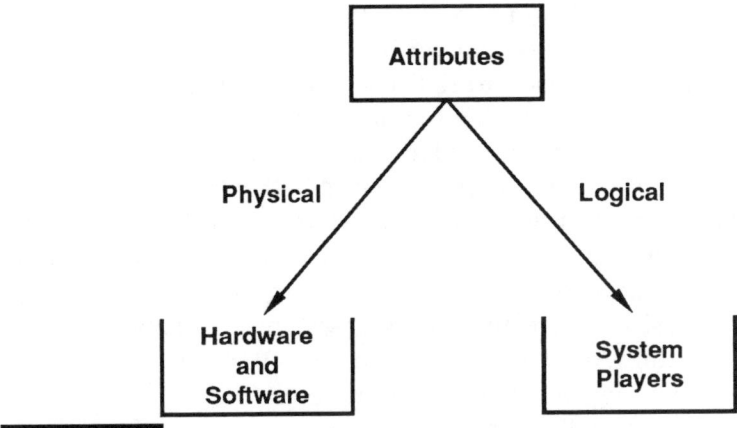

FIGURE 4-2: Logical and Physical Attributes

- Operator
- Supporter

See Figure 4-2 for a graphic representation of the split between physical and logical attributes.

HARD AND SOFT ATTRIBUTES

One of the primary objectives in the design of any information system is to reduce or eliminate redundancy of data. Considering how to supply and control redundancy in documentation systems led me to distinguish between hard and soft attributes.

Some relationships between system elements are revealed only when you consider specifying their attributes. Consider the relationship called "contains" and its inverse, "part of." Attributes that describe the "contains" relationship are hard, while those that describe the "part of" relationship are soft.

Let me give you some examples. A record "contains" several data items. A list of the data items is a hard attribute of the record. Without this information the record cannot be created. However, the record that a data item is "part of" is a soft attribute. A data item can be part of several records. You don't need to know which records it is part of in order to specify or create the data item.

There is no simple or logical way of ensuring that soft attributes are maintained. They are a form of redundant information. When you revise a record specification, adding a data item to the record, there is no immediate reason to revise the data item specification.

Soft attributes should not be included in specifications; only a pointer to this information is needed. Rather than keeping a list of the records that a data item is part of, it is better to scan all of the record specifications to find which records contain that data item. Then you can compile a *temporary* list for presentation in the data item specification as a soft attribute of the data item.

Similarly, consider the relationships "uses" and "used by." "Uses" is a hard attribute, while "used by" is a soft attribute. Here is an example, to make the concepts more concrete.

Programs use files. They read and write them, extract from them and revise them. Thus, a list of the files that a program uses is an essential part of its specification—a hard attribute. A list of the programs that a file is "used by" is a soft attribute. This soft attribute should not be a part of the file specification. Rather, your documen-

Programs \ Files	PAYMAST	HOURRATE	TIMESHT	PAYADJ	PAYSCHED	PERMAST
PAY101			I		I/O	
PAY104				I	I/O	
PAY105	I/O	I			I	
PAY106			I	I/O		I
PAY201	I	I/O		O	I	
PAY205	I/O			I		
PAY215	I/O	I/O		O		
PAY216	I/O			O	I	I

FIGURE 4-3: Melanson Chart

tation system should provide you with a current and temporary display of the programs that a given file is used by.

Finally, consider the relationships "creates" and "is created by." As an example, a program creates a screen. This is a hard attribute of the program. Inversely, a screen is created by a program, but this is a soft attribute of the screen.

In situations where each screen in your system is created by one (and only one) program, it may make sense to treat the "created by" or "source" of the screens as hard attributes and include them in the screen specifications. The same is true of reports and messages. However, I suggest that you treat the source of all screens, reports, and messages as soft attributes. This approach makes it easier to keep redundancy to a minimum and keeps your system designs flexible.

It is obvious that I am discussing capabilities that are possible only with a computer-based documentation system. The effort required to scan dozens or even hundreds of specifications in order to compile soft attributes prohibits a purely manual documentation system.

One common example of a manual approach to handling hard and soft attributes is the familiar cross-reference chart. The correct name for this graphic tool is the Melanson chart. Whatever the name, the tool is the same. This kind of chart shows the relationship between two system elements. Figure 4-3 is a sample Melanson chart, prepared for the programs and files of a hypothetical payroll system.

It is a simple matter to determine which files a given program uses. You need only read the program specification or program listing. Since the "uses" relationship is a hard attribute, the program must reflect the files it uses. The purpose of the sample Melanson chart is to record the soft attribute, the "used by" relationship between a file and the programs.

This manual approach to handling soft attributes calls for faithful maintenance of the chart. Each time a program or file is added to the system, each time a program is revised to use an additional file, the chart must be updated.

While Melanson charts are often a useful memory aid for small shops and small systems, the cost of maintaining them becomes prohibitive in other situations. In addition, there are dozens of other possible relationships between system elements that need to be recorded on such charts. Some examples are

- Data item to file
- Data item to form, screen, or report
- Message to program
- File to report
- Program to run

The Melanson chart is used one row or column at a time. You either want to know which files are used by a given program or which programs use a given file. With an automated documentation system, inquiries of this type can be answered by a simple list, representing a single row or column of the chart. You can specify which elements and which relationship you are curious about.

As you can see, documentation is a perfect application for a data base system that includes a query language.

COMMON ATTRIBUTES

All system elements have certain attributes in common. These attributes must appear in the specification, no matter which element you are specifying. Examples are the name, label, and purpose of the element. Let's discuss the common attributes before we examine individual element specifications.

NAME

People identify system elements by their names. Never underestimate the importance of naming and names. Names have the power to crystallize ideas, to clarify thought, and to aid understanding. It is important to create a meaningful name for each system element you specify. There are three techniques to keep in mind, techniques you are already familiar with.

First, remember your audience. Whatever it is that makes names meaningful, they must be meaningful to the people who use them.

Second, use the technique for creating definitions when creating names. After all, a meaningful name is often a capsule definition of the object it names. The technique is first to classify the object and then to differentiate it from other objects in that class.

Third, be prepared to test your names. Often, you can decide the name of a function or report by surveying your user community. When creating a new element, involve the users or other system players in the naming process.

LABEL

Many of the elements in computer systems must be identified to the software and hardware. I call this identifier the "label." For example, while people may identify a file by the name "Employee Master File," this name is meaningless to the software that actually creates and maintains the file. The software may need to refer to the file by its label, say "EMPLMAST." If your system products are implemented in multiple programming languages, or for several operating or hardware systems, you may need to assign a label for each version of the element.

The format of labels is out of your control, dictated by the software and hardware manufacturer. Take forms, for example. There is no problem with the name of the form. It is the same as the one printed on the form. The computer system does not need a label to identify the form, but the form may have other identifiers, such as a form control number. If this identifier is used by a forms department within your company, or by a printer, you cannot determine its format or values.

To your documentation system, the form control number is a label, an identifier, that is beyond your control. To ensure that you keep control of the information about and relationships between the system elements you specify, you need an identifier that is completely within your control: the element number.

NUMBER

Name, label, and number are all system element identifiers. The name identifies the element to people; the label to software and hardware. The *number* identifies the system element to your documentation system. I wish I had a better term for this identifier, for the "number" is seldom a purely numeric value. It usually includes alphabetical system identifier and element type codes. However, *number* is the best term I have been able to devise, and the phrase "name, number, and label" has a certain resonance and coherence.

You can think of the number as the identifier for the system specification, while the label is the identifier for the system element itself. Alternately, you can consider the element number as a record key in situations where each specification is a data base record.

You have complete control over the format and values of the element number. This allows you to build and link your documentation system without having to anticipate or respond to changes made by your software or hardware vendors.

The number is used to point to the location of soft attribute information. It is also used to link basic elements into higher-level elements. As an example, you could link several data items into a record. The record specification would include the numbers of its component data items as hard attributes.

The element number is the *primary* identifier within your documentation system. In brief, when you know the element number you can access the name, label, or any other attribute defined in the element specification. The element number is a hard attribute. It is the pointer that allows your documentation system to create and display all soft attributes.

This approach lets you select which attributes are displayed to a given audience, thereby making specifications more useful to that audience. For example, software builders need the labels and perhaps the names of the files used by the programs they are building. Programmers do not need to know other attributes defined in the file specification, such as a user-oriented description or the backup and retention planned for the file. By including only the file number in your program specification, you can let your documentation system determine which attributes of the file will appear as soft attributes.

The format of system element numbers depends on your approach to documentation system design and on how you plan to store and access element specifications. The simplest format is a pure serial number. You may also want to divide element numbers by system or even by element type within system.

I have found the following format to be generally useful: SSST999. The SSS portion is a three-letter system acronym. The T represents the element type code and is a single letter. See Table 4-1 for a suggested list of element type codes. The numeric portion is a pure serial number. For example, the fourth file created for a payroll system might bear the number PAYF004.

TEXT, TEST, AND MANUAL ELEMENTS

You will find three new elements in this table: the text, test, and manual elements. These represent some approaches to system documentation you may wish to explore by yourself.

It is possible to compile many useful reference manuals simply

Code	Element
D	Data Item
F	File
I	Form
E	Function
J	Job
Z	Manual
C	Menu
N	Message
M	Module
P	Program
R	Record
O	Report
Q	Run
S	Screen
B	Subsystem
X	Test

TABLE 4-1: Element Codes

by grouping element specifications and augmenting them with sections of narrative text. Such text and manual elements can be specified as you would any other system element.

The manual specification defines the manual itself. It may contain lists of system elements, or it may define a program to assemble and print the manual. Note that such manuals are created from the latest versions of the system specifications found in the System File.

Remember that some parts of a system test are worth saving against future revisions and testing. If you decide to save information on tests, the ideal place to store it is in the System File. This requires a test element in your system model, and hence a test specification. The test specification may be nothing more than a simplified version of your original test plan. It may list or point to stored files of test data.

PURPOSE AND DESCRIPTION

Each specification should also include a statement of purpose or a description of the element. What is the difference between these two attributes? Some definitions may help to clarify your thinking and guide your use of these two similar attributes.

Purpose: the object for which a thing exists or is done.

The purpose attribute is a concise summary of the primary purpose of the element. To keep this text concise, try to limit your statement of purpose to a single sentence or a short paragraph.

This attribute does two things. It gives the initial reader (the system builder) an overview and introduction to the element being created. It also answers later inquiries of the form, Which program creates the new Master File at year end? The purpose attribute is an expanded definition of the element. It gives you more information than the element name.

Description: a verbal picture of an activity or object.

A description is a textual approach to presenting information. It is a verbal image of the element being described. Again, this attribute should be a concise summary, useful to all the system players. Limit your descriptions to between one and three paragraphs.

The effectiveness of purpose and description statements depends (as always) on writing them for a specific audience. In some cases, you may need to write two statements of purpose, one for the technical system players, one for the nontechnical. As an example, you could state the purpose of a function in two distinct ways. One purpose would be written in technical terms that would help a system builder create the function. Another purpose would be written for the user and would be expressed in terms of the business problem the function solves for the user.

NOTES

Include an undefined attribute called "notes" in all of your element specifications. You can think of this as an expansion area used to hold information your documentation system could otherwise not accommodate.

The notes section can hold messages about pending revisions, record additional descriptive text, or explain deviations from shop or system standards.

I do not mention this attribute in the individual element specifications that follow. However, it is *always* included in every specification. I leave it to you to remember this attribute when designing your own specifications.

DOCUMENT CONTROL

Several other attributes must appear on each specification, attributes that pertain to document control. I will not repeat these in the discussions that follow. You must remember that these attributes belong with each specification you create. Here are the document control attributes.

NAME

It is important to include a name or title for each *specification*. This provides a quick way of distinguishing between similar specifications. It may also indicate where specifications belong in the System File. If the element number does not implicitly identify the system and element type, be sure the specification name does so.

PREPARED BY

Include the name of the person who wrote or revised the specification. It shows the reader whom to contact for clarification or additional information about the specification.

DATE

Show the creation or revision date on each specification. The date provides a quick method of distinguishing between different versions of the same specification. Specifications with later dates are assumed to be the most current and correct versions.

PROJECT NUMBER

By including the project number on each specification, you link the System File to the Project File. The project number is the number of the project that created or last revised the specification. Figure 4-4 illustrates how the project number links your system and project files. Such linking lets you trace the reasons, history, and costs behind revisions to system specifications.

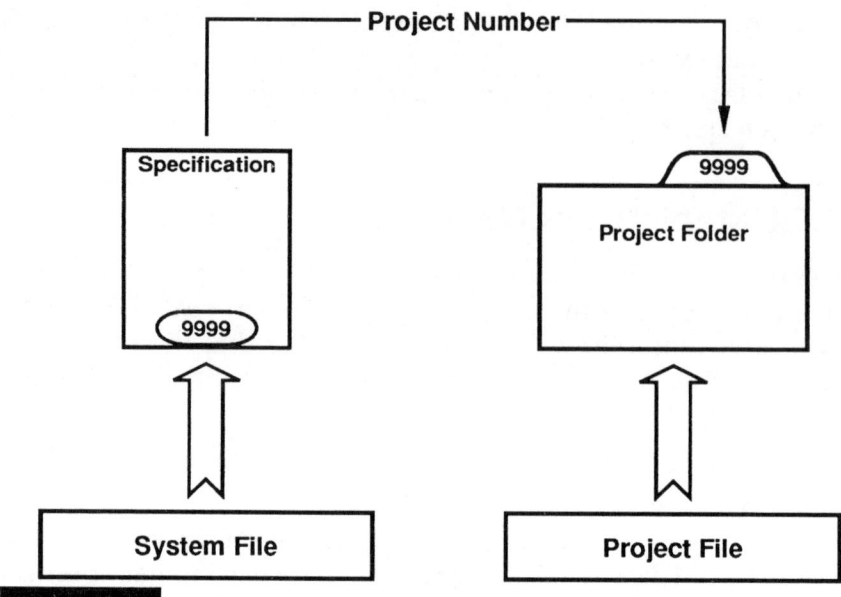

FIGURE 4-4: Linking Project and System Files

PAGE NUMBER

How you paginate system specifications depends on how they are assembled into documents. It is possible to omit this control information from individual specifications, adding it only when manuals are assembled. However, if an individual specification requires two or more pages, be sure to include pagination in the format "Page 9 of 9." This shows the reader the correct sequence and page count of the specification.

Taken together, the common attributes form a template for all system element specifications. The template is shown in Figure 4-5. I will use this template through the following four chapters, as we examine the specification of each system element in the system models.

DESIGNING SPECIFICATIONS

The creation of system specifications is a process of documentation. It will prove useful to examine the design of your specifications against the steps in the documentation process: plan, draft, edit, review, release, and maintain.

```
┌─────────────────────────────────────────┬──────────────┐
│     System Element Specification        │    Number    │
│                Name                     │    Label     │
└─────────────────────────────────────────┴──────────────┘
┌────────────────────────────────────────────────────────┐
│              Purpose or Description                    │
│                                                        │
└────────────────────────────────────────────────────────┘
┌────────────────────────────────────────────────────────┐
│                                                        │
│                                                        │
│                                                        │
│              Specific Attributes                       │
│                of the Element                          │
│                                                        │
│                                                        │
│                                                        │
└────────────────────────────────────────────────────────┘
┌────────────────────────────────────────────────────────┐
│                     Notes                              │
│                                                        │
└────────────────────────────────────────────────────────┘
┌──────────────┬──────────────┬──────────────┬──────────┐
│   Prepared   │     Date     │    Project   │   Page   │
└──────────────┴──────────────┴──────────────┴──────────┘
```

FIGURE 4-5: Specification Template

PLAN

You have already started planning your specifications by developing your system model. The system model defines a library of system specifications that you will create.

For each specification you must have a clear definition of the audience and purpose. State each specification's purpose and goals in terms of the information needs of the system players, the readers of the specifications and derived documentation. Determine the subject matter of your specifications by selecting which attributes about each element you will specify.

Part of the planning process is selecting the medium you will use. In this chapter I present the specifications as printed forms. This is primarily to help you grasp each specification as a whole. It is not intended to suggest that you limit your specifications to this medium. On the contrary, I encourage you to automate your documentation system, using online screens to capture and maintain your specifications.

DRAFT

During the process of drafting system specifications, you will develop the appropriate techniques for recording each attribute. I'll show you some simple and useful charting methods. In addition, I'll suggest some standards and conventions for recording attributes.

The text portions of the system specifications I suggest are few and small. You should have no difficulty with creating the text you need. You may wish to read Chapters 9 and 10 for suggestions on improving your text writing skills.

EDIT

Confine your editing efforts to creating an effective format for displaying specifications. This includes the screen and printed versions of each type of specification. Evaluating the accuracy and completeness of specifications belongs in the next step, review.

REVIEW

Before you finalize the design of each specification, review your efforts. Compare the specification to your plan for its purpose, audience, and subject. Test the specification by having it reviewed by its intended audience. Does it meet their information needs?

RELEASE AND MAINTAIN

Part of the design of your documentation system is a plan for the controlled release and maintenance of system specifications. Make sure you have a method of distinguishing production and developmental versions of the specifications. Make sure your design includes a method for distributing specification revisions to the appropriate system players in a timely fashion.

STORAGE AND RETRIEVAL

The design of your specifications also depends on how you plan to store and access them. There are two main approaches: global and system-by-system.

In the global approach, all specifications are created, stored, and accessed without regard to separate system products. This approach is useful when you are creating a "family" of systems designed to interface and interact with each other. The System File contains specifications for all elements used in all of your products.

The system-by-system approach distinguishes element specifications by which system product they apply to. Each product has a separate System File, holding specifications and derived documentation for only that system.

If you produce a printed version of your System File, organize the specifications to make access simple for the readers. This usually means separating the specifications into manuals or binders. If you use the global approach, divide the specifications into their element types. For example, you would create separate binders for form, screen, and report specifications. If you use the system-by-system approach, organize the specifications into separate binders for the different systems.

Within each binder, order the specifications by the identifier most commonly used by the readers. For example, a user is more likely to remember a data item name than its number or label. Consequently, when data item specifications are assembled into a data dictionary, they are sequenced alphabetically by data item name. On the other hand, a software builder is more likely to want a program reference manual organized by the program labels.

I will leave you to resolve the remaining design problems for your documentation system. Now it is time to examine the specifications and attributes of each element in the system models.

Perhaps a little reassurance is in order before you start. The number of elements and the lists of their attributes can seem overwhelming when you are first exposed to them.

First of all, realize that there are no new elements in any of the system models I have presented. You are already designing and building all of these elements in one form or another. Also, the elements actually represent categories into which information about your system can be divided. They are simply "slots" in which you store the information.

A second point to bear in mind is that there are no new attributes associated with the elements. You are already creating and using this information. The specification process discussed in this chapter is simply a systematic way of recording the information.

5

Specifying the Batch Function Group

This is the first of four chapters that detail the specification of system elements. We divided the elements into four groups: the batch function group, the online function group, the information group, and the exchange group. This chapter details the attributes used to specify elements in the batch function group. Here again are the elements in this group, presented in a structured list.

    Batch System
        Subsystem
            Transaction
            Job
            Run
                Program
                      Module

BATCH SYSTEM

As I have already pointed out, the batch system specification defines a logical entity. I don't mean to imply that information systems do not have a very real and physical existence. Some of their parts are purely physical. But the entire batch system is composed of so many varied elements that it is hard to think of it as a single object.

An additional reason to keep the system specification general and logical is that it must address all of the system players. This is the most diverse audience any system document need be written for. The purpose of the system specification is to convey an overview of the functions, structure, and operation of the system.

You can draw heavily on information in the product design document to create a system specification. Indeed, the product design itself can act as the system specification, with some removal of design details and the addition of a system chart.

To the logical design information in the product design you will need to add some physical attributes. The system model shows that a batch system is composed of subsystems. The system specification must identify those subsystems and show how they are related.

The format of the system specification includes both text and graphics. This format is common to several system elements, including run and screen specifications. You could treat the text portions of these specifications as one part and the charts as another, creating a System Specification A and System Specification B. This is useful when you produce text and graphics with different tools. Of course, all parts of the specification can also be considered as one single document. Figure 5-1 shows the first page of the batch system specification. The details of each attribute are discussed separately.

A word of caution about the figures you'll see in the next few chapters. I illustrate the specifications in Chapters 5 through 8 as if they were single-page forms. Of course it is often impossible to fit the required information onto a single page. These forms are intended to give you a quick, visual overview of the specifications.

NAME

Obviously, the name of the system should be meaningful to the user. This is also an important marketing consideration whether you are selling your product to the general public or to a department within your company.

The system name should give the user an idea of what the system does, what its primary purpose is. What business or information problem does the system solve?

NUMBER

The number is the identifier used by the documentation system. It is usually an acronym of the system name, in the format SSS. This

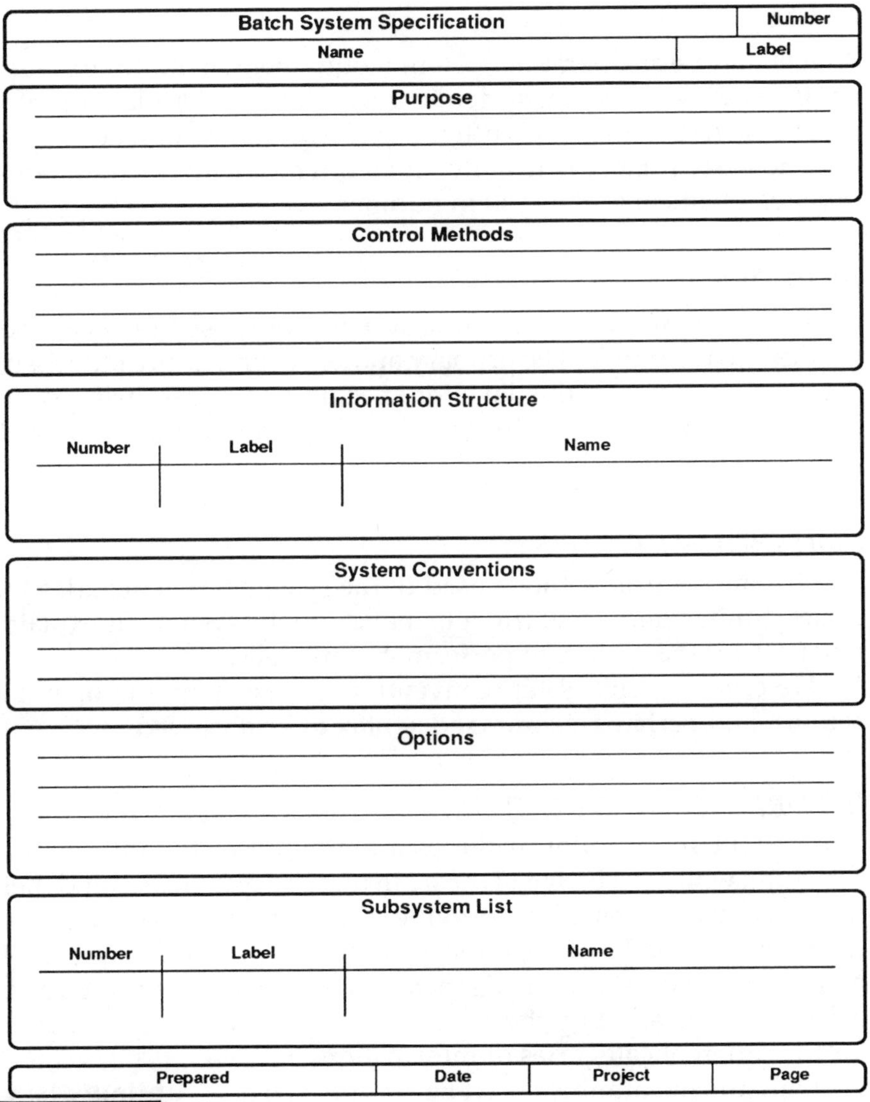

Batch System Specification

Batch System Specification	Number
Name	Label

Purpose

Control Methods

Information Structure

Number | Label | Name

System Conventions

Options

Subsystem List

Number | Label | Name

Prepared | Date | Project | Page

FIGURE 5-1: Batch System Specification

number may prefix all other system specification or element numbers.

This identifier can also be a short form of the system name, useful both to the users and to your technical staff.

LABEL

A label may be an operating system requirement in multiple system environments. It can also define a standard system label prefix. Application data file labels often begin with the system label.

The system label is usually an acronym for the system name, perhaps identical to the system number.

PURPOSE

Create a condensed version of the system's purpose from the product design document. The primary audience for this attribute is still the user, but even at this level of specification it can help you to distinguish among a multitude of small information system products in your shop.

CONTROL METHODS

Specify the control methods used in the system. This includes the cycles, timing, and event triggers that drive the system. It explains what causes the system to perform its functions.

Here, you specify system conventions for user requests, operator actions, and perhaps a command syntax to be observed.

INFORMATION STRUCTURE

The system specification includes a definition of the information structure, which is a listing of the main files the system uses and their relationships. This attribute provides the users and system builders with a simple model of the information processed by the system. It helps them understand, in a general way, the kinds and groups of information handled by the system. This attribute specifies names for the different categories of information.

Only the file numbers need be specified as hard attributes here. Using these, your documentation system can access the file specifications for the file names and descriptions. You may wish to supplement these with diagrams or text that show how the files interact.

SYSTEM CONVENTIONS

It is important to design and record the conventions used within a system. Specifying the system conventions helps project teams create and maintain the system.

This attribute records the general design principles and includes such conventions as these:

- Date formats
- Run or report requests
- File labeling
- Error handling

OPTIONS

Specify the system-wide options available. Such options are usually controlled by a parameter file. An example of a system option is the company name printed on reports. Factors, rates, and percentages to be used in calculations are another kind of system option.

This attribute specifies which options are available and shows how to exercise them.

SUBSYSTEM LIST

The batch system is composed of subsystems. Hence, its specification includes a list of the subsystems. Only the subsystem number need be specified as a hard attribute. The subsystem specifications will yield the label, name, frequency, purpose, or other attributes of the subsystem.

SYSTEM CHART

The subsystem list must be supplemented with a chart showing the relationships and connections between the subsystems. Users, builders, and supporters all need the information shown by the system chart.

The system chart takes the form of a block diagram. On it, each subsystem is shown as a single black box; only the input and output that connects the subsystems is shown outside of these boxes. I refer to this as "absolute" input and output.

Data flow diagrams work well for a system chart. Any simple block diagramming technique will do; even conventional flowchart symbols work well.

The system chart may refer to attached lists of transactions, reports, and so on, that are too long to include on the chart itself. Generate such lists by specifying only the appropriate element

104 • System Documentation

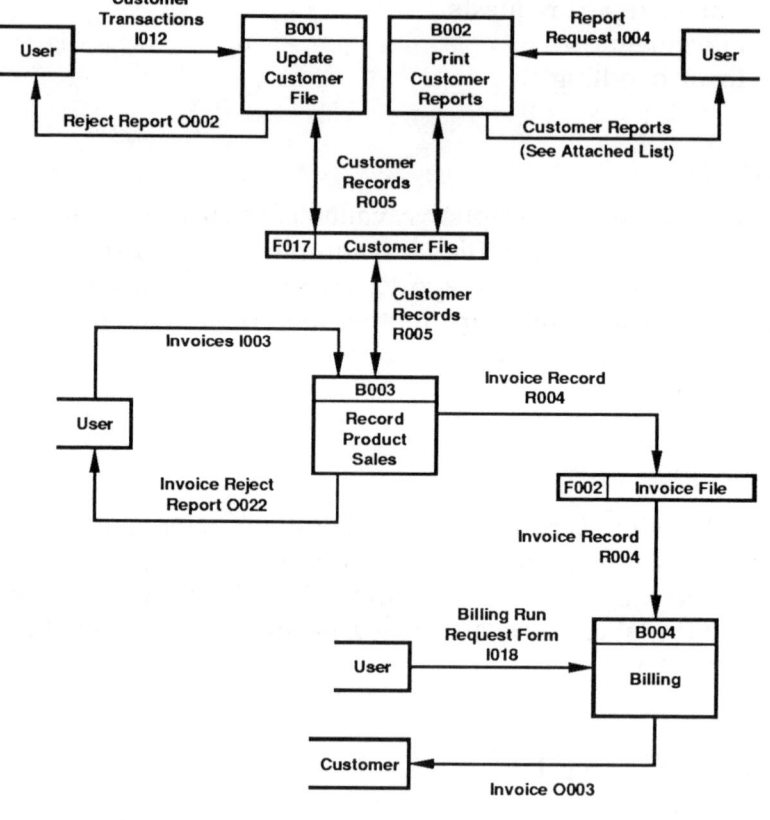

FIGURE 5-2: Batch System Chart

numbers, and let your documentation system provide names or labels as soft attributes. Figure 5-2 shows a sample system chart for a hypothetical batch system.

Each element shown on the chart is identified by a segment of its element number and by the element name. For example, the element in the upper left corner of the chart is an input form, number I012. This is the Customer Transactions form.

SUBSYSTEM

The subsystem specification has two distinct audiences and purposes. First, the designer uses it to decompose the user's overall information needs into discrete groups and to convey this partitioning to the system builder. Second, the user reads it to understand each subsystem in terms of the major functions of the system. In other words, the specification shows the user which subsystems meet which information needs.

Like the batch system, the subsystem is more logical than physical. It is a collection of transactions, jobs, and runs, which performs a single information processing task. The ideal format for this specification is a combination of text and chart. The text portion of the specification is sketched out in Figure 5-3.

NAME

The subsystem name should be meaningful to the user. When a batch system is not transaction-driven, the subsystem is the user's basic processing unit.

The subsystem name should identify the information need that the subsystem meets. This is not a technical or system-oriented name. Rather, it should be expressed in terms of the job the user is performing with the aid of the subsystem.

NUMBER

The subsystem number is the standard identifier used by the documentation system. It will have the usual format: SSSB999.

LABEL

The subsystem does not need a machine identifier, or label. This attribute may record an abbreviation or acronym of the subsystem name as a useful short-form identifier that the technical and nontechnical system players can use. For example, the label for a Month End Reporting Subsystem could be MER.

PURPOSE

The purpose section of the specification names and defines the

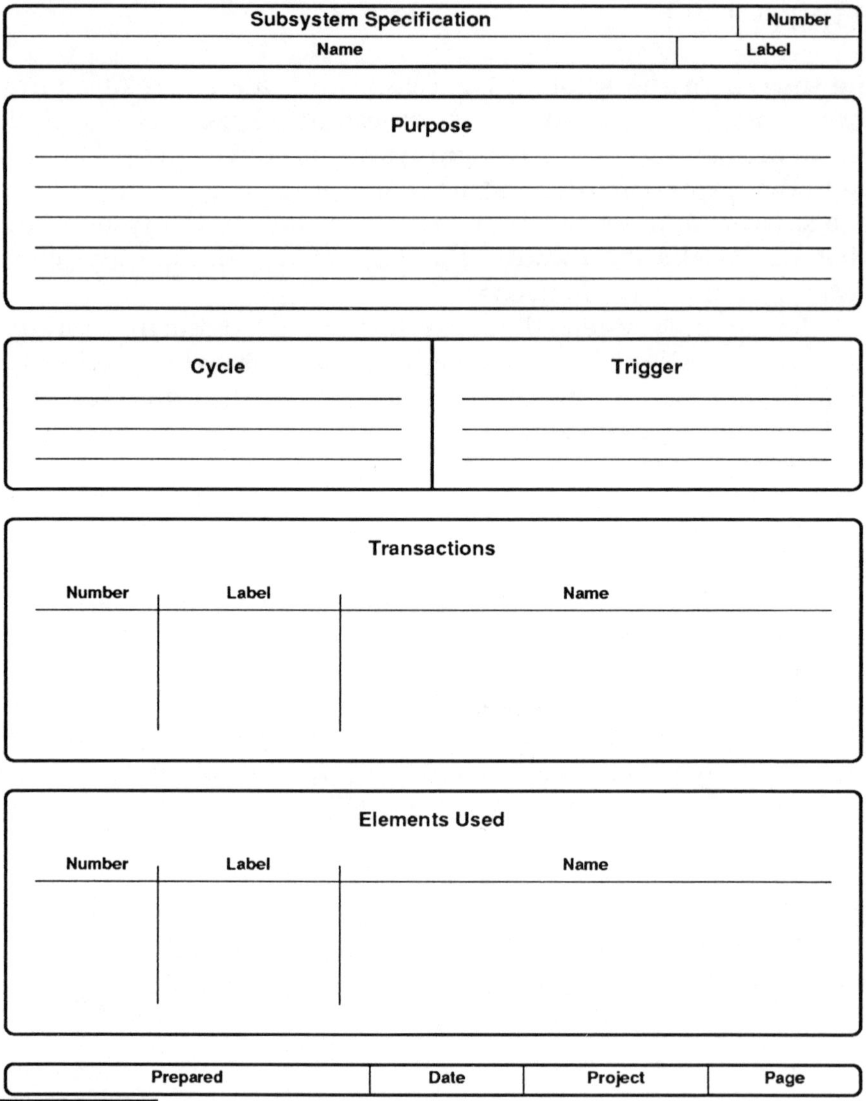

Subsystem Specification

Subsystem Specification		Number
Name		Label

Purpose

Cycle

Trigger

Transactions

Number	Label	Name

Elements Used

Number	Label	Name

Prepared	Date	Project	Page

FIGURE 5-3: Subsystem Specification

subsystem processing tasks and explains to the user exactly what the subsystem does.

These information needs can usually be met with the same statement of purpose, since the subsystem is strongly tied to the information needs of the user at a high level of system functionality.

The subsystem is a way of grouping one or more processing

functions that share some common factor, such as cycle, files used, or reports produced. Make sure you state the common factor in the purpose attribute.

CYCLE

Most batch systems operate on fixed cycles: daily, weekly, monthly, and yearly. The cycle attribute specifies how often and when the subsystem operates.

To specify the cycle you can use the format Number per Period, that is, the number of times the subsystem operates in the specified period—for example, 1 per Day, 2 per Month. Another common cycle for subsystems is "on demand," that is, whenever the user requests it.

TRIGGER

You may also need to specify the trigger events—the events that trigger operation of the subsystem. Trigger events include specific dates and system events. The trigger attribute can also be used to record the number of the triggering element, such as a request form or transaction.

TRANSACTIONS

If the system is transaction based, it is helpful to the users, support staff, and maintenance programmers to provide a list of the transactions handled by the subsystem. Specify only the transaction numbers as hard attributes. Your documentation system can provide the transaction label and name from the transaction specification.

ELEMENTS USED

Since a subsystem is a logical grouping of system elements, it makes sense to record the elements used. This attribute can take the form of a list, supplemented by the subsystem chart.

List the elements that compose the subsystem: form, job, run, file, and report. The numbers of these elements are hard attributes of the subsystem. They are needed to build and operate the subsystem. Specify only the element numbers, and let your documentation system supply additional, soft attributes.

108 • System Documentation

SUBSYSTEM CHART

Note that the "elements used" attribute does not show the relationships between the elements. The list of elements used must be supplemented by a subsystem chart. See Figure 5-4 for a sample subsystem chart.

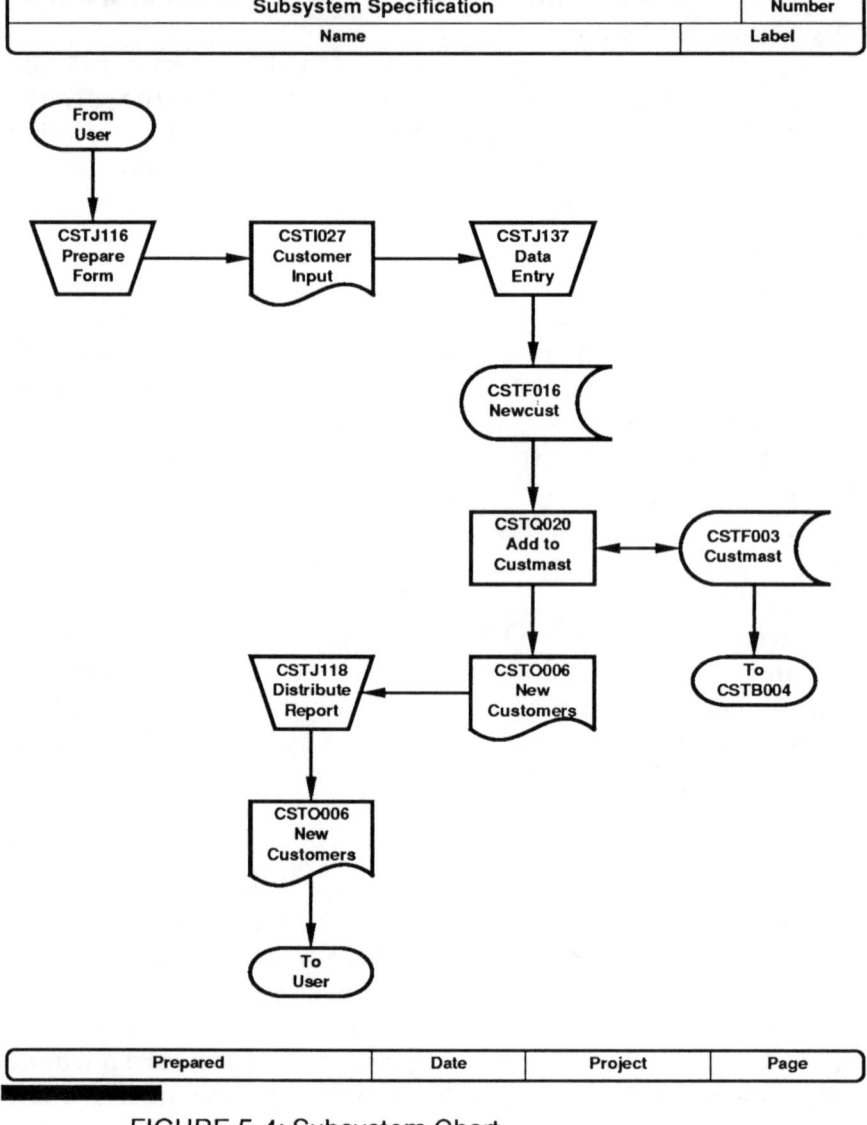

FIGURE 5-4: Subsystem Chart

The subsystem chart reduces the elements of the subsystem to black boxes. It shows only absolute input and output from the runs connecting the elements.

Remember that, except in extremely unusual situations, the user will be the ultimate source and destination of all information in the subsystem. Exceptions occur when system maintenance or operating functions are grouped into one subsystem. Here, the source and destination of the subsystem information may be files or other subsystems.

The data flow diagram is a useful charting technique for subsystems, although most of the subsystem is physical rather than logical. If you use a data flow diagram for the subsystem chart, specify the element numbers as hard attributes but display the physical element labels wherever possible. For example, process boxes in the chart will represent either jobs (processes done by people) or runs (processes done by machines). In addition, consider using labels for the files and forms, supplemented with their names.

The "elements used" attribute can also be given as an appendix to the subsystem chart. This list of elements shows the name, number, and label of each item on the chart. Such a list can make the chart useful to both users and builders.

You may want to automate the production of several different forms of system chart. To do this, specify the symbols of the chart itself, identified only by their element numbers. Your documentation system can then print the chart with either numbers, labels, or names, according to the specific audience for which a version of the chart is being prepared.

TRANSACTION

Like subsystems, transactions are primarily a logical grouping of physical system elements. Transactions exist in the mind of the user.

You can specify transactions as system elements in their own right or as an alternate way of recording information found in the job and run specifications. Transactions are another perspective on system information. They are analogous to the functions of an online system.

Transaction specifications are primarily addressed to the user. They show the user how to conduct exchanges of information with the system. See Figure 5-5.

110 • System Documentation

```
┌─────────────────────────────────────────────────┬──────────┐
│         Transaction Specification                │  Number  │
├─────────────────────────────────────────────────┼──────────┤
│                    Name                          │   Label  │
└─────────────────────────────────────────────────┴──────────┘
```

Purpose

Method

| Step | Description |

Results

| Action | Number | Label | Name |

Processing Path

| Number | Label | Name |

| Prepared | Date | Project | Page |

FIGURE 5-5: Transaction Specification

NAME

Specify a transaction name that is meaningful to the user. Use the definition technique to classify and differentiate transactions by their names.

NUMBER

The documentation system identifier for transactions is their number. This can have the format SSST999. With large systems or families of products you may need to expand on this format in order to accommodate more than a thousand different transactions.

Resist the temptation to code or segment the numerical portion of your transaction numbers. There is no value in grouping system elements into clusters for documentation purposes. Keep to a simple, sequential numbering scheme. Rely on other specified attributes and on your documentation system to select and sequence transaction specifications according to your needs.

LABEL

If your system's transactions are mainly logical, there is no need for transaction labels. You may find this attribute a useful place to specify the code that identifies the transaction record.

PURPOSE

The audience for the statement of the transaction's purpose is the user. System builders do not use the transaction specification per se to build software.

Describe the processing tasks or objectives that the user can accomplish by using the transaction. Address the user directly. A good format for this attribute is "Use this transaction to..."; for example, "Use this transaction to add new clients to the Client File."

You can list the kinds of options available for the transaction, but do not go into detail. Remember to keep the statement of purpose short and concise, since it will also be used to answer inquiries of the form, "What transaction should I use to...?"

METHOD

The method attribute specifies the steps the user must follow to perform his or her part of the transaction. This may be a single job number that points to a specified manual procedure, such as completing and submitting forms. Otherwise, use the format shown in Figure 5-5 and define the procedure as an ordered list of steps.

RESULTS

Whereas the purpose attribute defines the processing tasks or goals of transactions in a general way, the results attribute lists their specific outcomes. Results can include system control, data manipulation, and reporting. This attribute answers such questions as

- What files, records, or data items are revised?
- How does the system respond?
- What reports are produced?
- Where are the changes I make reflected?

A good format for this list is Verb Noun. The verb shows the action performed on each element. The noun is the name of the system element affected by the transaction.

When you use this format, specify the verb and the system element number as hard attributes of the transaction. Let your documentation system provide the names of the system elements.

PROCESSING PATH

A definition of the processing path followed by the transaction is optional. This attribute is useful to builders and supporters when solving problems with specific transactions. It is an ordered list of the programs or modules that process the transaction. You need only specify the program or module numbers in correct sequence. Your documentation system will provide additional soft attributes, such as name and label.

This attribute is optional because the same information is also found in the run chart specification. You may want to design your documentation system to translate the run chart into a sequenced list of programs, thereby eliminating redundancy.

JOB

Jobs are physical elements. They are an important (but often neglected) part of the design of batch systems. Jobs are performed by users, data entry operators, and computer operators. Even if you do not formally design and specify jobs, this category of specifications can act as a handy storage place for memos and notes.

The audience of the job specification can be any system player. The purpose of the specification is to give the reader detailed instructions on the performance of the job. It shows the reader how to do the job. Figure 5-6 pictures the job specification.

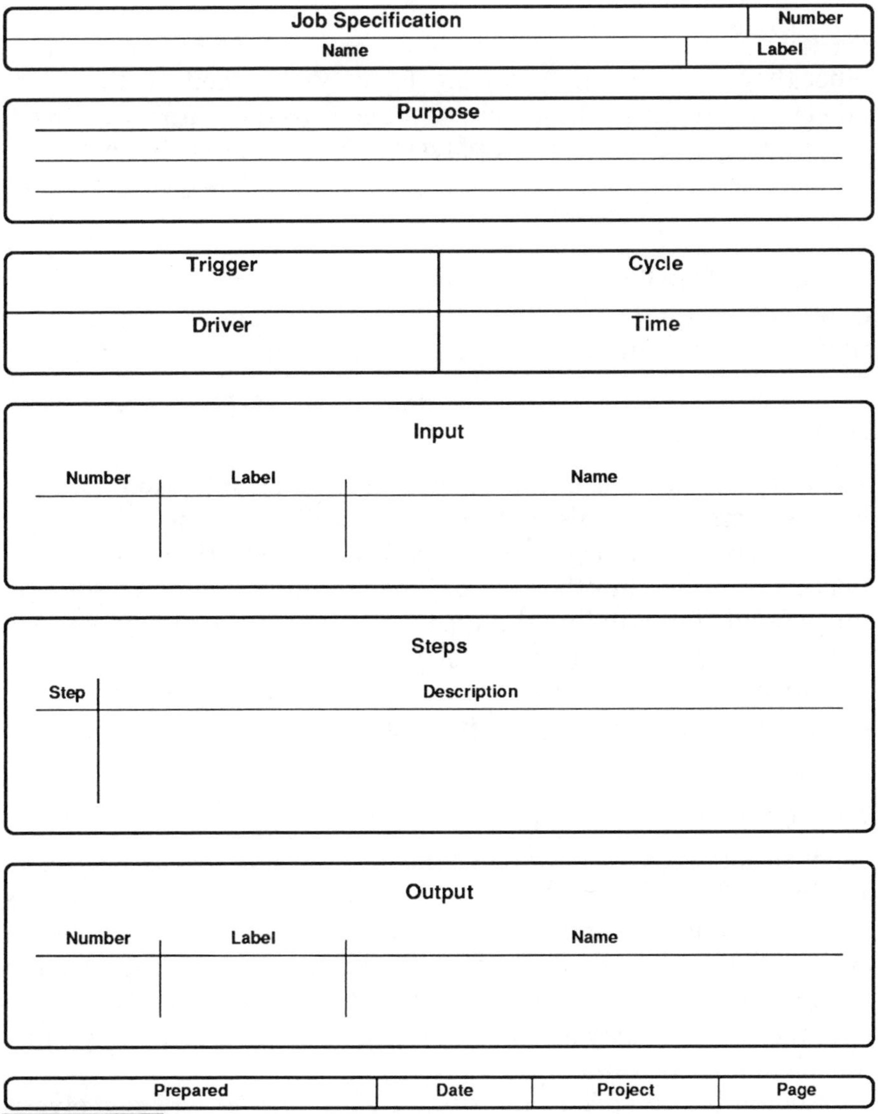

Job Specification	Number
Name	Label

Purpose

Trigger	Cycle
Driver	Time

Input

Number	Label	Name

Steps

Step	Description

Output

Number	Label	Name

Prepared	Date	Project	Page

FIGURE 5-6: Job Specification

NAME

Since the audience is the person who performs the job, the job name should be meaningful to that person. A good format is Verb Noun. The verb describes the action the person performs. The noun is the object, usually a system element, that the job acts on.

NUMBER

Since there is no machine portion of a manual procedure, there is no label for a job. Thus, the job number becomes the primary reference and identifier for the system players. The format is SSSJ999.

LABEL

The job label attribute can be used to record an acronym, short form, or other alias for the job name. If job specifications are stored in text files, you may want to record the file label here.

PURPOSE

The purpose attribute of the job defines the reason for doing the job. It summarizes the goals that the reader will accomplish.

This attribute is also used to answer such questions as, How do I accomplish X? In other words, the system players can scan the purpose attributes to find the appropriate job or to confirm that they are about to perform the right job.

Address the reader directly, using the format "Use this job to...." Again, the format Verb Noun is useful.

TRIGGER

What situation or event initiates the job? Specify this as the trigger attribute. Triggers can take the form of user information needs, dates, or system events, such as error conditions. This attribute augments the cycle attribute, described below. For example, it may not be enough to know that a given job must be performed two times each month. You may also need to specify the exact dates on which the job should be done.

Remember to specify the trigger as the *reader* will perceive it. Triggers can also be specified by system element numbers, as in the case of an operator receiving a console message.

CYCLE

Most batch system jobs are performed on a regular cyclic basis. The job cycle is specified in the same format as is the subsystem cycle, namely Number per Period. The cycle answers the question, How often should I do this job?

Do not confuse the cycle with the trigger. An example will help distinguish between the two. Consider a monthly backup job. The cycle of the job is one per month. However, the backup cannot be made until monthly processing has ended. Thus, the trigger would be Completion of SSSQ024 Monthly Summary Reports.

In addition, you can use this attribute to organize reference manuals into daily, weekly, monthly, and yearly procedures. Remember to include the "on demand" option.

DRIVER

Who performs the job? This is specified by the driver attribute. If you design the users when you design the system environment, use the same terminology to specify the job driver. Thus, the job driver may be specified as Level One User, System Administrator, and so on. Note that the audience for the job specification and the job driver are the same person.

TIME

The job time attribute is an estimate or average of how long it takes to do the job. It helps both users and EDP operations departments to schedule their work. Job time can be expressed as an absolute value (1 hour 30 minutes) or can include a volume factor (10 minutes per form, 30 minutes per thousand records).

INPUT

The input attribute is a form of checklist that tells the readers what materials or information they will need to perform the job. It can be defined by descriptive text or by a list of elements, such as forms or reports. Specify only the element numbers as hard attributes of the job. Let your documentation system present names and labels from the appropriate element specifications.

STEPS

The heart of the job specification is an ordered list of the steps the driver must perform. Address the readers directly, taking into account their level of experience, background, and knowledge.

OUTPUT

The output attribute is similar to the input attribute. It is a checklist of what the job produces. It can take the form of descriptive text or can be a list of element numbers (with labels or names added as soft attributes).

Here you specify such elements as completed input forms and run request forms. Data entry specifications can also be recorded as jobs. In this case, the output includes a data file on magnetic media.

RUN

There are two audiences for the run specification: the system builder, who must construct the run, perhaps coding it in an operating system language; and the computer operator, who uses the specification to conduct the production run. The run is a purely physical system element. It is a machine procedure.

This specification combines both textual and graphic attributes. It includes a chart, as described in the next section. It may also include a third component, printed listing of the finished software code. Figure 5-7 shows the textual portion of the run specification.

NAME

The name is a capsule definition of the run's purpose, expressed in physical terms. Since the system operators conduct the run, the name should be meaningful to them.

NUMBER

The run number is the standard documentation system identifier, of the form SSSQ999. Few system players will use this identifier. Since the run is a physical element, its label is more commonly used as an identifier.

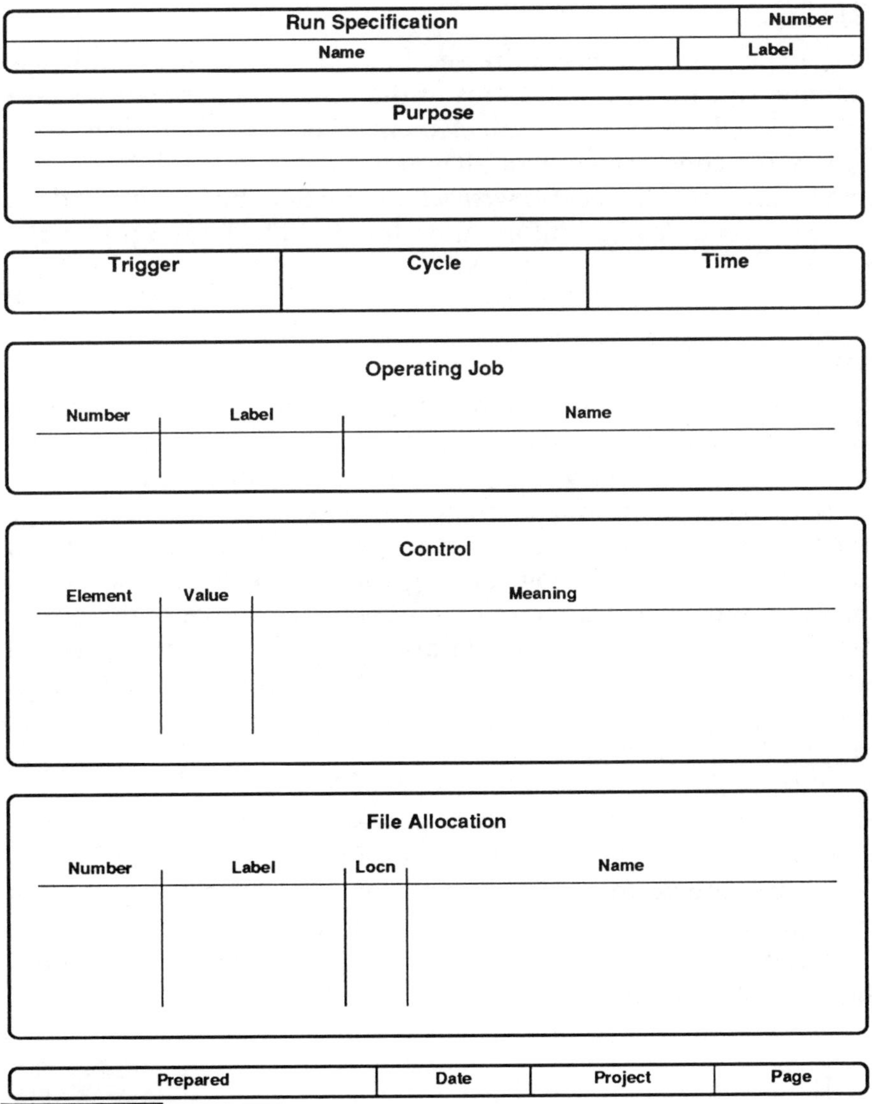

FIGURE 5-7: Run Specification

LABEL

The run label is a hard attribute required by the operating system to identify the run code. It is the label of the file that contains the cataloged run instructions. Operators invoke or initiate the run by using the run label.

PURPOSE

The purpose attribute is addressed to a purely technical audience. State the run's purpose in terms of the processing operations performed on files and the system elements produced. Be sure to keep it short and concise even though you write it in physical terms and for a technical audience. Show *what* the run does but not *how* it does it. Leave such detailed information for later attributes and for the run chart.

TRIGGER

Runs are conducted and controlled by operators, so these system players need to know when to start them. The trigger attribute shows operations staff what situation or event initiates the run.

Remember to specify the trigger event as it is experienced by the reader. Consider the case of a run that is used to reorganize an indexed master file. The logical trigger for the run is that the file has become fragmented, but the operator does not experience this event. Rather, the operator receives an application or operating system message, which should be specified as the trigger event for the run.

CYCLE

Batch system runs follow the same processing cycles as subsystems. Specify the run cycle using the usual format Number per Period. When runs are performed on specific dates or upon completion of prerequisite runs, this information can be specified as the trigger.

The run cycle helps operations staff schedule their work, as does the next attribute, time.

TIME

When it is possible to specify the average time it takes to perform a run, do so. Otherwise, run time may be expressed as a function of processing volumes, such as number of transactions or records.

OPERATING JOB

The run specification may provide operators with all the information they need to conduct the run. If they must perform additional manual procedures, specify the procedures by listing the operating job numbers. This attribute lets you connect such jobs as control-total logging, journal proofing, and file backup to a particular run.

You can provide the operators with a reference manual that includes a section of job specifications. Alternately, you may want to design your documentation system so that it includes the entire job specification with the run specification.

CONTROL

Operators are responsible for setting the correct run time variables for each run. The control attribute specifies these options and shows the operator how to select them.

The format of the control attribute depends on how you implement run time options. These may be set in a parameter file, supplied on control cards, or entered in a series of console monitor exchanges.

Use this attribute to record the impact of computer system parameters, such as the system date and time.

FILE ALLOCATION

The operator also needs to know the file allocation for the run—which files must be set up on which devices. Specify the file number and location as hard attributes, and let the documentation system provide the file label and name as soft attributes. The file allocation also appears on the run chart, so you may decide to omit it here.

If your runs handle file setup via console messages, you can specify the message numbers here. Message specifications can be grouped into a single operator reference manual or can be provided as soft attributes of each run specification.

LISTING

When the run has been created and tested, you can store a printed version of the run code as part of the run specification. In a batch production environment, it is convenient to produce and maintain such listings in the System File.

RUN CHART

The run chart is a valuable overview of the run. It helps the builders construct the run code. It shows the operators, in simple graphic form, what the input and output files are and where they are located.

120 • System Documentation

The charting technique shown in Figure 5-8 collapses all the information into a very compact form with a few easy-to-understand charting conventions. I designed it so that the run chart could be created and maintained on a series of 8½-by-11-inch sheets. The sheets can be joined edge to edge to form a complete chart. Originally this technique was part of a purely manual documentation system, but it also works well when automated.

NAME, NUMBER, AND LABEL

The name, number, and label on the run chart are the same as those for the run specification. These identifiers are hard attributes of every specification.

Page numbers are also important with this technique, since the separate pages of the run chart are assembled into a specific sequence to create one complete chart.

As the example chart shows, standard (or slightly altered) flowchart symbols appear in the central area of the form. These are

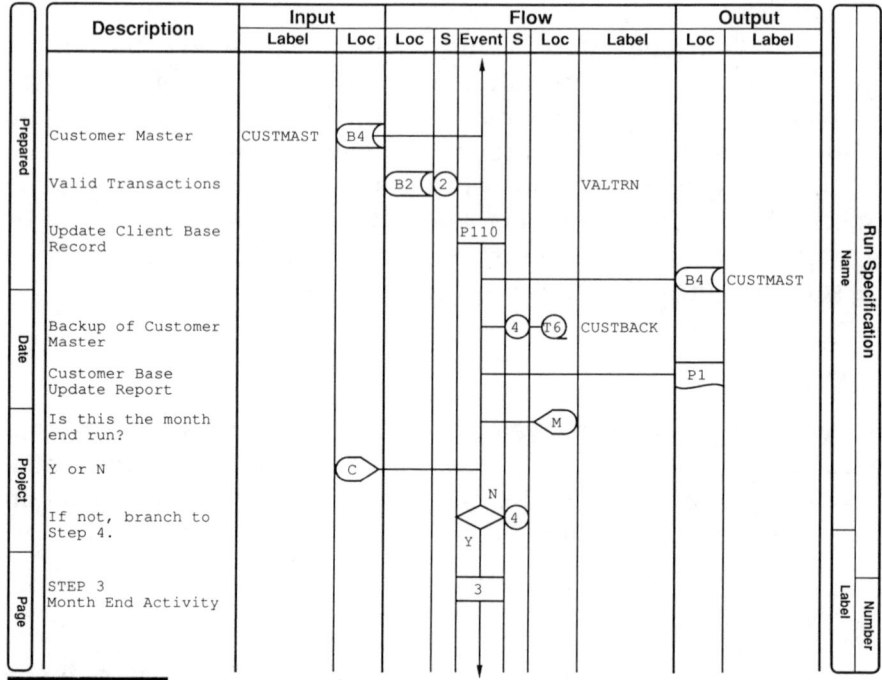

FIGURE 5-8: Run Chart

Symbol	Element
⌷	Disk
⌾	Tape
▢	Diskette
▭	Program or Step or Operating System Command
◇	Decision
○	Step or Branch Point
⌓	Report
⌬	Monitor

TABLE 5-1: Run Chart Symbols

supported by descriptive text. Table 5-1 explains the charting symbols used. Each column of the chart is discussed below.

DESCRIPTION

The Description column of the chart holds the names of any system elements shown as symbols on the chart. These include

- Program
- File
- Console screen or message
- Report

It also shows the sequence of processing steps. Steps are identified by a step number and have a descriptive name. If the run itself contains decision points and branches, the decision criteria are also listed. The column also holds any comments needed to clarify run processing.

INPUT

The Input column shows the label, symbol, and location (peripheral device identifier) of what I refer to as absolute input. This is input that comes from outside of the run itself, as opposed to files that are created by, and then read back into, the run.

The label is recorded in the Label column. The "Loc" column shows the symbol for the physical device. The device identifier is written within the symbol. For example, the first item in Figure 5-8 is a disk file labeled CUSTMAST. It should be mounted on device B4 for this run.

FLOW

The column labeled Flow shows the flow of processing control through the run. There is only one vertical line connecting the steps and elements of the run. This is the run flow. The Flow column is divided into several other columns.

The first Loc column shows the symbol and location of relative input. This is input that does not come from outside the run but is created during an earlier step in the run. For example, the first relative input for the run pictured in Figure 5-8 is the disk file VALTRN. This file is located on disk drive B2.

Both columns titled S contain step or branch symbols and numbers. These show the source of relative input and the destination of relative output. They also show branches or jumps of the run control flow within the run.

The Event column shows processing events in the run. The symbol and labels for the program and operating system command and the decision symbol appear in this column, along with the run flow line. The first event in Figure 5-8 is the program P110, Update Client Base Record.

The second Loc column shows the symbol and location of relative output from the run. This output never actually leaves the run itself. Rather, it is used as input in a later step. As in all location columns on the chart, the symbol contains the peripheral identifier, so both the medium and the allocation of each file are shown. For example, the tape file CUSTBACK is located on tape drive T6.

The Label column shows the labels of all relative input and output elements. The symbols and labels of the relative and absolute input and output are separated on the chart so that the operator can scan the columns to determine file allocation and setup requirements for the run.

OUTPUT

The last column on the chart, Output, contains the symbol, location, and label of absolute output from the run. Two absolute outputs from the run are shown in Figure 5-8: the disk file CUSTMAST, located on drive B4, and the report Customer Base Update Report, printed on line printer P1.

PROGRAM

Programs are physical system elements. Or are they? In reality, there is no clear distinction between logical and physical system elements. Yes, you can touch a program listing, but you cannot touch the source or object code files. You cannot see a program and can only deduce its existence from the effects of its operation. However, because of our long and close association with programs, we tend to think of them as physical elements.

The audience for the program specification is the system builder, who uses the instructions to create and revise programs, the basic building blocks of software. Figure 5-9 is a representation of the program specification.

Let me remind you how the program specification is used. It is *not* simply completed by the designer and handed to the builder. Rather, the specification is a communication vehicle for both of these system players. They mutually specify the program as it is built.

The designer starts by specifying the general objectives of the program: its purpose, the files it uses, the desired control features, and perhaps a tentative structure. In other words, the designer specifies *what* the program must do.

The builder works within the guidelines specified by the designer but can alter the guidelines to create an effective solution to the processing problem. As design details of the program emerge, the builder completes the technical details of the program specification.

It is best to let individual project team members decide how much or how little the designer should specify the program.

NAME

The program specification has a single audience, the system builder. The program name should be meaningful to the programmers who

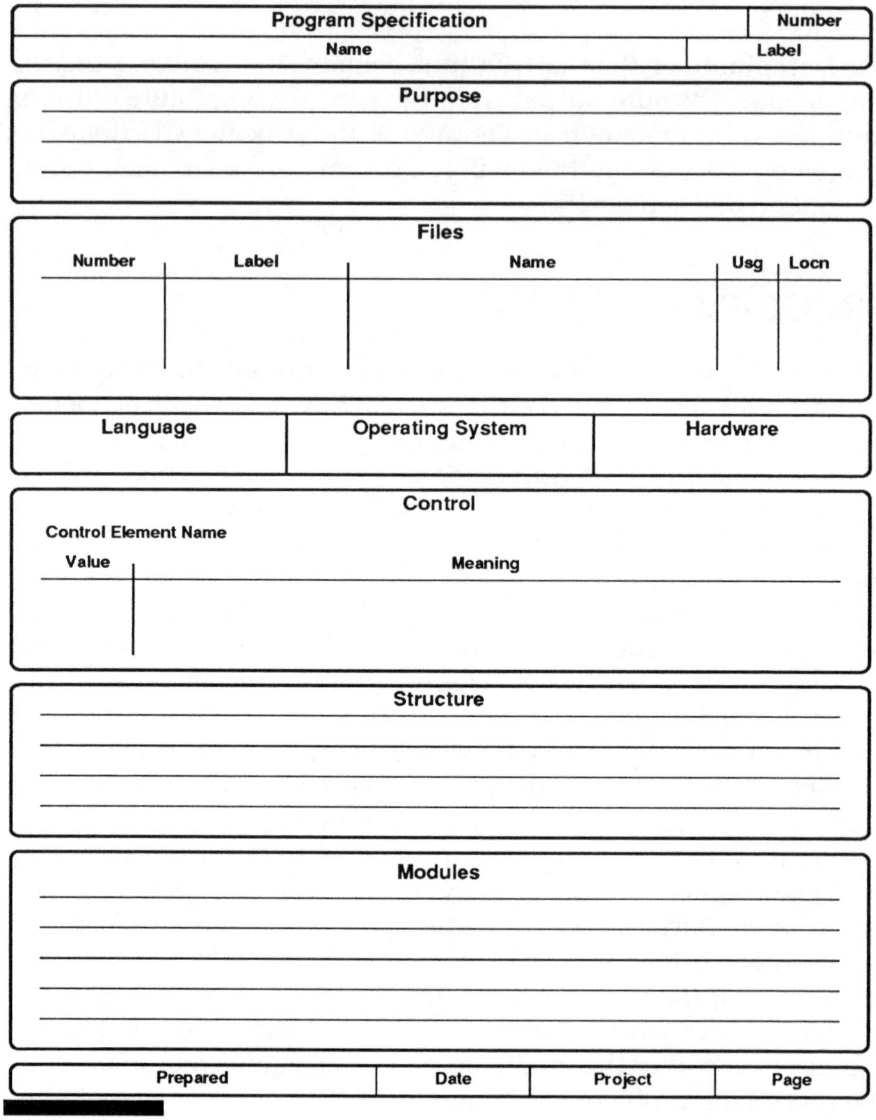

FIGURE 5-9: Program Specification

will build and maintain the program. Program names can take the familiar form Verb Noun, or they can define the major processing function of the program.

NUMBER

The program number identifies the program for your documentation system.

Software builders like to divide program labels into groups. For example, all the daily programs are numbered in the 100s, monthly programs are 200s, yearly programs are 300s, utility programs are 400s, and so on. The benefit of this approach is that the program label shows the builder roughly where the program fits into the system. The drawback is that such schemes must be recorded and communicated to all the builders who create or maintain the system. It is all too easy for newcomers to unknowingly violate unwritten labeling standards.

Resist the temptation to group or cluster program specifications by their program numbers. There is no corresponding benefit for the effort. Other elements, such as runs or subsystems, show how the elements of the system are connected.

The format of the program number is SSSP999. The numeric portion is a pure serial number, devoid of segments or codes.

LABEL

Since programs depend on the operating system and hardware to exist and function, their machine identifiers, or labels, are critical. Further, the program label is the primary identifier used by software builders. When you create printed versions of your program specifications, organize and file them by label for the convenience of your programming staff.

The format and value of a program label, like all labels, are only partially within your control. You may need to design your specifications and documentation system to handle multiple labels for each element. This is especially true when you implement your products in different programming languages, or for multiple operating and hardware systems.

PURPOSE

The purpose attribute tells the programmer the primary object of the program. It keeps the programmer on track, just as it does the writer. It is an overview and introduction only. Do not let your purpose paragraph wander into a description or program narrative. Tell *what* the program does, but not *how* it does it.

Remember that this brief definition of the program's function can also answer "inverted" queries on the System File. For example, you might scan the purpose of several program specifications to answer a question such as, Which program adds the line items on the invoice and calculates sales tax?

Here is a technique you can use when writing the purpose of a program. Visualize the program standing before you in the form of an obedient little robot, like R2-D2 from the movie *Star Wars*. The robot is about to perform a specific task for you with its limited intellect and initiative. You address it, saying, "Program, I want you to...." What follows is your statement of purpose for the program.

FILES

The files attribute shows all input and output for the program. In a print spooling environment, it is easy to think of output reports as just another kind of file. Even when your programs print reports directly, it is useful to specify them as output files for the program. Other printing details about reports are recorded in the report specification.

Specify the file numbers, usage, and location as hard attributes. Let your documentation system provide additional soft attributes such as label and name.

The usage attribute shows how the program uses the file. Usage can be a physical attribute, defined by the programming language you use. In cases where your system or shop uses multiple languages, it is easier to devise a logical scheme of usage codes. Table 5-2 suggests one possible scheme.

The location attribute defines the peripheral device on which the program can expect to find or place the files it uses. Remember that file allocation is the responsibility of the run, not the program. Programs supported by runs do not need to interact with the operator to establish the correct file allocation and setup.

Code	Usage
S	Source, Read Only
D	Destination, Write Only
R	Random Access, Read or Write
X	Source/Destination, Read or Write
F	Father/Son Generations
C	Copy

TABLE 5-2: File Usage Codes

LANGUAGE/OPERATING SYSTEM/HARDWARE

The three attributes language, operating system, and hardware record information about how the program is implemented and the operating environment for which it is designed. They are useful to the builder who must create or maintain the program. They are also important planning aids at the global or shop level, especially when different versions of the system products are being developed for different brands of hardware.

CONTROL

If the program has options or requires run time variables, these are specified in the control attribute. Program control may involve parameter files, system flags, or console dialogs.

The general format for specifying program control is to list the element, its possible values or settings, and the meaning of each. You can vary or supplement this format according to how program control is actually implemented.

Run time variables may be the responsibility of the program, but they are more commonly established by the runs that support it. Program control, however, is not redundant information. It appears in the program specification to show the program builder what options are needed. Program control information is repeated in run specifications to show which specific program options are needed in a given run. The builder of the run uses control information from the program specifications to define the run control.

STRUCTURE

So far, we have not specified how the program is to be created or how it performs its processing functions. The content and format of such specifications depends on how you build programs. The method presented here assumes that you use, or are at least familiar with, the techniques of structured programming. The specification shown in Figure 5-9 uses two attributes to specify structured programs: structure and modules.

The structure attribute shows the control structure of the program. You can use an organization chart to show the program structure, but I prefer the structured list technique, the same technique I used to present the system models. Since programmers are familiar with coding record layouts as structured lists, they understand program structure lists almost intuitively. Structured lists are easy to create, revise, and produce. Here is an example.

> Control
> >Setup
> >Determine transaction type
> >>Add record
> >>Change record
> >>Delete record
> >
> >Error handling
> >Close

MODULES

The second attribute used to specify structured programs is called "modules." Note that modules included in a program specification are specific to that program. Global modules are specified as system elements in their own right.

When a global module is used by a program, specify the module number as a hard attribute of the program specification. Include a list of called or global modules at the beginning of the modules attribute, or make this a separate attribute.

The modules attribute is a textual or graphic description of each module named in the structure attribute. Specify the processing functions for each module in the program. Several techniques are useful here.

Perhaps the easiest technique for specifying module processing is structured text. This is a logical form of English used to communicate between software designers and builders. It resembles a high-level programming language.

Structured text uses four types of term: instruction, decision, loop, and branch. Instructions are data processing commands. They specify reading or writing records, arithmetic manipulations on data items, moving values from one field to another, and the like. They are written as single lines of text.

Decisions test the values of data items and show processing instructions for each outcome. As the result of a test, you may specify instructions or branches. Decisions can be expressed in the familiar if/then/else form or as cases.

Loops define iterative processes. The loop process is repeated until a specified condition or test is met. Loops can be specified in several forms. You can place the test statement first or last in the list of process steps. Counters that control the loop can be specified explicitly or may be implicit to the loop statement.

Branches are module control commands. They transfer control to a labeled point in the module.

Figure 5-10 is an example of the structured text used to specify a module. It shows how each of the four terms is used. Of course, you may elect to develop your own unique version of structured text.

Decision tables are a concise way to specify complex decision logic. Figure 5-11 shows a sample decision table. As you can see, the table is divided into four parts. The left side is called the stub, the right side the entry. The top half of the table shows the conditions that are tested. The bottom half shows processing actions taken as a result of the tests.

In addition to structured text and decision tables, you can specify module processing functions with diagrams. Simple block diagrams are best. When you feel you must use a flowchart, try to limit it to a single $8^{1}/_{2}$-by-11-inch sheet.

If your programs are not structured, you must find other techniques for creating program specifications. One approach is to partition program functions into different groups of logic rather

```
Module 2
01   Do until end of Transaction File
02      Read transaction Record
03      If Transaction Code EQ, A, C, or D
04         Then continue at 09
05         Else set Error Flag to 15
06            Perform Module 9
07            Go to 02
08      End If
09      Case Transaction Code
10         Case 1 EQ A
11            Perform Module 3
12         Case 2 EQ C
13            Perform Module 4
14         Case 3 EQ D
15            Perform Module 5
16      End Case
17   End Do
```

FIGURE 5-10: Structured Text

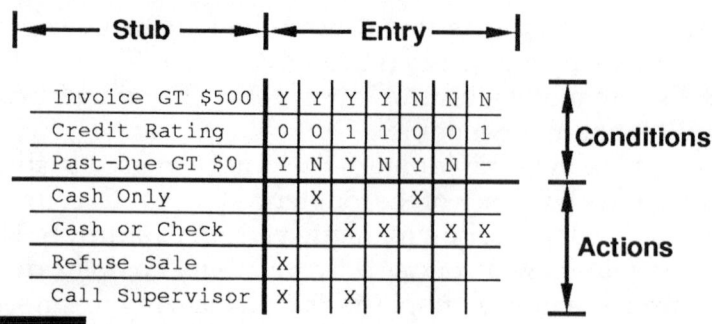

FIGURE 5-11: Decision Table

than into different modules. For example, you can specify program logic under the following three headings:

Iterative logic describes the overall program control. It shows which routines or processes are repeated for each record or transaction.

Validation logic describes the testing of data item values. It shows how error conditions are handled.

Processing logic describes how valid transactions or data items are manipulated. It shows how values are changed, how records are written, and how report lines are produced.

I have seen many techniques for program specification used successfully. Each has its own strengths and weaknesses. Which technique you decide to use depends as much on the preferences of the system designers and builders in your shop as it does on the relative merits of alternative techniques.

The least successful program specification techniques I have ever used are program narratives and overall program flowcharts.

Program narratives, large blocks of text, intimidate software builders. The diversity of program logic makes it difficult to organize the narrative in any sensible order. The English language imposes its own confusing logic and syntax on the subject of program logic and processing. Finally, program narratives are difficult to revise and maintain. Minor revisions to a program are easily lost in the text of the narrative.

Program flowcharts seem to work best for small programs or modules within programs. They can be a valuable development aid when sketched by a programmer but are not suitable for permanent specifications. The reason I discourage their use is that they are too difficult and expensive to create, produce, and revise.

LISTING

Once the program has been created, you may want to include a listing of the source code as part of the program specification. In a batch production environment, it is convenient to produce and maintain program listings in the System File.

MODULE

Like the program, the module is a physical system element. Modules may be called by programs as they are executed. They may also take the form of commonly used routines stored in copy libraries and copied into a program when it is compiled.

Note that only global or system-wide modules need to be specified as individual elements. Specifications for other types of modules are included in program specifications.

The audience for the module specification is the system builder who creates or maintains the module. Designers may also refer to the specifications of existing modules to learn which functions are already available.

The module specification shown in Figure 5-12 does not include a list of programs that use the module. This information may be useful, but it is not a hard attribute of the module specification. Instead, each program specification lists the numbers of the modules used by the program. Your documentation system can scan the program specifications and compile a "used by" list for display as a soft attribute on the module specification.

NAME

The name is a capsule definition of the function of the module. Make module names meaningful to the technical system players, the people who work with the modules.

NUMBER

The module number is the standard identifier used by the documentation system. Its format is SSSM999. You will need to modify the system identifier portion of this number (SSS) when modules are used in several different systems. Your company acronym makes an ideal system identifier for globally used modules.

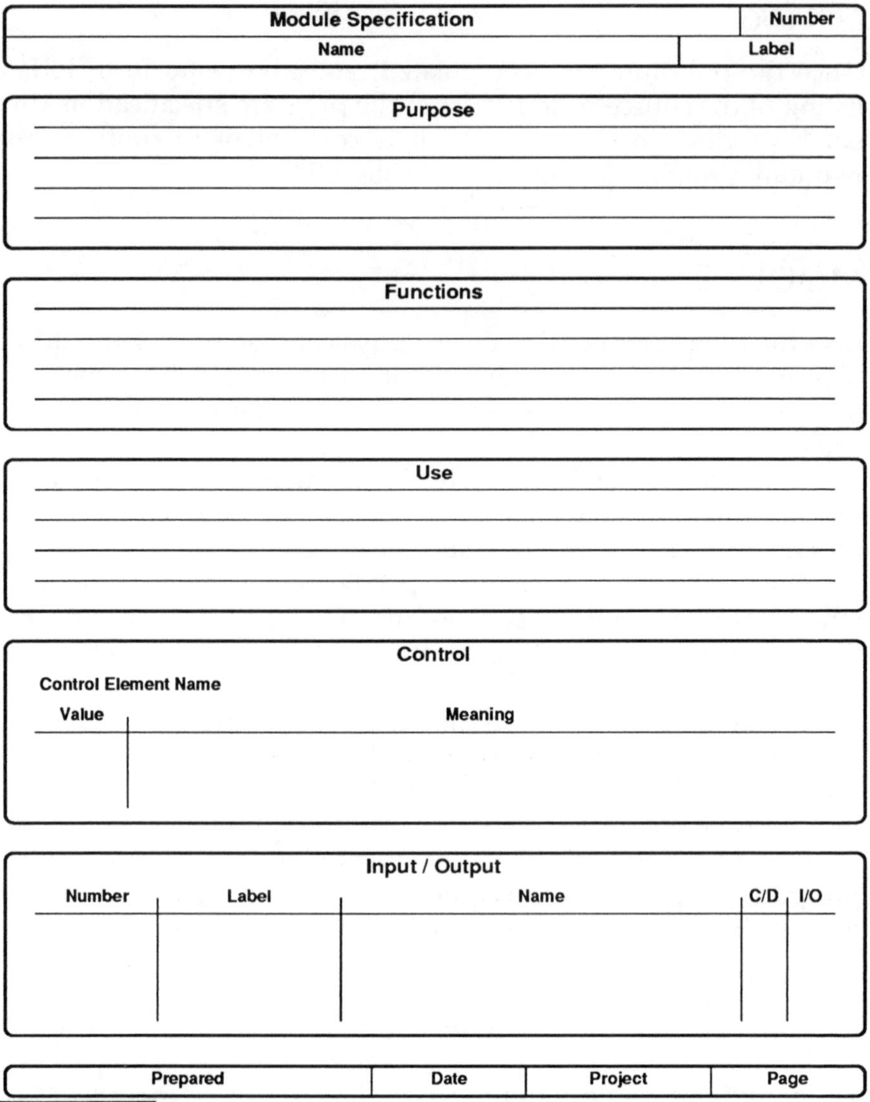

Module Specification	Number
Name	Label

Purpose

Functions

Use

Control

Control Element Name
Value   Meaning

Input / Output

Number	Label	Name	C/D	I/O

Prepared	Date	Project	Page

FIGURE 5-12: Module Specification

LABEL

The label is the machine identifier of the module. The format of the label depends on how modules are actually called or used by your software. The label may identify a file that contains the module code, or it may be the identifier used by a copy library system.

PURPOSE

The purpose attribute states the primary function performed by the module. This statement of purpose helps software builders to create and maintain the module. It also augments the definition provided by the module name and helps designers answer questions of the form, Do we have a standard module that handles X?

It is useful to make the "what versus how" distinction when writing the module purpose. Show *what* the module does. Reserve your discussion of *how* the module performs its tasks for the next attribute.

FUNCTIONS

The actual processing task (or tasks) performed by the module is specified in the functions attribute. This is a textual description, perhaps supplemented by tables or simple diagrams.

Specify the module functions just as you would in a program specification. The same techniques apply: structured text, decision tables, and flowcharts.

USE

The use attribute shows software builders how to use the module. It describes how a program calls, copies, or invokes the module and also specifies any communication protocol that the calling program must observe.

CONTROL

Like runs and programs, the module may have options that are controlled by run time variables. Specify module options and control by listing the control element names and numbers, their possible values, and the meaning of each value or setting.

INPUT AND OUTPUT

Modules perform specific processing functions on data. Consequently, the module specification includes an input and output attribute, which lists (as hard attributes) the element numbers of the files, records, or data items that the module reads and writes. When control information and data are provided to the module separately, this attribute can be used to specify which elements provide control information. You can revise the attribute to suit the nature and format of all information passed to the module and returned from it.

6

Specifying the Online Function Group

This is the second of four chapters that detail the specification of system elements. This chapter covers the online function group. Here is a structured list of the elements in this group.

    Online system
        Menu
            Function
                Program
                      Module

The online function group includes some elements we have already discussed in the last chapter, Specifying the Batch Function Group. Program and module specifications for online systems differ slightly from those for batch systems. However, the menu and function elements and their specifications are unique to online systems. Let's examine the elements and their specifications one by one.

ONLINE SYSTEM

The online system is a logical entity. Like the batch system, it includes both physical and logical elements; and like the batch system, it is difficult to think of as a single, physical thing.

The online system specification must meet the needs of a diverse audience. Virtually all system players will need the general information contained in this specification. Its purpose is to show the system players an overview of the system, its structure, and its functions. The system specification defines what the system is, what it does, and how it is put together.

The specification contains much of the information found in the product design document. It is simply organized and presented in a different fashion. The online system specification does not include a system chart because the relationships between the system elements and functions are manifested in the menu structure of the system itself.

Figure 6-1 shows the online system specification. We'll examine each attribute of the system shown on the form.

NAME

The system name should be meaningful to users and to potential users. That is, there are important marketing considerations involved in selecting a name for the system. The name should express the primary function or application of the system to the user.

NUMBER

The system number is the identifier used by your documentation system. It is usually an acronym of the system name. In my element numbering scheme, the system number is the SSS prefix for all other element numbers.

LABEL

There may or may not be a need to provide the system with a machine identifier. When the system appears on a menu with other systems, the label may be the code the user enters to select or invoke the system. Alternately, the system label may be the operating system command that invokes the system.

PURPOSE

Rely on the product design document to create a brief statement of purpose for the system. Remember that the audience for this statement of purpose is diverse, and write in terms that the least informed reader can understand.

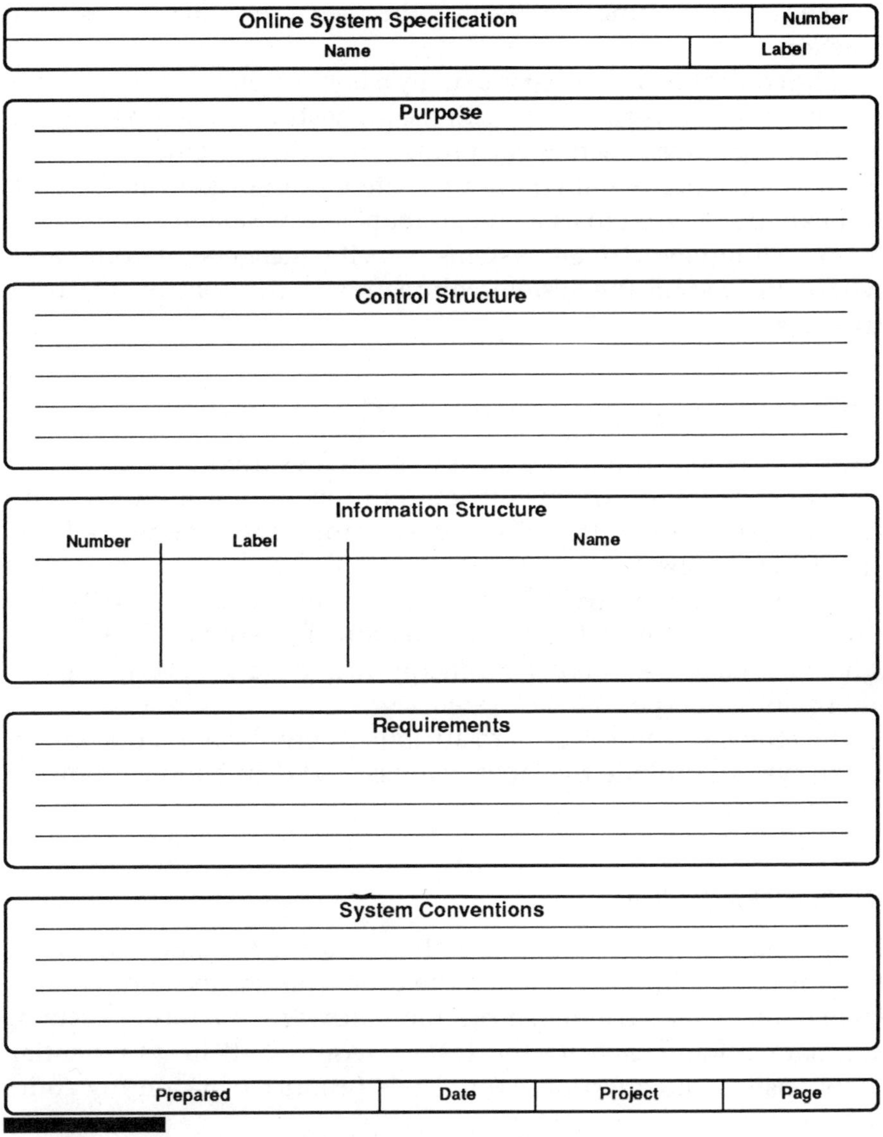

FIGURE 6-1: Online System Specification

CONTROL STRUCTURE

Online systems are either command-driven or menu-driven. In either case, the system specification should include an overall summary of the system control structure.

For menu-driven systems, use a structured list that contains all the system menus and all the functions on each menu. This list can be used to determine the "route" the user must take to reach a function.

The control structure list is usually a one-for-one mapping of the system's menu screens. Start with the highest-level menu and work down to the lowest, listing each function in the system.

This attribute is sometimes presented as an organization chart and may be referred to as a "menu map" of the system.

For command-driven systems, specify the general command syntax and list all the system commands in the control structure attribute.

INFORMATION STRUCTURE

The information structure is a list of main files used by the system. Include a definition of this attribute in the specification. If your system uses a path or tree directory structure, specify it in the form of a structured list.

The information structure provides the users and system builders with a simple model of the information processed by the system. It helps them understand, in a general way, the kinds and groups of information handled by the system.

List the file numbers as hard attributes here. Let your documentation system provide file labels, names, and descriptions from the file specifications.

REQUIREMENTS

When your system products are offered to the general microcomputer user, it is important to tell the user what the system requirements are. This attribute shows the hardware, operating system, and data storage capacity the system requires. It helps potential users answer the question, Would this product work on my computer system?

Choosing the target software and hardware environment for an online system is as much a marketing process as a technical process. Once a decision is made, the environment (or multiple environments) must be specified. The designer and builder need this information to complete all phases of system development.

SYSTEM CONVENTIONS

The system specification is the best place to record system-wide conventions. Project teams need to know the "ground rules" of the system before they can create or revise it.

This attribute specifies naming and labeling conventions for the system. It may also include generic layouts for display items like screens, reports, and messages.

MENU

The menu, a logical element, is a group of system functions roughly analogous to the batch subsystem. Menus are usually implemented as screens but need not be. In the case of command-driven systems, menus are purely logical categories of functions. The menu specification is shown in Figure 6-2.

The system designer and builder use the menu specification to organize both their work efforts and the system functions. The user can gain summary and overview information about system functions from it. Menus are a means of linking the functional elements of a system. They may parallel the system's menu screens or may provide the details of an individual area of the control structure.

NAME

A menu is a group of functions. The menu name should define the group for the user. In well-designed systems, functions and menus parallel the business tasks of the user. Thus, menu names should help the user associate a group of system functions with one aspect of his work.

For menu-driven systems, the name of the menu should be identical to the header displayed on its menu screen.

NUMBER

The menu number is the documentation system identifier. Its format is SSSC999.

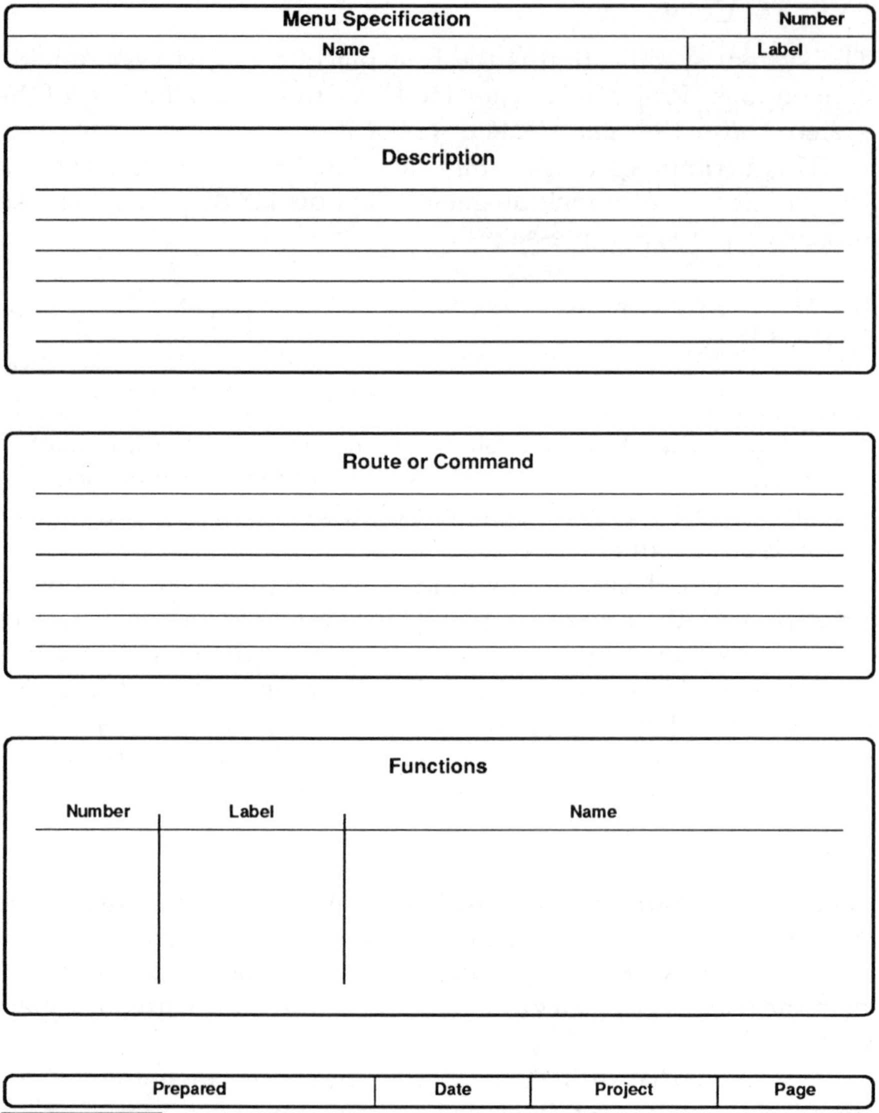

Menu Specification		Number
Name		Label

Description

Route or Command

Functions

Number	Label	Name

Prepared	Date	Project	Page

FIGURE 6-2: Menu Specification

LABEL

The menu label is an acronym for the group of functions, not the label of the screen that displays the menu to the user. Use this attribute to specify which program executes or invokes the functions for the user.

DESCRIPTION

The menu description expands on the name of the group of functions. It explains why the functions have been grouped into this menu, specifying their common feature or purpose.

Dividing system functions into menus may be a purely logical device, a technique to help the user understand the system. The description attribute is a textual explanation of the menu.

ROUTE OR COMMAND

The route or command attribute tells the user how to execute the functions on the menu. For menu-driven systems, the route is the course the user must "navigate" through the menu screens to arrive at this group of functions. For example, consider an equipment leasing system with the following control structure:

Main Menu
   Enter New Leases
   Print Coupons
   Cash Receipts Menu
     Enter Cash Receipts
     Print Deposit Listing
     Apply Cash Receipts
   Calculate Late Charges
   Print Customer Statement
   Display Customer Status
   Report Menu
     Print Amounts Due
     Print Accounts Overdue
   File Maintenance Menu
     Lease File Maintenance
     Receivable File Maintenance
     Receipt File Maintenance
     Backup and Restore Files
     Change System Parameters
   Exit

The route for the Cash Receipts Menu is

Main Menu
   Cash Receipts Menu

The route for the Print Deposit Listing function is

Main Menu
   Cash Receipts Menu
      Print Deposit Listing

As you can see, routes can be extracted from the overall control structure of the system. If you are creating add-on documentation for an existing system, you can create the control structure attribute by systematically exercising each menu selection in the system. It is then a simple matter to extract individual routes.

For command-driven systems, the route may be a list of instructions the user must follow before performing any of the functions on the menu. Examples are changing the working directory and selecting a group of application data files.

When the command syntax is not consistent for the entire system, the command attribute of the menu specification shows conventions for this group of functions.

FUNCTIONS

Since a menu is a group of functions, a list of the functions is an important attribute of the specification. Record the function numbers as hard attributes of the menu. Additional attributes of each function, such as name, label, and purpose, are available from individual function specifications and can be displayed as soft attributes on the menu specification.

FUNCTION

A function is primarily a logical element. As perceived by the user, a function is a single processing task that the system performs. One or more modules or programs may perform the function when it is implemented. Thus, a function is one or more physical elements grouped together to perform a common logical processing task.

Consider some examples from the control structure shown earlier in this chapter. The Main Menu could be implemented as a single program, with each first-level menu (Enter New Leases, Print Coupons, Cash Receipts Menu, Report Menu, etc.) as a separate module in the menu program.

Other functions on the Main Menu, such as Enter Cash Receipts or Print Deposit Listing, would probably be implemented as separate programs, called from the Main Menu program.

Finally, functions on the Report Menu typically would be implemented as short chains of extract-sort-print programs.

As you can see, functions can represent a variety of physical elements. However, each function is a single logical element to the user, who needs information about that element and neither knows nor cares how many modules or programs come into play to print the Accounts Overdue report. The function specification shows the user what the function does and how to request, select, or otherwise invoke the function. Program and module specifications show the builders how to create and implement the function.

You may already be familiar with function specifications in the form of operating system reference manuals. In these, the system commands (functions) are listed in alphabetic order. Each command is presented in the form of a function specification. See Figure 6-3.

NAME

Function names are created strictly for the user. They should define the business or processing task that the function accomplishes. A good format for function names is Verb Object. The verb is usually a processing or control instruction (enter, calculate, revise, print). The object is a system element (employee, finance charge, master file, report).

NUMBER

The documentation system identifies the function by its number. The format for function numbers is SSSE999.

LABEL

As logical elements, functions do not need a machine identifier, or label. You can use this attribute to record the acronym, mnemonic, or code by which the user selects the function from a menu screen.

PURPOSE

You may need two different statements of purpose for the function, one addressed to the user, the other to the builder or supporter. The designer can start by writing the technical purpose of the function.

Function Specification		Number
Name		Label

Purpose

Tech: _____

User: _____

Route or Command

Steps

Step	Description

Processing

Number	Label	Name

Elements Used

Number	Label	Name

Prepared	Date	Project	Page

FIGURE 6-3: Function Specification

Later, a writer can create the second statement of purpose in nontechnical terms.

The user needs to know, in summary form, what the function is and does. It is helpful to visualize the user sitting at his terminal, browsing through the functions shown on the system menus. The user pauses at this particular function and asks what it is used for. Your reply is a statement of the function's purpose. Good formats are "Use this function to…" or "This function lets you.…"

This attribute also answers questions of the form, How do I get the system to X? It helps the user select functions and confirms that the selection is the correct one.

ROUTE OR COMMAND

For menu-driven systems, show the route the user must follow to reach the function. See the section on menu specification above for a discussion of routes and their notation.

For command-driven systems, show the syntax and options of the command for the function. Table 6-1 shows a commonly used convention for command syntax notation.

STEPS

Some functions can be executed in a single step. The user simply selects them from a menu or enters a single command. Other functions involve a sequence of interactions with the system, or commands with variables and options. The steps attribute shows users exactly how to perform their part of the function.

For menu systems, this attribute takes the form of a chronologically ordered description. Tell the user what will happen when the function is selected. It is also important to keep the user in control of the function at each step. Show the options and exit points at each step in the function. Show where files are updated.

Remember that the user will experience only the features of the

Notation	Meaning
UPPER CASE	Command to enter or Key to press
lower case	Variable text to enter
[ ]	Optional entry
< >	Required entry
{|}	Choices
/	Or
…	Multiples

TABLE 6-1: Command Syntax Notation

system, the elements of the user interface. Examples of system features are screens, messages, and reports. Do not detail the processing or calculations that are "invisible" to the user.

For command-driven systems, this attribute lists the variables and options shown in the command attribute. Explain each variable and option available.

PROCESSING

The next attribute, processing, links the logical and physical aspects of the function. Processing is specified by the designer and used by the builder to implement functions as single or multiple programs. This attribute is essential when a function is spread over several programs or perhaps requires a special sequence of module processing within a program.

List the program or module numbers in the correct sequence (if sequence is applicable). These hard attributes act as pointers to the program and module specifications.

ELEMENTS USED

The function specification includes a list of elements that the function uses. Functions can use any of the following elements: file, record, data item, screen, message, and report. Specify the numbers of these elements as hard attributes. Let the documentation system provide soft attributes, such as names and labels. Include messages that appear in message lines or windows on the user's screen, but reserve the specification of dialogs for screen specifications.

PROGRAM AND MODULE

We have already examined the specification of programs and modules as elements in the batch system function group. With two exceptions, the specification of online programs and modules is the same.

The first exception is that online programs and modules become responsible for their own file allocation. They interact directly with the user to ensure that the files they use are placed on the correct physical devices.

The second exception is that program and module control information (options and run time variables) is secured directly from the user, usually in the form of prompts or dialogs.

In either case, prompts and dialogs are not defined in the program and module specifications. Rather, they are defined as part of screen or message specifications. The control attribute of the online program and module specification becomes a list of message or screen numbers. These are the messages and dialogs the program uses to set up files or acquire run time variables.

For online systems, specify all input and output elements, including screens, reports, and messages, as if they were files.

7
Specifying the Information Group

This is the third of four chapters that detail the specification of system elements. We have come to the information group. The elements in this group, shown in the following structured list, are common to both batch and online systems.

File
    Record
        Data item

FILE

The file specification has two audiences. The user reads portions of the file specification to learn how information is grouped in the system and how processing functions affect different files. The builder uses information in the file specification to build the files via programs.

    Note that this discussion covers only data files stored on magnetic media. You may need to develop other forms of the specification to define the attributes of files stored on paper, microfilm, or other nonmagnetic media.

    Files are a physical element. In fact, a file is literally a physical

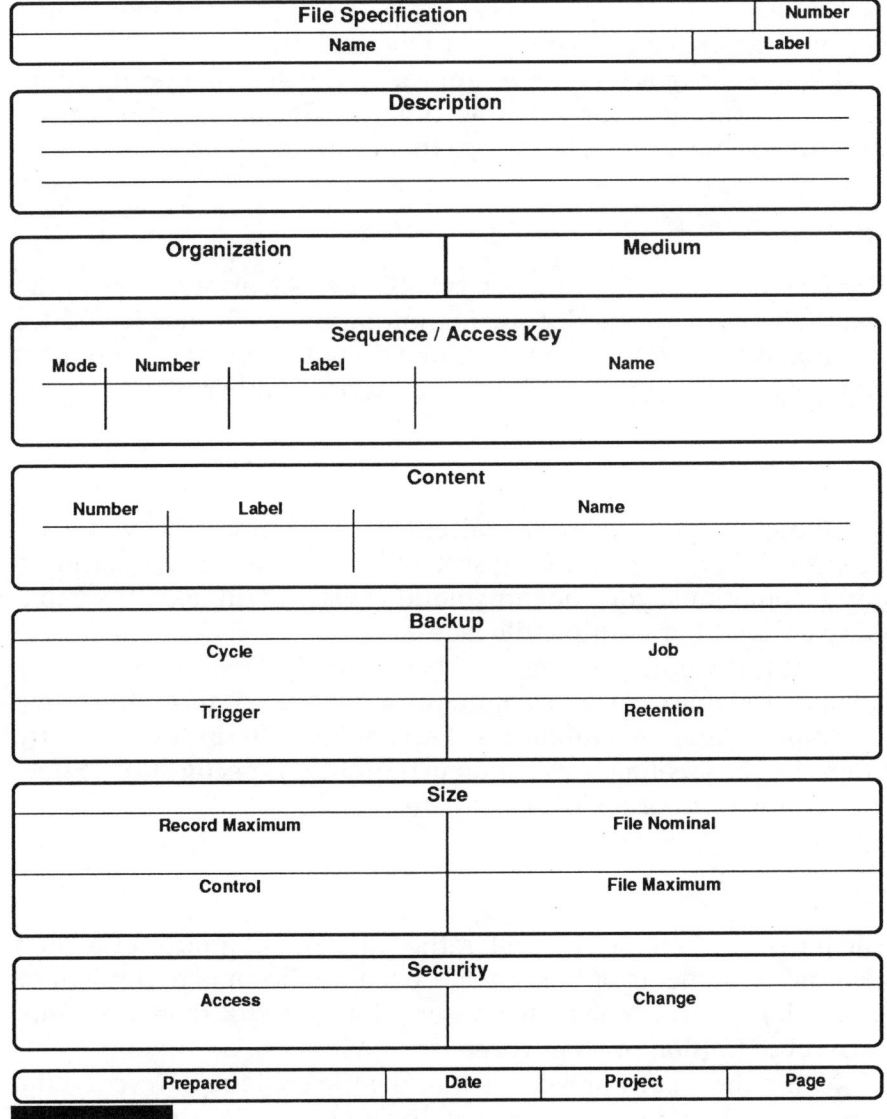

FIGURE 7-1: File Specification

collection of related records. Figure 7-1 shows the file specification sheet.

NAME

Since file names are used by all the system players, it makes sense to create them with the most important player in mind—the user. The file name should identify the category of records contained in the file, in terms that are meaningful to the user.

Remember that file names appear in the system specification. They help the user form a conceptual model of the information structure of the system, so choose them carefully.

NUMBER

The format for the file number is SSSF999. As always, this is the identifier used by the documentation system. Do not introduce additional codes into the number, and do not segment file numbers into groups. Keep the number a pure serial number.

LABEL

The file label is a machine requirement. Its format and value are determined by your operating system and hardware. For multiple implementations, your documentation system will need the capability of handling multiple file labels.

As if this were not complicated enough, file labels may actually contain variables. It is a common technique to allow the same software to serve several different sets of files. In this case, be sure to specify the labeling convention in the system specification. Show the generic form of the file label here.

DESCRIPTION

The purpose of all files is similar; they all contain groups of related records. Statements of their purpose tend to become redundant or trivial. It is better to relax into a description of the file than to attempt a useful definition of its purpose.

Name the record or records that the file contains. Describe the role this group of information plays in the system. Where it will help the system players (particularly the users) to understand the information structure of the system, describe how the file interacts with other files or system functions.

ORGANIZATION

File organization can be a physical attribute, the options determined by the programming language, operating system, and hardware

Code	Organization
D	Direct
H	Hierarchical
I	Indexed
N	Networked
R	Relative
S	Sequential
O	Other

TABLE 7-1: File Organization Codes

used to implement the system. It can also be specified as a logical attribute.

To specify organization logically, you must design a scheme that is independent of the implementation environment. A logical scheme for defining file organization is useful when you develop different versions of your system for different languages or operating environments. Table 7-1 illustrates such a scheme.

MEDIUM

There are only a few media on which files can be stored, so this attribute is best specified using a "checkbox" approach.

Your documentation system should allow you to specify the file medium by selecting options from a menu or by entering a medium code. The name or description of the medium is provided by the documentation system as a soft attribute. Allow for a checkbox to specify "other." In this case, you will also need to enter a description of the medium.

A suggested list of file media and codes is shown in Table 7-2.

Code	Organization
C	Cartridge Tape
F	Floppy Disk
D	Hard Disk
M	Mass DASD
R	Reel Tape
O	Other

TABLE 7-2: File Medium Codes

Note that, by my definition, a specific file exists on only one medium. When records are transferred to another medium, as when a disk file is backed up to tape, a new file is created. The tape version of the file should be specified separately from the disk version. This approach encourages you to assign distinct identifiers to each distinct version of a file.

You may decide to relax this restriction and specify each medium on which the file is stored. If the file has a different label on different media, list the media and labels in the notes section of the specification.

SEQUENCE/ACCESS KEY

The sequence/access key attribute defines the data items by which the records in a file are sequenced, and as a result, accessed. The sequence/access key may consist of one or more data items. For example, an employee master file containing only one type of record would be sequenced and accessed by the employee number. If the file holds several record types for each employee, the sequence/access key would be the concatenation of employee number and record type.

As you might expect, only the data item numbers need be specified as hard attributes. Other information about the data item can be displayed as soft attributes by the documentation system.

You will also need to specify the sequence mode. A coding scheme for sequence modes is shown in Table 7-3. All you need to show with this attribute is whether the records are stored in ascending or descending order of the sequence key, and whether or not the signs of data item values are taken into account.

Note that changing the sequence of the records creates a different file because a file (by my definition) can have only one sequence.

Code	Organization
UA	Unsigned Ascending
UD	Unsigned Descending
SA	Signed Ascending
SD	Signed Descending
FF	Entry Order (FIFO)
LF	Reverse Entry Order (LIFO)

TABLE 7-3: Sequence Modes

Collections of records sorted into different sequences should be specified as separate files, with separate file numbers and labels. This may be necessary even if the change in sequence is only perceived on a logical level. For example, you may need to specify files with multiple access keys as if they were actually separate files.

CONTENT

In most cases files contain a single type of record. If this is universally true for your systems, you may decide to absorb the record specification into the file specification.

However, it is possible for a file to contain several record types. It is also possible for a record to be stored in several different files. In situations like this, it is best to simply specify the record numbers of the records in the file and define the records separately in their own specifications.

Specify the record numbers as hard attributes. The record number allows your documentation system to associate the record specification, and hence even the data item specifications, with the file.

BACKUP

As EDP professionals have learned, file backup is so important that it is almost a sacred ritual. The file specification includes details about the backup procedures for the file. Backup attributes include the cycle, trigger, job number, and retention.

The cycle attribute specifies how often the file is backed up. Use the same format for backup cycle as for the subsystem or run cycle: Number per Period.

The trigger attribute shows the situation or event that initiates the backup. You can use this to record specific dates, message numbers, prerequisite runs, and so forth. If you specify a manual procedure to follow when backing up a file, the cycle and trigger attributes may be recorded in the job specification.

The job attribute specifies the manual procedure followed to back up the file. Of course, file backup may also be performed by a run (in a batch system) or a function (in an online system). Use the job attribute to record the numbers of either of these elements.

The retention attribute shows how long each backup is kept. It may specify a scheme of rolling generations, such as, "Save the last three monthly backups."

SIZE

There are several facts about the size of a file worth specifying or recording. These include the record maximum size, control size, nominal file size, and maximum file size.

The record maximum size is a physical attribute. Your programming language may or may not require that you specify this attribute in program file definitions. When record sizes are mandatory, record this attribute in bytes. You can design your documentation system to extract the maximum record size from record specifications and display it as a soft attribute of the file specification.

Control size is similar to the record maximum size; it is a physical attribute demanded by some languages and operating systems. Control size is also referred to as the "blocking factor." Again, specify this attribute in bytes. System builders may need to convert the record maximum and control sizes into units other than bytes, but bytes have the advantage of being universally understood.

Nominal and maximum file size are logical attributes. They are "information only" design guidelines. The nominal size is the number of records the file is designed to handle in normal operation. The maximum file size is a type of system limit. It is the number of records the file can accommodate before some intervention is required. Files reaching their maximum size may need to be reorganized or to have historical information removed.

SECURITY

Specifications for all elements in the information group include the security attribute, which specifies the security clearance needed to access or change the file, record, or data item. Since security features are built into the system software itself, the format and values for this attribute cannot be generalized. You must determine them according to your particular system design.

RECORD

Records are physical system elements. The record maps the logical data items onto the physical fields of computer storage media. The primary audience for the record specification is the system builder, who uses it to code programs that read, revise, and write the records.

Record specifications also serve a secondary, nontechnical audi-

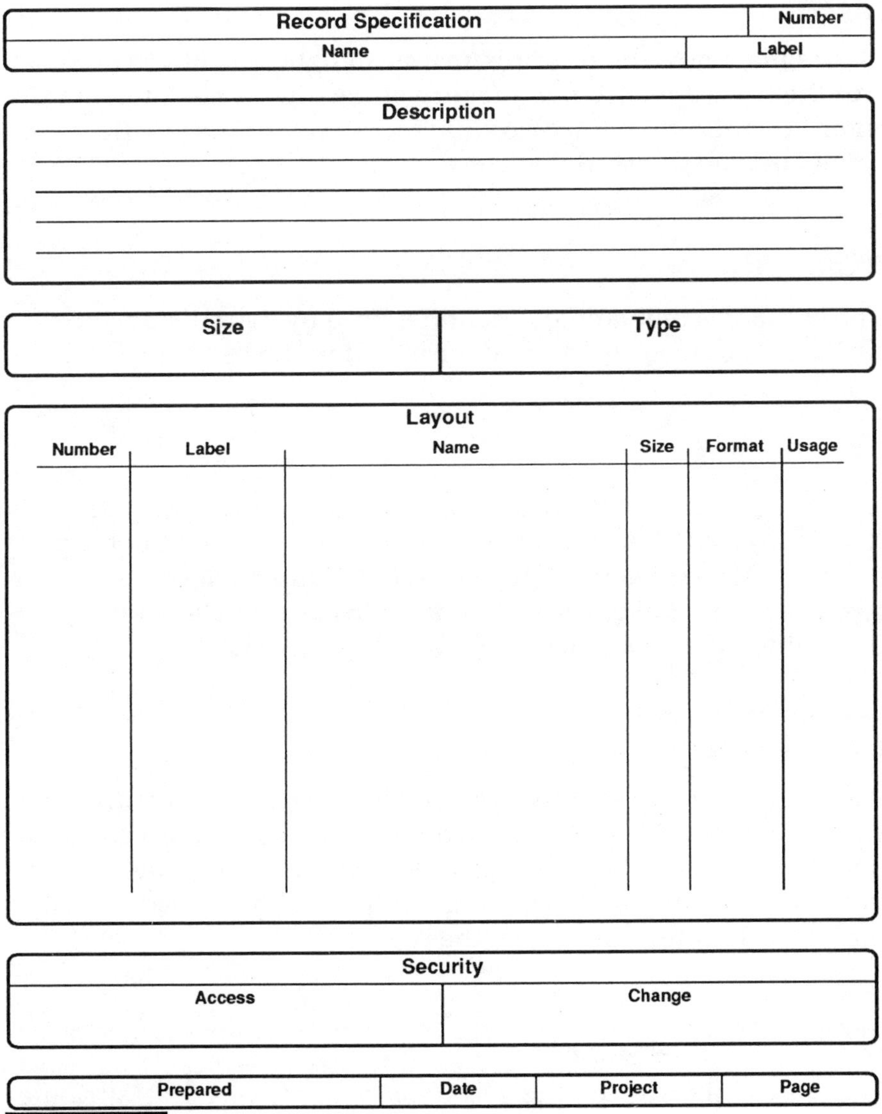
Record Specification | Number
Name | Label

Description

Size | Type

Layout
Number | Label | Name | Size | Format | Usage

Security
Access | Change

Prepared | Date | Project | Page

FIGURE 7-2: Record Specification

ence. They can be a useful way to identify and define groups of data items, such as transaction records, master file records, and history records. Figure 7-2 shows a record specification that meets both the physical (technical) and logical (nontechnical) information needs of the readers.

NAME

If possible, make the record name meaningful to both the builder and the user. Identify the category of data items contained in the record by their common object (inventory record) or function (personnel update transaction record).

NUMBER

The number is the standard identifier used by your documentation system. The suggested format for record numbers is SSSR999.

LABEL

Data base systems require a record identifier or record type code. Record these as the record label attribute. File systems do not require record labels. However, you can record transaction codes or type codes here for convenience. Use the label attribute to show something about the *record*, not the *file* in which it is stored.

DESCRIPTION

All records have the same basic purpose, storing groups of data item values. It is more useful to write a brief description of the record than to attempt specification of its purpose. Strive to make the description meaningful to both technical and nontechnical readers. State the general content and use of the record.

SIZE

The maximum size of the record is a hard, physical attribute. Whatever units your programming language requires, specify record size in bytes.

TYPE

This physical attribute shows whether the record size is fixed or variable. A checkbox approach is the best way to specify it. Use the label or notes attributes to record other record typing schemes.

Format: S99T9

Part	Meaning
S	Sign
99	Size in Bytes
T	Type Code
9	Decimal Places

Code	Meaning
A	Letter
N	Number
X	Character

TABLE 7-4: Field Format Codes

LAYOUT

The essential attribute of the record is its content and field definition, commonly called the record layout. The layout shows how the data items are mapped onto fields. Specify only the data item numbers as hard attributes. List them in the correct sequence, as they appear in the record.

The field portion of the layout specifies the physical storage areas that hold the data item values. Since field definition varies from language to language, it is best to use a logical scheme for specifying fields. The field definition scheme I use divides each field into three attributes: size, format, and usage.

Specify the size of the field in bytes. This is the actual physical size of the field, not the size of the data item stored in it. The field size is determined by the format and usage attributes.

The format attribute shows how the stored values are to be interpreted. See Table 7-4 for a format coding scheme. The format specifies the number and arrangement of the characters stored in the field.

The usage attribute shows how the characters are fitted into the bytes of the field. See Table 7-5 for a suggested list of usage codes.

Code	Usage
B	Binary
E	Edited*
P	Packed
S	Scientific
X	Unpacked

*Edit mask for printing.

TABLE 7-5: Field Usage Codes

SECURITY

Finally, the record specification includes the security attribute. As with files, the format and values of the record security attribute depend on your application system.

DATA ITEM

Information is a value in a context. "Nine" is not information. "Shoe size" is not information. "My shoe size is nine" is information. A data item is a definition of the context and allowed values for one piece of information in your system. Data items are purely logical elements.

Both the user and the builder need the information documented in data item specifications. The user reads data item specifications (or portions of them) to understand the meaning of the information displayed by the system. The user may need to know the meanings of codes, the number of characters allowed in a description, or how certain values have been calculated by the system. The builder reads data item specifications to determine the validation tests, display headings, and editing masks to be coded into programs.

When assembled into a data dictionary, the data item specifications form one of the most generally useful system documents. The data item specification is shown in Figure 7-3.

NAME

The general rule is to make data item names meaningful to the user. Some data items are strictly internal to the system—they are never displayed to the user. For these, make the data item name meaningful to the builders who will create and maintain the system.

Specifying the Information Group • 159

Data Item Specification	Number
Name	Label

Description

Used In

Number	Label	Name

Values

Picture	Source
Unit of Measure	Default

Code List or Calculation

Validation

Security

Access	Change
Display Heading	Edit Mask
Contains	Alias

Prepared	Date	Project	Page

FIGURE 7-3: Data Item Specification

The data item name is the preferred display heading for data item values. This header appears on screens, in messages, and on reports. Thus, there is a conflict between meaning and brevity in data item names. Do not sacrifice meaning for brevity. The specification contains other attributes (display heading and alias) that are intended to record shortened versions of the data item name.

NUMBER

The data item number is the standard documentation system identifier. The format is SSSD999. The only deviation from standard may occur in very large systems, or families of systems, where there are in excess of a thousand data items.

Do not use the number as a program label or display heading. Do not build in additional codes. Keep this as a pure, serial number identifier.

LABEL

The data item label is a field label; it is the program identifier of the fields that store data item values. Depending on how your system is implemented, you may need to store several different labels for each data item.

I consider the inside of a program to be the domain of the programmer. The creation and use of field labels should be under the programmer's control. The only concession I ask of programmers is that they use the specified label for input and output file definitions or record layouts. From this starting point, the program code can be used to interpolate to the labels of working storage fields.

You can save hours of troubleshooting by using the solid base of label names provided by the data item specifications. Working storage areas can use the standard field labels if you add a common prefix, such as "WS." The trade-off here is between creative freedom and maintenance costs.

DESCRIPTION

The specification includes a description of the data item rather than a statement of its purpose. The description shows both the purpose and use of the data item, in terms the user can understand. That is, the description defines the data item in business or application terms, not system terms.

Include a definition of the data item that classifies and differentiates it. Some examples:

Employee Number: a numeric code that identifies a specific employee and is the reference key for all information about that employee.

Receivables Check Amount: the dollar value of a check received as payment, to be applied to an outstanding invoice.

If you use a logical data typing scheme (such as the one described under "Picture," below) you can omit the data type from the description attribute. The data item type (code, amount, etc.) will be defined in the picture attribute.

USED IN

The Used In attribute is soft. It is not defined in the data item specification but is generated and displayed with the specification by your documentation system. I have shown this soft attribute in Figure 7-3 to remind you that it is one of the most useful soft attributes you can design into your documentation system.

The Used In list shows users where the data item is displayed and in which records or files it is stored. This helps the user access and maintain information. The list also helps maintenance designers and builders plan revisions to the system and allows support engineers to determine the impact of subsystem or function processing.

The Used In attribute can include any system element whose specification includes the data item number. The most useful elements to include routinely are file, screen, and report.

PICTURE

Picture is a term I borrowed from the Cobol programming language. It was simply too appropriate to pass up. The picture is a logical attribute, defining the number and arrangement of characters that express the data item values. The physical aspect of data item storage is defined in the record specification, not here.

I took the name for the picture attribute from Cobol, but not the coding conventions. My coding scheme is shown in Table 7-6.

UNIT OF MEASURE

The unit of measure defines part of the context of data item values. In most cases, the unit of measure is obvious. I started specifying it only after a painful experience with an inventory control system. Item: Paint, battleship grey. Quantity: 20. Question: How much grey paint do we have—20 gallons, 20 quarts, or 20 eight-ounce spray cans?

Format: S99T9

Part	Meaning
S	Sign
99	Size in Bytes
T	Type Code
9	Decimal Places

Code	Meaning
X	Character
C	Code
D	Date
F	Flag
A	Letter
N	Number

TABLE 7-6: Data Item Picture Codes

SOURCE

The source attribute shows who supplies data item values to the system and who is responsible for maintaining these values. The source can be specified as a hard or soft attribute. Treating the source as a hard attribute, you might specify one of the defined users (for example, Level One Terminal Operator), a department within a corporation, or perhaps the operator. If the source is specified as a soft attribute, your documentation system could scan the System File and compile a list of transactions, programs, or functions that supply or revise the data item values.

DEFAULT

The default value of a data item is the value the system assumes or generates when the user does not supply a value. When the default value is zero or spaces, specify zero or spaces. Reserve use of the term *none* to show that there is no default value. That is, when the user *must* supply a value.

CODE LIST OR CALCULATION

Besides knowing what values are allowed for the data item, users need to know how system-generated values are calculated. This information is specified as the code list or the calculation attribute.

If the data item is a code or flag, list each value and show its meaning. Calculated values require a little more thought and planning. It helps to make a distinction between the logical and physical methods of calculating the data item values. The logical method, expressed as a simple formula involving other data item names and constant factors, is recorded here for the benefit of the user. The physical method, expressed as an algorithm, as a decision table, or in structured text, is recorded in a program or module specification for the benefit of the builder.

This is the ideal place to anticipate and answer such user inquiries as, "How does the system calculate the subtotals on my Accounting Summary Report?" or "Why doesn't the sales tax on the invoice agree with my pocket calculator?"

VALIDATION

The validation attribute shows routine checks and tests performed by the system. Of course, there is the ever-popular "none," but more rigorously engineered systems will include such validation tests as

- Data type
- Range, maximum, or minimum
- Date format and range
- Comparison to other data items

This attribute is intended to inform the user but can also be used to supplement program specifications. You may decide to specify the number of the program or module that performs the validation.

SECURITY

If your system includes data security down to the field level, specify the security requirements as an attribute of the data item.

DISPLAY HEADING

Form captions, report column titles, and screen item headers are an important feature of the user interface. These display headings identify the values the system displays to the user. They are the context that converts data into information.

As I said earlier, the data item name is the ideal display heading.

It conveys the complete meaning of the value to the user. When the data item name is too long to use as a display heading, the correct abbreviation or condensed version of the name is specified here.

Specifying the display heading ensures its consistent use throughout the system. Consistent display headings increase the user's confidence and decrease the user's learning time.

You may wish to provide for multiple versions of the display heading. Each version should be a logical shortening of the data item name. Remember: The fewer versions you use, the simpler the user's learning task.

When you assemble data item specifications into a data dictionary, the display headings should be converted to additional entries in the dictionary. These need only point to the data item, using the format See Data Item Name.

EDIT MASK

The edit mask attribute is similar to the picture attribute but defines how the data item values are *displayed*. Unlike the picture, the edit mask is part of the user interface. Edit masks should be designed to make the system displays easy to read and use. It helps to adopt a standard scheme for specifying edit masks, such as the one shown in Table 7-7.

You may need to specify multiple edit masks for some items. A familiar example is check versus journal printing. An amount printed on a check needs an edit mask that includes leading dollar signs or asterisks. These are referred to as *check protect* characters.

Code	Organization
+	Display all signs
−	Display negative signs
CR	Display CR or DB
DB	Display DB only
X	Character
9	Number
.	Decimal Point
,	Comma
Z	Zero suppression
$	Dollar sign
*	Check protect
B	Space character

TABLE 7-7: Edit Mask Codes

The same amounts when printed on an accompanying journal would have an edit mask that simply shows the dollars and cents amount of each check.

CONTAINS

In the system models we have examined, there is no group of information larger than a single data item yet smaller than an entire record. The contains attribute lets you define such intermediate-sized groups of data items.

For example, you could define a data item called Record Key as containing the data items Record Type Code, Transaction Code, and Transaction Date.

ALIAS

Hopefully, you will never need to use the alias attribute to record alternate versions of the data item's name. In a machine environment there are no aliases. You either name the element correctly or you do not. Your users have greater processing abilities than your software and hardware, but you must not abuse their ability to handle aliases. The ability is there, but it is not free. Aliases increase the user's learning time. They also increase the user's perception of the complexity and difficulty of your system. When your system uses a diversity of aliases, the user perceives it as lacking consistency and integrity and may suspect similar shortcomings in the design and construction of your software.

The most frequent chore in writing add-on documentation is the selection (or creation) of the preferred names of data items. Are Customer ID, Record Number, Client Code, Master Key, and Reference Number really all the same data item? Which name should I use consistently throughout the documentation? You can compile lists of aliases and include them in a data dictionary or glossary. Unfortunately, this only improves the documentation, not the system.

Record aliases here if you must. Include them as "See Data Item Name" entries in your data dictionary, glossary, or index. But also think of alias lists as "hit lists." With each revision to your system, eliminate the aliases.

Use this attribute selectively. Record only true aliases of the data item name. Multiple labels needed for implementation in different languages are not really aliases and should be recorded in the label attribute.

8

Specifying the Exchange Group

This is the last of four chapters devoted to the details of specifying elements. We have reached the last item in our list of element groups, the exchange group. This group consists of the elements used to exchange information between the system and the user: form, screen, report, and message. These elements are all part of the user or human interface of a system. Appropriate care should be taken in designing and specifying them.

The exchange group elements are partially or completely designed early in the development process so that the user can experience the features of the system before it is actually built. The design step produces at least a list of the contents and a rough layout for each exchange element used in the system.

These parts of the user interface need not be designed by technical experts. In fact, nontechnical project team members can produce more effective designs for forms, screens, and reports because they can focus on the user's needs and on human factors. They are not distracted or limited by technical considerations.

As a compromise approach, nontechnical staff can design and specify the format and layout of exchange elements; technical staff can finish the design and specification process by supplying the technical attributes for each element.

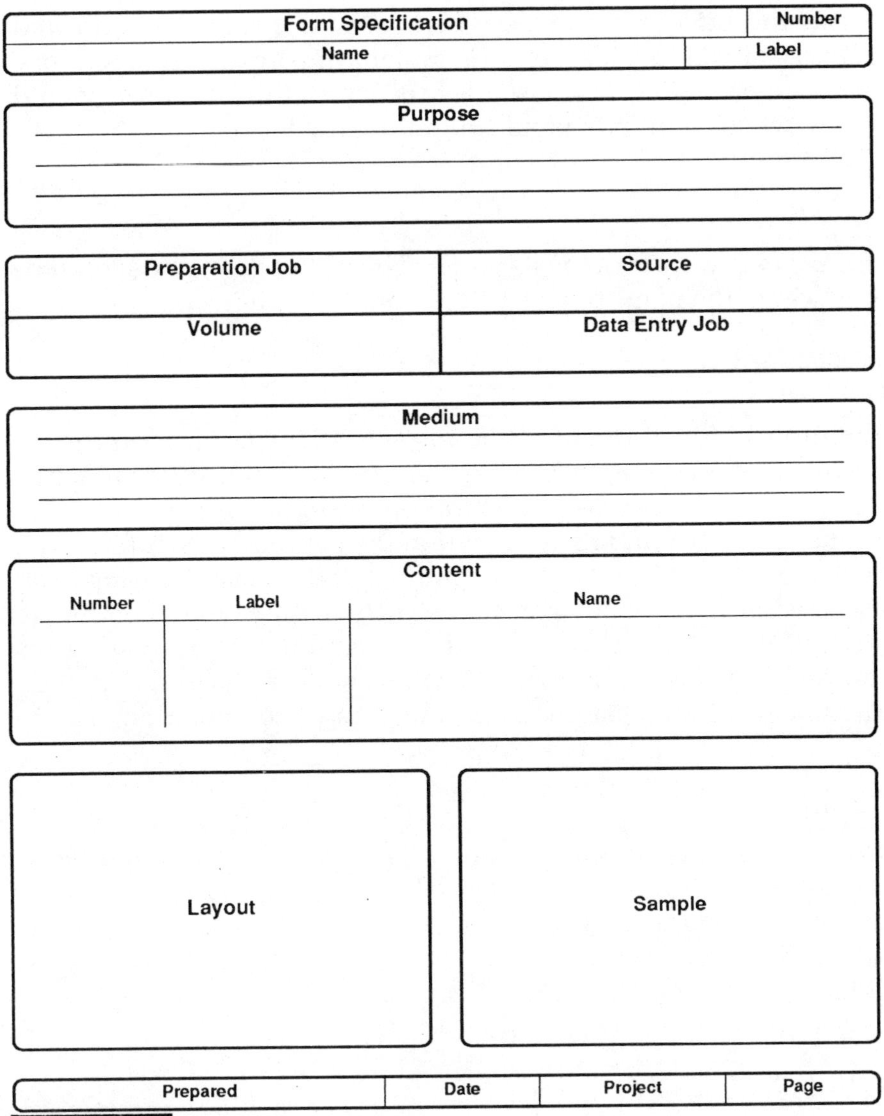

FIGURE 8-1: Form Specification

FORM

Recall that a form is a source document prepared by the user that acts as input to the system. Forms are physical elements and are confined to one medium—paper.

Figure 8-1 illustrates the form specification. This document shows the builder (form designer) how to create the form and includes attributes that help the system implementers, operators, and supporters. It also specifies the procedure the user should follow when completing and submitting the form.

NAME

Users identify the form by its name. The text of the name should be identical to the name or title printed on the form itself.

NUMBER

The form number identifies the form and its specification for the documentation system. This number need not appear on the actual input form. In most cases the form producer or supplier will print a control number and revision date at the bottom of the input form. Such identifiers are out of your control, but this is no hardship. You use the form number, which is strictly within your control, to identify the form. This means that a vendor or corporate forms control department can revise the value, or even the format of their identifiers, without serious impact to your documentation.

LABEL

The form control number, or any other identifier outside of your control, is recorded as the form label. This identifier is usually printed on the form itself. In fact, the form label can become the identifier most commonly used by people. Do you know the name of the W-2 form?

PURPOSE

Define the purpose of the form from the user's perspective. What does the user accomplish by using the form? Forms can serve one or more of the following general purposes:

- Capture information
- Convey information or instructions
- Request action from others
- Initiate actions or processing functions
- Record historical information

The statement of purpose can take the format Verb Object. The verb is chosen from the list above. The object can be a system function or element. For example, forms can be used to request reports, initiate subsystem operation, or capture data items that comprise a master file or transaction record. Forms are also used to convey user options or run time variables to the operator. They can record system control totals for later analysis and review.

PREPARATION JOB

The form specification can include detailed instructions for using the form. However, it is more convenient to record the preparation job number as a hard attribute of the form specification and specify the preparation job separately.

This approach lets you separate the information needed to create the form from the information needed to use it.

SOURCE

The source attribute specifies who is responsible for completing and submitting the form or batch of forms. In a batch environment, this shows the data entry operator whom to contact for scheduling, legibility, or verification problems. It also shows to whom the forms should be returned after data entry is completed.

Normally, the user designated as the source of the forms will also be specified as the driver of the preparation job.

VOLUME

The volume of forms used by the system can be expressed in two ways: as the number of forms used in a given period or as the number of forms required per processing volume.

The first format, Number per Period, is the same as that used to specify cycles. It is useful only when the number of forms used is relatively independent of processing volumes. The volume of forms used only in connection with system cycles can be specified this way. Examples are forms used to request or record.

The second format, Number per Element, is useful when the volume of forms used depends on the number of elements (such as transactions or records) processed.

This attribute helps the user or the operations department control the inventory of forms. It can also help the data entry department schedule their work.

DATA ENTRY JOB

The form specification points to the data entry specification or job used to convert the data to magnetic media. Specify the job number as a hard attribute, allowing the documentation system to provide additional soft attributes from the job specification itself.

It helps the data entry operator to identify the form in the job specification too. Remember to specify the form number as the input required for the data entry job.

MEDIUM

Forms have only one medium; they are printed on paper. The medium attribute specifies additional production details about the form. Depending on the purpose, handling, and storage of the form, you may want to specify

- Form size
- Number of parts or copies
- Distribution of each part
- Color of paper for each part
- Color of ink
- Weight and finish of stock
- Drilling or padding

You may need to enlist the support of a professional form designer to determine these details. Once specified, production details should be recorded here for future reference.

CONTENT

The content of the form must be expressed as a hard attribute. Specify the number of each data item that appears on the form.

Specifying the content of the form makes it possible for the form designer to create the layout of the form. The data item specifications show the character size and display heading of each data item. You can provide the form designer with the appropriate data item specifications or include the character sizes and headers as soft attributes on the form specification.

A list of the data items contained in the form also makes it possible to plan revisions. "If we expanded the part number to twelve characters, what changes would we need to make?"

LAYOUT

The form contains more than data items. It has lines and boxes, blank and shaded areas. The form may group several related items into one block and establish a new name for that group of items.

Forms can be collections of identical lines, one line per record or transaction. They can also be designed to capture common information in a single block, supported by multiple lines of variable details.

This kind of information is specified in the form layout. The layout is a representation of the finished form but does not closely resemble the finished form. It is used by a graphic artist or printer to produce the form. Consequently, it contains additional technical information that does not appear on the form itself.

Forms are features of a system. They are elements of the user interface, seen and touched by the users. Form design is a critical aspect of system design. For this reason it is advisable to enlist the advice and assistance of experts.

If you design your own forms, remember these important points:

- Include the title (name) and control number (label) on the form.
- Put the reference number (the data item by which the forms are sequenced, stored, or accessed) where it will be readily visible, usually in the upper right corner.
- Order the items on the form from left to right and top to bottom in the sequence followed by the user when filling in the form.
- Use boxes and rules to guide the user's eye and hand, but keep them to a minimum. Use plenty of white space for a visually attractive form.
- Put detailed instructions or long code lists on the back of the form to minimize clutter.
- Use checkboxes wherever possible.
- For handwritten forms, allow between 0.20 and 0.25 inches of vertical space for each line, between 0.10 and 0.20 inches for each character.
- Include the character size of each item in the header (also called the caption). Alternately, show the number of charac-

ters by using boxes or pips (short vertical lines that divide a horizontal line).
- Include boxes that show who prepared the form, the date it was prepared, and a batch number where applicable.

SAMPLE

The form layout serves technical purposes; it shows how the form is created. For this reason, it may not give an accurate impression of the final appearance of the form. Thus, the specification also includes a *sample* of the form. The sample shows exactly what the form looks like. Fill in the sample just as the user would. Use hypothetical but realistic values for each item on the form.

Samples are an excellent way to bolster the confidence of novice users. The sample is a hard attribute of the form specification, but it can be included with the preparation job specification as a soft attribute.

Note that the form specification shown in Figure 8-1 calls for layouts and samples to be attached, not for 2-by-3-inch reduced versions to be printed on the specification itself!

SCREEN

Screens are logical elements. They are groups of information presented on a monitor. Screens can occupy either the full display area or a smaller box or window on the monitor, perhaps appearing inside another screen.

The screen specification shows the builder how to create the screen. It shows the user what data items, menu selections, or lines of dialog appear on the screen. Figure 8-2 illustrates the attributes of the screen specification.

NAME

The screen name is the text that appears on and identifies the screen. Since screens are elements of the user interface, it is important to make the screen name meaningful to the user. The name should be a capsule definition of the screen's purpose or use.

It is important to use screen names consistently. First, the text of the specified name must be identical to the text displayed on the screen. This lets the user relate his experience of the system to

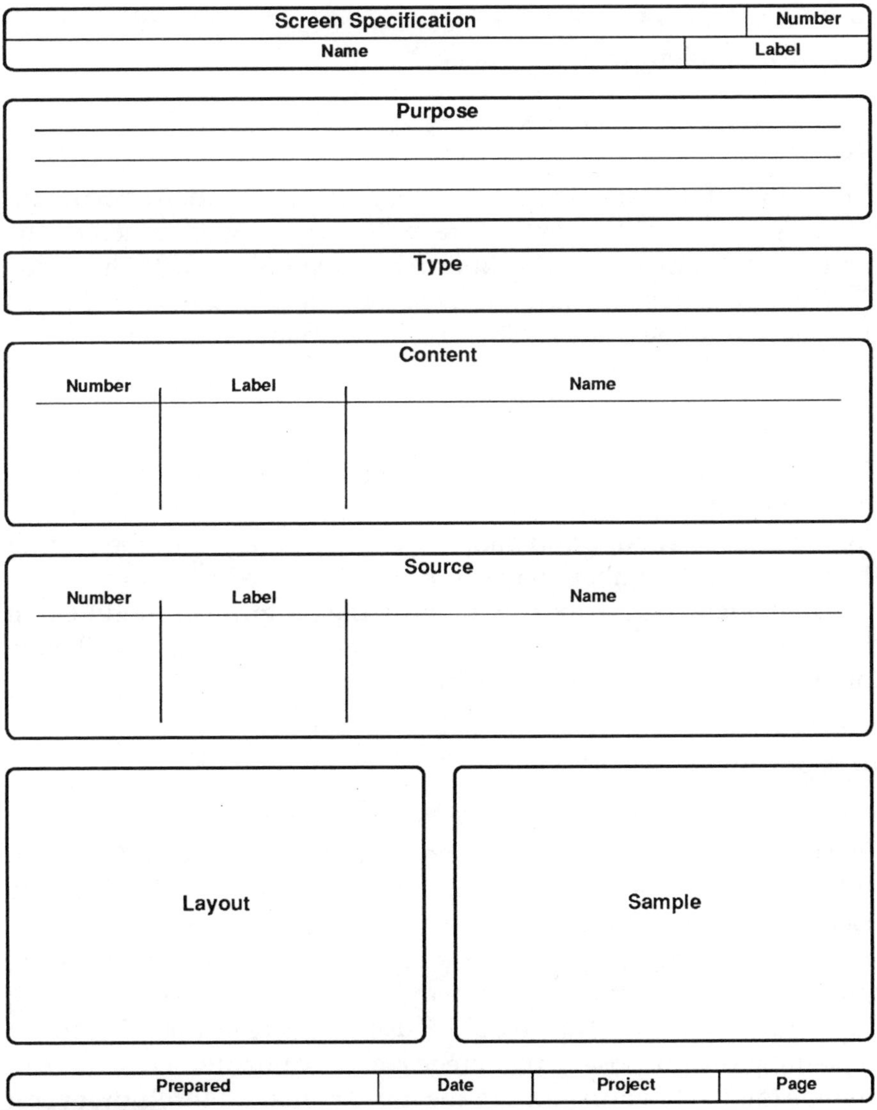

Screen Specification

Screen Specification		Number
Name		Label

Purpose

Type

Content

Number	Label	Name

Source

Number	Label	Name

Layout

Sample

Prepared	Date	Project	Page

FIGURE 8-2: Screen Specification

supportive documentation. Give each screen in your system a unique name. Second, the system screens must refer to each other by using their names exactly as specified. An example will illustrate the need for this consistency.

From a menu screen the user selects a function called Add New Customer. In response, the system displays a screen titled Customer File Maintenance. The user is left to wonder: "Did I press the right key? Is Customer File Maintenance an alias for Add New Customer? Is there a problem with the system?"

NUMBER

The format of the screen number is SSSS999, the standard documentation system identifier for the screen. It is a good idea to include the screen number in the heading line of the screen, along with the name. This lets the users and supporters access specifications (or derived documents) in the System File for details about the screen.

LABEL

The format and value of the screen label depend on how screens are implemented in your system. The label could identify the file that holds the screen image and data maps. Alternately, the label, rather than the screen number, may serve as a displayed identifier.

Do not use this attribute to identify the program or module that displays the screen. See the discussion of the source attribute below for an explanation of this prohibition.

PURPOSE

You may need to create two statements of purpose for each screen. One is addressed to the builder and states the purpose of the screen in technical or system processing terms. The other addresses the user, showing what function the screen accomplishes for the user.

When writing descriptions or statements of purpose for the user, I find it helpful to actually picture the user sitting before me, asking a question such as, What would I use this screen for? I start by explaining the purpose of the screen conversationally. (Yes, this can involve talking to yourself). I refine my explanation through several repetitions, finally arriving at the written version.

TYPE

Screens can be classified by their function and their size. See Table 8-1 for a coding scheme for screen types.

Screens perform one of three functions and are typed accordingly as menu, data, or talk.

Menu screens display a list of selections. They allow the user to

Format: FS

Part	Meaning
F	Function Code
S	Size Code

Function Codes

Code	Meaning
D	Data
M	Menu
T	Talk

Size Codes

Code	Meaning
F	Full
L	Line
W	Window

TABLE 8-1: Screen Type Codes

select another menu, a data screen, or a function for execution; for example, the user may return to a higher-level menu or exit from the system. Menu screens are linked together to form the hierarchical structure of the system.

Data screens act like the reports and forms of a batch system. They either display or accept data item values.

Talk screens let the system conduct a dialog with the user. The system uses talk screens to solicit additional or optional information about functions selected by the user. Talk screens can also be used to inform the user of problems or errors and can prompt the user to take appropriate actions.

Screens can also be classified, according to their display size, as full, window, or line. Full screens occupy the entire display area of the monitor. Windows occupy only a portion of the monitor display area. They can be of any width or length; their dimensions are specified in the layout. Line screens occupy a single line on the monitor. They usually run the full width of the monitor and display messages or prompts.

CONTENT

The content of a screen is a hard attribute. It must be known before the screen can be built. Specify the number of each element contained by the screen, allowing your documentation system to add appropriate soft attributes.

Different system elements appear on different types of screens. Menu screens contain other menus, data screens, or functions. Data screens contain data items. Talk screens contain messages.

SOURCE

The source attribute identifies the system element that produces the screen, such as a program or module, or even a batch system run.

Menu and data screens are often produced by a single program. It is rare for talk screens, especially those that display error messages, to have a single source. I suggest that you treat the source of *all* types of screen as a soft attribute. Do not specify the screen's source, but let your documentation system compile a list of sources by scanning the System File.

Whichever approach you use, make sure you can work backwards from the screen to the program. When the user experiences a problem with a screen, the solution lies in the processing element that creates the screen.

Another way to link display elements (screens, reports, and messages) to their source is by a "signature." You can display the number or label of the source program as a variable portion of the display element. When a screen, report, or message is "signed" by the program that produced it, the user can provide you with the link you need.

LAYOUT

Screens are a prominent feature of the user interface. Screen design should not be left to the builder. The layout lets the designer create and communicate the appearance of the screen to the builder.

Screen layouts can be created on ruled forms. More commonly, they are "painted" by the designer during a session with an interactive screen generator. It is important not to lose the distinction between "what should be" and "what is" in such situations.

Even if you use a screen-generating utility that creates all of the code needed to make the screen fully functional, make sure you can extract the screen layout and store it in the System File.

Here are some important points to remember when designing screens.

- Always include the name and number in the heading line.
- If the name and number do not identify the system, display the system name or label in the heading line.
- Display the system identifier, screen name, and screen number in the same place on all screens.
- Use the specified display headers for all data items shown on screens.
- Use the specified function names as the selections on menu screens.
- Avoid cluttering screens with too much information.

See Chapter 15 for more detail on designing screens.

SAMPLE

The screen layout shows the builder how to create the screen, but it does not show the user what the screen typically will look like; therefore, a sample should be included as an attribute of the screen specification. Show the screen as the user will actually see it. Use typical values for displayed data items. You may need to include several samples to show variable or optional features of complicated screens.

If you failed to include sample screens in your product design document, be sure to create them now. Screens are a critical component of the user interface. As such, they are invaluable as marketing, training, and support tools.

REPORT

The report specification is illustrated in Figure 8-3. This document is addressed to the builder and to the user. It shows the builder how to create the report. It shows the user what information the report contains, how to request the report, and how to interpret it.

Reports are physical elements, primarily because they are confined to the printed page.

178 • System Documentation

```
┌─────────────────────────────────────────────┬──────────────┐
│           Report Specification              │    Number    │
├─────────────────────────────────────────────┼──────────────┤
│                   Name                      │    Label     │
└─────────────────────────────────────────────┴──────────────┘

┌──────────────────────────────────────────────────────────────┐
│                         Purpose                              │
│                                                              │
└──────────────────────────────────────────────────────────────┘

┌──────────────────────────────────────────────────────────────┐
│                   Sequence and Breaks                        │
│   Mode   Number      Label              Name          T  P  │
│                                                              │
└──────────────────────────────────────────────────────────────┘

┌──────────────────────────────────────────────────────────────┐
│                         Content                              │
│      Number       Label                 Name                 │
│                                                              │
└──────────────────────────────────────────────────────────────┘

┌──────────────────────────────────────────────────────────────┐
│                    Print Specification                       │
│ Paper Code or Form Size:                                     │
│ LPI:                          │ CPI:                         │
│ LPP:                          │ CPL:                         │
└──────────────────────────────────────────────────────────────┘

┌───────────────────────────────┬──────────────────────────────┐
│      Distribution Job         │          Volume              │
└───────────────────────────────┴──────────────────────────────┘

┌──────────────────────────────────────────────────────────────┐
│                         Source                               │
│     Number        Label                 Name                 │
│                                                              │
└──────────────────────────────────────────────────────────────┘

┌───────────────────────┬───────────────────────┐
│                       │                       │
│        Layout         │        Sample         │
│                       │                       │
└───────────────────────┴───────────────────────┘

┌───────────────┬───────────────┬──────────────┬──────────────┐
│   Prepared    │     Date      │   Project    │     Page     │
└───────────────┴───────────────┴──────────────┴──────────────┘
```

FIGURE 8-3: Report Specification

NAME

Like all elements in the exchange group, reports are part of the user interface; consequently, report names should be meaningful to the user.

The report name should tell the user what purpose the report serves or what category of information it contains. The title or header printed on the report must be identical to the specified report name. Do not be slipshod in naming reports. Demonstrate the integrity and consistency of your system in all aspects of report design and specification.

Here is a case study that illustrates the importance of making report names meaningful to the user. It involves an online mortgage servicing system. Certain adjustments to the Master File were accumulated in a transaction file. The system administrator applied these revisions to the Master File once each month, essentially in a batch mode.

The program that applied the transactions created a report named Revisions to Master File. This program performed two main functions. First, it validated the transactions themselves. Second, it applied the valid transactions to the Master File.

The program could be run in two modes. In the first mode, the program passed the transaction file, performed its validations, and reported the results in the Revisions to Master File report. This allowed the system administrator to correct or delete erroneous transactions. In the second mode, the program repeated its validations, updated the Master File, and again produced the Revisions to Master File report.

The report always looked essentially the same, no matter which program mode created it. On days when the system administrator performed several validation and correction runs, keeping track of the reports became difficult.

The solution was to specify the program as producing two different reports, one named Master File Revisions Pending, the other Revisions Made to Master File. Of course, the programmer perceived the two reports as the same report. The only difference was that the report title changed to reflect the program's mode of operation. The user, however, perceived the reports as being separate and distinct.

This solution required only simple changes to the program code. It also required revision of the original report specification and the creation of a second report specification, essentially identical to the original. A comment in the notes area of both specifications linked them for control purposes.

NUMBER

Report numbers are an excellent short-form identifier. Print the report number in the heading line of the report, along with the report name. The standard format for report numbers is SSSO999.

LABEL

Although they are physical elements, reports seldom need machine identifiers, or labels. If your system has a print file spooling utility, the label can specify the spool file identifier for the report.

PURPOSE

Reports serve a variety of purposes. These include, but are not limited to, the following functions. A report can

- Survey or analyze system data
- Provide the user with reference information
- Report the progress, status, and results of processing
- Initiate corrective or administrative action
- Summarize or detail system data
- Act as a source document for the user, as in the case of checks or invoices

These general statements of purpose can be made specific for a particular report. Express the report's purpose strictly in terms of the application or business function it performs for the user.

SEQUENCE AND BREAKS

Not all reports take the form of listings, but for those that do, the report sequence is an important hard attribute. Specify the report sequence just as you would a file sequence, by listing the data items that compose the report key. Specify only the data item numbers, allowing your documentation system to provide the labels and names. In addition, you need to specify the sequence mode, as shown in Table 7-3.

You will find that the key that defines the report sequence also determines total and page breaks. The T and P columns on the specification are flags that show which breaks in the report key cause total or page breaks. The P column can also indicate breaks in the

Code	Total Break
S	Subtotal
T	Total
G	Grand Total

OR

Code	Total Break
T1	Lowest Level
T2	Second Level
...	Etc.
TN	Highest Level

TABLE 8-2: Report Total Break Codes

report part, which may entail their own page or heading changes. Report parts are discussed under the layout attribute, below.

You can also establish a logical scheme for coding the type or level of each total break. See Table 8-2 for an example.

CONTENT

What information does the report contain? Each data item printed on the report is listed in the content attribute. As usual, only the data item number need be specified as a hard attribute. The number can be used to access the label and name of each data item. In addition, a special version of the report specification can include the data item code list or calculation information.

PRINT SPECIFICATION

The print specification defines several parameters that are used to print the report. This attribute shows the paper code or form size of the stock on which the report is printed. It may also include information about the number of parts or copies required.

The remaining print parameters depend on your system and on the hardware environment. These may include

- Lines per inch
- Lines per page
- Characters per inch
- Characters per line

DISTRIBUTION JOB

When a centralized operations department produces all system reports, the operators need instructions for preparing and distributing them. The report preparation and distribution procedure is specified as a job. Record the distribution job number as a hard attribute of the report specification.

The distribution job includes instructions for decollating, bursting, and binding the report, and may give instructions for extracting and recording control totals printed on the report. The job specification also shows who receives each copy of the report, how it is sent to the users, and any critical scheduling or security procedures.

You can specify operator proof or control steps for financial systems in this attribute, provided they are simple. More complex proof processes should be specified as part of the operating job in the run specification that produces the report in question.

VOLUME

The volume attribute gives both operators and users a rough idea of how big the report is. You can define the report volume as an average number of pages or as a number of pages per volume of transactions or records.

SOURCE

Builders and supporters need to know which *physical* elements—programs and runs—produce the report, in order to conduct troubleshooting and revision projects. Users need to know which *logical* elements produce the report. They request reports by requesting subsystem runs or by selecting functions. In both cases, the documentation system provides a list of the report's sources as a soft attribute. It scans the system file for logical and physical elements that specify the report as output.

LAYOUT

The report layout shows not only the content but also the organization of the report. It contains the technical information needed to create the report.

The layout specifies the location and headings for each group of data item values and expresses the construction details of the report in a concise format. It may include construction details for specific types of form, such as checks or tax reporting forms.

Reports are features of the user interface. They deserve your best design efforts. Here are some pointers to bear in mind.

Use the specified display headings for each data item. The user can use the display heading to access information in the data item specification (or data dictionary or user manual index).

Each page of the report should have a uniform heading line that includes the report number, report name, reference item, and page number. The reference item is the identifier by which the report is stored and accessed. It distinguishes different versions of the report. The date is a commonly used reference item.

Break complex reports into different parts. Report parts correspond to breaks, or changes in the report key. Each report part should have a heading line including the part number, part name, part variables, and page number.

The part number identifies and sequences the report parts. Part numbers can be assigned to the defined options of a report, or they can be assigned sequentially as the report is produced.

The part name is a descriptive title. It shows the user the purpose and content of the report part.

Part variables are items that further identify the information in each part. The part name and variables are often intermixed.

The page number can appear in either the report heading or the part heading. Number the report or part pages sequentially. For example, consider an Items at Reorder Point report produced by an inventory system. The report is sequenced by the following key:

Factory
  Storage Room
    Part Number

The report has a page break for each change in Storage Room and Factory, so that it can be distributed to the appropriate supervisors. This report would be broken into parts, one part per Storage Room.

The part name includes the factory name and storage room number as variables. Here is how the report and part headings for this report are printed:

```
INVO214        Items at Reorder Point          21JUN89
Part 12        Factory: URBAN Room: 3          Page 42
```

Include a summary or control totals part at the end of each report. This part shows the files used to compile the report, the totals of record counts or hash totals, and the options or run time variables used. The control totals part can include the "signature" of the program that produced the report, that is, its name and number or label.

SAMPLE

Report layouts seldom resemble actual reports, so the report specification includes a sample. The user can review sample reports to get an overview of what is available. Report samples can be used to test critical form designs for correct preprinted information, print alignment, and the like. They are also useful marketing and training documents.

Be concise when creating a sample, but show all the important features of the report. Show the report and part headings, at least a quarter page of the report body, and all total breaks. Create multiple sample pages to show various options.

MESSAGE

Messages, the text that appears on screens and reports, are logical system elements. The message specification shows the builder how to create dialogs, advise the users or operators of problems, or prompt them for information or action.

Message specifications can be massaged into manuals or appendices that show the users and operators how to interpret and respond to system messages. The message specification is shown in Figure 8-4.

NAME

The message name is a short form of the message text. It is used primarily by the designer and builder and should be meaningful to them. The users identify messages by their number and text, as these (not the name) are displayed.

NUMBER

The message number is the identifier used by the documentation system. It is also the reference key; message manuals or appendices

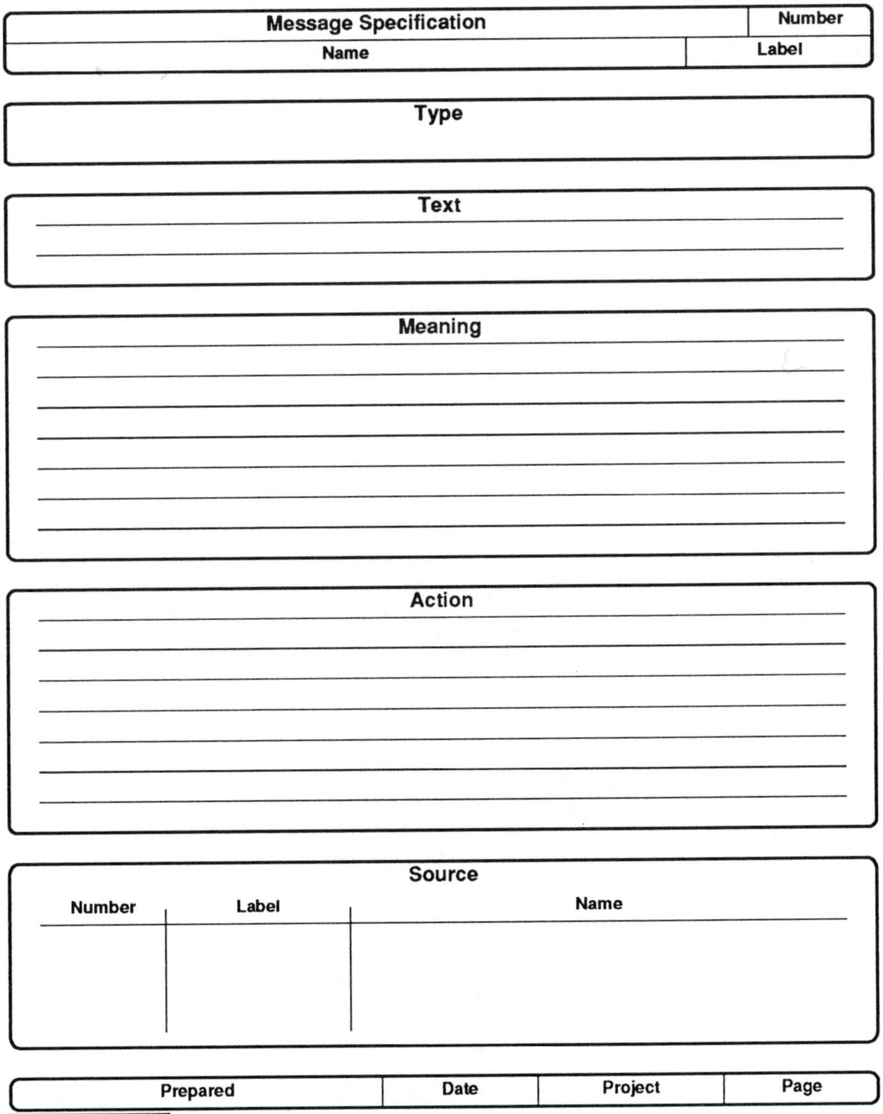

Message Specification form

Message Specification		Number
Name		Label

Type

Text

Meaning

Action

Source

Number	Label	Name

Prepared	Date	Project	Page

FIGURE 8-4: Message Specification

are organized in message number sequence. The message number format is SSSN999. If you use the same message throughout several systems, assign a general or global system prefix.

Display the message number with the text of note, warning, or error messages. This identifies the message as belonging to your application system, not the operating or host system. It also directs the reader to supportive documentation.

LABEL

Because messages are logical elements, they do not require a machine identifier, or label. If your system stores and accesses message text from a common file, the label can specify a record key. Resist the temptation to record the source program label as a hard attribute.

TYPE

Messages can be categorized into three types: dialogs, prompts, and displays. They can be further categorized into levels of problem: notice, warning, or error. Table 8-3 suggests a coding scheme for message types.

A dialog is conversation between the user and the system, consisting of a series of two or more message lines. Dialogs walk the user through a complex decision process, usually involving the selection of options for a function. The message specification for a dialog shows the logic branches and outcomes for the conversation. Use the same techniques to specify a dialog as you would to specify program logic: flowcharts, structured text, or decision tables.

Format: FL

Part	Meaning
F	Message Function Code
L	Problem Level Code

Message Function Codes

Code	Meaning
D	Dialog
T	Display (Text)
P	Prompt

Problem Level Codes

Code	Meaning
E	Error
N	Notice
W	Warning

TABLE 8-3: Message Type Codes

A prompt is a single message line used to secure a single value or a simple decision from the user. For example, a prompt similar to "Enter selection" usually appears at the bottom of menu screens. When a print function pauses to allow the user to set up the printer, the system displays a prompt such as, "Press any key to start printing."

A display is composed of one or more lines of text used to advise the user of unusual situations in system processing. Like prompts, displays require a user response, but this is usually simply an acknowledgment. Displays are categorized by the problem level code more often than dialogs or prompts.

Notice, warning, and error displays perform similar functions. They advise the user and wait for acknowledgment. Notices advise the user of unusual or unexpected situations. Warnings alert the user to a potential problem that may require corrective action but does not halt processing. Errors advise the user of problems that prevent the system from processing and must be corrected before the system can continue.

TEXT

The text attribute specifies the actual text of the message exactly as it will be displayed. If you elect not to display a message number or signature, the message text becomes the sole identifier of the message. Reference or support documents will list messages in alphabetic order by the message text.

The message text may include variables such as the number (signature) of the source element, file labels, physical device identifiers, record keys, and the date or time.

MEANING

The meaning describes the situation or problem that caused the system to display a prompt, note, or error message. It explains the text of the message fully, defining and interpreting any variables, and is addressed to the reader of the message.

ACTION

The action attribute, also addressed to the reader of the message, defines the steps the reader should take in response to the message.

SOURCE

Who sent the message? All possible sources are listed as a soft attribute of the message specification. Note that the source attribute defines the *possible* sources of the message. It cannot define the actual source of a message displayed in a particular instance. The software element that issues the message should include its "signature" as a variable in the message text. The signature can be either the number or label of the run, program, or module.

9

The Basics of Technical Writing

In the last four chapters, we explored *what* needs to be documented. It is time to focus on *how* to create the text and graphics that make up documentation. The next four chapters are devoted to the creation of text and graphics, and to their organization and integration into system documents.

System specifications call for surprisingly little text. You can specify most system elements with no more than a few sentences or paragraphs. All they require are statements of purpose or descriptions. But even here, there is always room for improvement.

To move beyond individual specifications to longer documents and manuals, you will need to create larger blocks of text and graphics. By using the in-line approach, you build a base of system information in the System File. You can extract this information and massage it into the documents and manuals you need by organizing the raw information, creating supportive text and graphics, and assembling the whole in a useful sequence.

In this chapter we'll examine basic tools and techniques for this kind of technical writing. In the following chapters we'll look at some specific techniques for creating text and graphics, and also at some structures that incorporate both.

THE IMPORTANCE OF EFFECTIVE COMMUNICATION

As we have seen, the purpose of documentation is to communicate information about a system among the system players. Communication is essential among the members of project teams and between the system developers and users. Those who prepare the documentation must be able to communicate effectively. Writing, at least the form of writing used in system documentation, is not a talent. It is a skill. It can be improved and developed through learning and practice.

Most technical system players, especially software builders, have already proven their ability to learn how to write effectively. Programmers learn coding languages. These involve specific terms, rules for combining terms into valid instructions, and techniques for organizing instructions into groups. The same principles apply to the English language.

THE PURPOSE OF TECHNICAL WRITING

System documentation requires a specialized form of writing called technical writing. Technical writing is always intended to inform, never to entertain; it is not poetry or fiction or essay. It is objective, not subjective. All technical writing depends on communicating information concisely and clearly.

Technical writing can serve several purposes. It can be analytic, developmental, instructive, directive, archival, or even promotional. We write analytic prose when we create overviews or statements of purpose. Product designs and system specifications are developmental forms of technical writing. Job specifications or user manuals are purely instructive forms of documentation. The content of the Project File is both directive and archival. Marketing literature is a form of promotional technical writing. In fact, all technical writing serves each of these purposes. In a specific document, one purpose will be foremost, but the other purposes are still being served in the background.

> **PROBLEM:** "I wouldn't even test a system with a manual that looks like this, never mind buy it!"
>
> **SOLUTION:** The system documentation is part of the user interface.

Bring the user and reference manuals up to the same level of quality as other elements in the user interface. Increased sales or increased user acceptance may be attained by enhancing the features that users often see first—the user manuals.

RULES OF GRAMMAR

Relax. We won't review or even discuss grammar in this text. Learning about grammar is not the easiest or best way to improve your technical writing skills. Here is my rationale for this controversial approach.

Rules of grammar are not legislated, enacted, and enforced. They are extracted from our continually evolving use of language. The rules are an attempt to capture and formally express the conventions we use in written or spoken communication.

Rules as rules have no value. Their only value is that they express the conventions we use to communicate effectively with our readers. If English is your native language, you already have an intuitive knowledge of these conventions. Further, the problems you are likely to encounter in technical writing are not solved by applying simple rules.

Consequently, it is easier to improve by studying examples and by practice than by learning rules of grammar. Your sole and ultimate rule must be that you convey factual information using conventions that your reader expects.

TECHNIQUES OF TECHNICAL WRITING

Techniques are the methods and tools you use at any level of technical writing. Basic techniques include the following:

- Simplicity
- Consistency
- Appropriate sentence length
- Coherent paragraph construction
- Use of alternate sentence or paragraph structures

Let's look at other techniques that you can use throughout the writing process.

PARTITION AND CLASSIFY

Classification and partitioning are methods of dividing. Partitioning divides a single thing into its component parts. Classification divides a group of things into smaller, distinct classes. We examined these techniques as they applied to the development of your system model. They can also be applied to the information you want to develop into a system document.

Which method of division you choose depends on your subject. If you want to describe a batch system, for example, you would start by partitioning it into its major functions: daily, weekly, monthly, and yearly subsystems. You could further partition each of these parts by specific daily, weekly, or monthly functions.

However, if your task is to document the 312 commands of an operating system, you would classify the commands by dividing them into smaller categories, such as file handlers, device drivers, batch instructions, and so on.

Whether you decide to partition or classify also depends on your purpose. For example, if your task is to design the user manual for an online system, you could partition the system into groups of functions that relate to specific user tasks, such as entering data, revising data, and printing reports. However, if your purpose is to organize dozens of reports in the report section of the manual, you may need to classify the reports according to their content or use.

Whether you classify or partition, there are some common ground rules to follow.

1. Apply partitioning to a single item.
2. Apply classification to a group of items.
3. Partition or classify according to your purpose.
4. Make each part or class complete and exclusive.
5. Define each part or class in clear, objective terms.
6. Choose the clearest format for expressing your partition or classification (list, table, or figure).
7. Make parts and classes of equal rank parallel in form.

DEFINITIONS

Defining means giving a precise meaning to a term. Clarity in writing begins with clarity in thinking. Be sure that you and your reader have a clear understanding of the meaning of your terms. Always define terms before discussing them.

Two types of definition are useful in technical writing and system documentation: parenthetical and sentence definitions.

In parenthetical definitions, you give the reader a synonym or explanatory phrase for the term you are defining. Put it in parentheses immediately after the term. Here are some examples:

> The monitor (display screen) of your terminal...

> The system date (the date you enter when booting your computer) defines the report date.

Sentence definitions can involve one or more sentences. A sentence definition has a specific format: (1) the name of the item or term you are defining, (2) the class or group to which the item belongs, and (3) a list or discussion of the features that distinguish the item from other items in the class. Here is an example.

> Printer: a computer output device that displays information in printed form on paper.

When you classify the item, be precise. Make sure the item reflects all attributes of the class you name. The reader expects your classification to tell him the general features of the item. Using a narrower classification yields a more specific meaning. For example, a printer could be classified as a piece of computer hardware, but this would not distinguish it from such input devices as keyboards or light pens. When you differentiate the item, make sure you separate and distinguish it from every other item in its class. Consider this definition.

> Input Form: a sheet of paper with preprinted headings and lines.

This definition does not distinguish the input form from report forms, which can also have preprinted headings and rules.

Do not be circular in sentence definitions. The name of the item should not appear again in either the class or distinguishing features.

A less common form of definition is the expanded definition. This includes the elements of the sentence definition, plus one or more of the following:

- History and background
- Example

- Graphic illustration (diagram, picture)
- Analysis of parts
- Comparison and contrast to similar items
- Basic operating principle
- Special materials or conditions.

CONVERSATIONAL STYLE

I taught myself technical writing largely by imitating the work of other technical writers. Unfortunately, I emulated the wrong kinds of documents and manuals—military standards and scientific journals. These use an impersonal or scientific style of writing that will not serve you well when documenting information systems. It took years for me to realize that a conversational style is not only easier to use but also more effective.

Write to your readers as if you were talking with them. Use first and second person pronouns (I, you, we, us) freely. Use contractions (you're, can't, won't) as you would in normal conversation.

The following examples demonstrate the differences between impersonal and conversational styles.

> Impersonal: After the report is received by the requester, it should be checked for correct date ranges.
>
> -versus-
>
> Conversational: After you get the report, check the date ranges.

> Impersonal: It is recommended that the backup procedure be performed on a daily basis.
>
> -versus-
>
> Conversational: We recommend that you back up every day.

As you can see, the conversational style is more direct and clear. It often requires fewer words. The informal tone of this style invites readers to read, rather than erecting a barrier between them and the information they need.

Be conversational, but not humorous, flippant, or sarcastic. Make your technical writing style simple, honest, and sincere.

TROPES

Tropes are figures of speech that liken one object to another. The simile, metaphor, and analogy are all forms of trope. In technical writing, tropes are used to instruct, not for artistry or entertainment.

Tropes compare terms or situations with which the reader is familiar to new or unfamiliar concepts. This lets the reader apply existing knowledge or experience to a new situation.

You are probably familiar with the analogy drawn between a roadmap and a menu map. Making menu selections is like making a turn in the road. This simple analogy allows the reader to draw several useful conclusions about how a menu-driven system works:

- I must always be somewhere on the menu map when I'm using the system.
- I travel through the menus to get to my destination.
- The menu selections are either destinations or turning points.
- There is a specific route that leads to each destination.

There are three criteria to follow when using tropes. First, they must be transparent; that is, the known part of the trope must be familiar and obvious to the reader. It is not helpful to tell a computer novice that your report generator acts just like a data base system. Second, they must be natural; the trope must apply sensibly and readily to the new idea. A word processing system may perform analogously to a space shuttle launch, but the analogy is bound to be difficult and strained. Third, they must model correctly; in other words, the trope must support the points of comparison you are trying to make but should not imply incorrect associations. If you tell your reader that using an input screen is just like filling in a form, the reader will expect to be able to go back and change entries before the form is completed.

Well-designed tropes can help readers, especially users, learn about your system. They can even be the focal points for system design. Obvious examples include operating systems that treat the monitor as if it were a desktop, and background utilities that provide such desk accessories as a calculator, notebook, calendar, and address book.

EXAMPLES

Readers like examples. You don't need an elaborate psychological survey to prove this point. Simply note your own reaction to the examples given in this book.

Examples give the reader an easy way to learn and to acquire and apply information. When using reference texts, we all tend to look for examples similar to our particular situation. We can then apply the example without having to read any further. The more specific and concrete the example, the better for the reader.

Consider the following instruction for entering a command, supported by an example.

> Install the print drivers by entering this command:
>
> f:INSTALLPD h
>
> f = label of your diskette drive
> h = label of your fixed drive
>
> For example, if your diskette drive is A and your hard drive is C, you would enter
>
> A:INSTALLPD C

CASES

A case is a group of related and consistent examples. Cases bring all the advantages of examples, plus benefits of their own. For example, in a payroll system, the same employee or group of employees would appear on all the input forms, screens, and reports of the system. More precisely, information about the same employee would appear first on specification layouts and later in tutorials or user manuals.

Cases show the reader how the system transforms and displays information at each step in processing. The reader can learn how the information is interrelated.

There are two important rules to observe when designing and using cases in your system documentation.

First, control the continuity of all examples, throughout all the system documentation. This is easier if you treat the specification layouts in the System File as the only hard source of example information. Changes to the specifications will automatically radiate through the derived documentation.

Second, match the case material to the audience. Examples for a spreadsheet system should use accounting or planning information. This is familiar material to the intended user.

Cases are also a useful way to create test information. Cases can be used to build examples one on the next in order to test detailed logic or processing conditions of the system.

WRITING BETTER

Writing better means using techniques that make it easier for you to write. It also means using techniques that make what you write easier to read.

Learning to write better means learning new skills and developing existing ones. Learning the basic rules of grammar may help, particularly if you motivate yourself by taking a class in grammar or writing. You must also practice what you learn.

A more efficient way to improve your writing skills is to analyze and emulate the work of other technical writers. Study the manuals you use at your own site and manuals written for diverse products. For example, your automobile owner's manual probably uses many of the techniques I discuss in this book. Study all the examples of technical writing around you. Learn what works and what does not work.

Although it may be painful (at first), you can learn much by submitting your efforts to a professional editor. This not only improves the quality of your system documentation but also points out your weaknesses.

You can improve your writing by observing the following guidelines for effective documentation.

First, organize your documentation effectively. The organization and sequence of information in system documentation should be supported by judicious use of headings, page layout, and graphics.

Be concise. The reader usually turns to documentation to answer a pressing question, and you must provide the answer as quickly and effortlessly as possible. Eliminate padding and needless preliminaries. Provide only the information the reader needs, in the most efficient format.

Keep your writing simple. Use simple words and phrases. Use paragraphs to group sentences effectively.

Keep your system documentation strong by using the active voice, concrete words, and examples.

Be consistent. Establish patterns for the reader that show what is the same and what is different. You set your reader's expectations and maintain or frustrate them by your consistency.

Use terms consistently. Avoid multiple terms, aliases, and synonyms. When you describe a file as being opened, selected, and accessed, you imply that different things are happening to the file.

Figuring out that these terms refer to the same activity takes work and time for the reader.

Be consistent in your use of phrases. Describe identical procedures with identical phrasing and text. For example, if each subject describes how to select an item from a menu, use exactly the same text each time. Consistency builds your reader's confidence about your system and about his or her ability to learn and use it.

Make your documentation readable. Readable text never has to be read twice. Eliminate jargon and slang that is unfamiliar to the reader. Use short sentences and short paragraphs.

WORKING METHODS

KNOW YOUR PURPOSE

I cannot overemphasize the importance of knowing your purpose *before* you put pen to paper (or fingers to keyboard). System documentation can be useful only if its purpose is clear. Knowing your purpose answers a multitude of questions and simplifies the decisions you must make.

Consider this problem. Should you repeat data item descriptions (type, size, etc.) with every screen in a procedure section or define them once in a data dictionary appendix? If your purpose is to maximize the convenience of the section for the reader, you will repeat the descriptions wherever they are needed. If your purpose is to reduce maintenance costs for the section, you will put them in a data dictionary.

PERSPECTIVE

I observed a peculiar phenomenon in one batch mainframe shop in which I worked. Most of the staff started as operators. When they were promoted to programmers, they created programs and runs that were easy to operate. When programmers were promoted to analysts, they created systems that were easy to program and maintain. It was only when outsiders were hired as analysts that we began to create systems that were easy for the users to use.

Having the ability to take on the user's perspective is essential to developing usable systems. The same is true of technical writing. It is only when you assume the reader's perspective that you can write effectively.

Learning to shift perspectives is difficult at best. Some people seem to have a natural talent for this kind of "head swiveling." Others can learn only from experience. If you suspect a weakness in this area, take the time to sit down with a first-time user. Observe the user's reactions to your system and your documentation. How does the user use the manual? Can the reader find the needed information quickly and easily? What kind of questions does the user expect your documentation to answer? The same technique can be applied to any system player who reads what you write. The best training would be to take on the role of each and every system player. Failing this, be prepared to seek and acquire the feedback you need in order to gain your reader's perspective.

INTERNAL BLOCKS

Technical writers encounter blocks. You may find yourself sitting before a blank page or an empty screen, with a deadline looming but no text being created. Blocks, I have found, are generally one of two types: internal or external.

Internal blocks are those that occur between your thinking and your writing. I would like to share three unusual but useful techniques for overcoming internal blocks. To clarify ideas at the sentence and paragraph level, I talk to ghosts. I envision the reader sitting before me and carry on an imaginary conversation. I present the information in the best verbal form in which I can express it. I listen to the reader's questions and note imaginary grimaces about unclear phrasing. I repeat the same discussion over and over until it is clear enough in my mind to write.

The second technique applies to internal blocks between the outlining and writing processes. For some reason, it is easy to convince myself that I have a workable outline when in fact I have not. Before I begin writing the text, I use the outline as my reference cards and (in my imagination) deliver a speech on the whole subject. This process reveals errors and deficiencies in the outline before I begin writing.

The third technique applies to internal blocks that result from a state of decision overload. When you are drafting text, do not distract yourself with decisions about organization, style, or terminology. The secret is to plan ahead. Spend at least as much time planning as drafting your work. Do not try to write perfect text the first time. You will probably agree that it is easier to edit than to revise and easier to revise than to draft. In other words, it is easier to improve what is written than to write it in the first place. Use this technique to eliminate internal blocks. Write the worst text you have ever written, but write something. Later, you can revise and edit it into acceptable form.

Sometimes the best place to begin is not at the beginning, but in the middle. Introductions and overviews are particularly difficult to write, so save them for last. Start in the middle and write your way out.

EXTERNAL BLOCKS

External blocks are those that occur between you and your sources of information. Taking the in-line approach to system documentation is a big help with external blocks. Most of the information you need resides in the System File.

When you must interview system designers and builders for information, observe a few simple rules.

1. Don't waste anyone's time. Come to the interview prepared. Know as much about the system as you can beforehand. Study the System File documents that have been completed, such as the product design and system specifications. Know your writing task and the exact information you need from those you interview. Have a list of questions you need answered.

2. Take notes. People resent supplying you with the same information repeatedly. Once they tell you, it is your responsibility to remember.

3. Keep the interview on track. Be diplomatic, but make sure you get the answers you need in the time set aside for the interview. It is your meeting, and you must control it.

Some people find it easier to correct a "dummy" draft than to answer questions in an interview. A dummy draft shows the organization, subjects, and topics you plan to write about. This draft does not contain the final, accurate details. Rather, it has blanks, question marks, or even imaginary facts you invent.

As another alternative to an interview, consider creating a written list of questions for your subject to answer. People who prefer to work alone, or who have difficult schedules, find both dummy drafts and lists of questions a convenient way to provide you with information.

MOTIVATION

Motivating writers to write is the domain of psychologists and managers. However, there are a few helpful ideas I have picked up over the years.

Keep yourself and your staff motivated by setting several easily attained objectives, rather than one large distant goal.

Motivation varies in direct proportion to proprietary interest. Proprietary interest is proportionate to the amount of involvement and control you have in a writing project. Keep yourself and your staff motivated by assigning responsibility for a document or group of documents to specific individuals. Within this overall structure, let the writers determine their own approaches, structures, and work methods.

Finally, attitudes are contagious. To keep yourself motivated, you must isolate yourself from negative attitudes. Discourage talk that is disdainful of your readers, your peers, or your managers.

10

Creating Text

In Chapter 9 we discussed some general techniques for technical writing. In this chapter we'll focus on creating text. We'll work through three levels of text: words, sentences, and paragraphs.

Recall the steps in the documentation process I defined in Chapter 2: plan, draft, edit, review, release, and maintain. The tools and techniques discussed in this chapter pertain to the second step, drafting. In Chapter 13 we'll cover the entire documentation process again as we learn how to design and extract manuals. Since the drafting step applies to all aspects of documentation, not just to the creation of manuals, we'll examine it in some detail here.

WORDS

WORD CHOICE

Use simple words. Good writing does not require big or fanciful words. Disregard any praise you may have received for your extensive vocabulary. Your purpose is to communicate simply and clearly to your audience.

Use words that are concrete and specific. Rather than saying "Respond when you are ready," say "Press the return key to start printing." Use concrete words that are derived from sensory images—the content of the user interface.

Use words that are objective rather than subjective. For example:

Subjective:
This report takes a long time to prepare and print, so we suggest you do it at a slow time.

-versus-

Objective:
This report takes 45 minutes to prepare and print. Schedule it for a time of low activity, perhaps at lunch or at the end of day.

The first version gives your subjective opinion of how long it takes to print the report. It suggests scheduling in abstract terms, leaving the reader to puzzle out what is meant by a "slow time." The second version corrects these faults.

JARGON

Jargon is a vocabulary of shorthand words used by a group of specialists. Jargon can save time and effort in communication, but only if the terms are clear to both the writer and the reader. Jargon is best left to the spoken language or to documents internal to the specialist group.

Jargon can be particularly intimidating to nontechnical system players. It is safe to assume that users will be familiar with the jargon of their business or application. It is not safe to assume they will be familiar with information system terminology.

When you create or use jargon, be aware of the costs involved. Make sure that the savings in writing time will not delay the reader.

Define any terms that are new or unfamiliar to your reader. Be consistent in your use of terms.

ACRONYMS AND ABBREVIATIONS

Use acronyms and abbreviations wisely. They are like jargon: You must make sure that they help your reader, not you. Acronyms and abbreviations are codes. They stand for something else: a phrase or a word. When commonly used, they acquire a meaning of their own. This short-form notation can help your reader. However, uncommon acronyms or abbreviations can actually hurt your reader; they reduce reading speed and comprehension.

These codes are used primarily to save space. Again, I caution you, never save space at the expense of your reader's understanding or ease of reading.

The only justifiable use of acronyms is when they identify terms that are global to the system. The obvious example is the system name. It is reasonable to use the acronym HDB to represent the Hyper Data Base system in all your system documentation.

Parenthetical definition is a good way to introduce acronyms. Here is a sample.

> The Hyper Data Base (HDB) system supports multiple query languages.

To increase readability, I have adopted the policy of introducing each acronym three times, using the parenthetical definition format. When an acronym appears four or fewer times, I delete all of them, leaving the terms fully spelled out in each case.

There are also valid reasons to use abbreviations. When you do so, check your spelling and punctuation in a dictionary. If you are coining an abbreviation, use the first letters of the word and truncate. For example, abbreviate *document* as *doc*, not *dcm*.

Be consistent in your use of abbreviations. They should be recorded in your style sheet or documentation standards manual.

USAGE

Usage is the way in which a word or phrase is used to express a particular idea. Good usage is the customary manner of using words in speaking or writing. Your usage must match that of your reader and must be consistent. As I write, the correct usage of "backup" is as a noun, not a verb. However, if technical writers continue to advise users to "backup on a regular basis" this usage will soon become acceptable.

Check your dictionary for correct usage and spelling.

CAPITALIZATION

It is reasonable to capitalize words that name concrete system elements. For example, I have capitalized System File wherever it appears in this text. This convention can become overwhelming and distracting in text that names several system elements. Use your discretion.

EMPHASIS

When words need special emphasis, they can be underlined, set in italic, or boldfaced. Underlining is the conventional way of instructing typesetters to set a word or phrase in italic type. Be moderate in your use of any of these devices. They lose strength and distract the reader when overused.

TERMS AND NOTATIONS

The introduction to a manual or guide is the ideal place to define special terms and notations used throughout the document. I find it convenient to define the terms *press*, *type*, and *enter* in the introduction of online system user manuals. You could also include a summary of format notations for command syntax or a table of symbols used to represent keys.

SENTENCES

ROLE OF SENTENCES

A sentence should contain one complete thought. This is not to say that the thought must be a simple one. Sentences can be definitions. They can express equalities or more complex relationships between two or several terms. They can be instructions.

Sentences unavoidably involve us in rules of grammar. We must consider the voice, tense, and structure of sentences. Before we do so, let me make a few general comments about sentence style.

STYLE AND ATTITUDE

Avoid trying to impress your reader. Try to communicate plainly and simply. Compare these two pairs of examples for readability.

> Replacement of the erroneous information must be effectuated.
>
> -versus-
>
> Replace the information that is wrong.

> In connection with various requests for special reports received by our programming department, it became of interest to investigate report generating software.
>
> -versus-

Requests for special reports led us to study report generators.

If you can appreciate the improvements in the second version of each sentence, you will readily grasp the concepts of voice, tense, and structure.

VOICE

A sentence can be in active or passive voice. In most cases, technical writing should take the active voice.

The active voice has this structure: actor, action, object (subject, verb, object). For example:

The operator mounts the correct disk pack.

The passive voice has this structure: object, action, actor (object, verb, prepositional phrase). Example:

The correct disk pack is mounted by the operator.

Whichever is first in the sentence, actor or object, gets the most emphasis. It is fine to use the passive voice to emphasize objects, but beware. In the passive voice, the actor can easily disappear. Consider this example:

The correct disk pack must be mounted.

Mounted by whom? The sentence gives no indication of who the actor is. Disappearing actors are not a problem in the active voice. Even when the actor is understood rather than expressed, it is clearly the reader who fills that role. Here is the revised version:

Mount the correct disk pack.

Always use the active voice for instructions.

VERB TENSE

Use the present tense for most of your system documentation writing. Set the main topic for discussion in the present tense, and adjust the tense of other events or actions around the main topic.

Here are two versions of the same set of instructions. The first version uses a variety of future tenses.

3. Next, you will enter the employee number.
4. The system will display the information screen.
5. If the employee status has been set to "inactive," the system will have masked all financial information.

-versus-

3. Enter the employee number.
4. The system displays the information screen.
5. If the employee status is "inactive," the system masks all financial information.

It may take some practice to get comfortable with writing in the present tense, as in the second version of the instructions shown above. The result is worth the effort. Your writing becomes simpler and clearer.

SENTENCE STRUCTURE, LENGTH, COMPLEXITY

Avoid overly complex or overly simple sentences. While a short, simple sentence is a good way to emphasize an important idea, a series of them is choppy and hard to read. It is difficult for your reader to piece together related ideas when they are separated into different sentences. Here is an example.

> There are some drawbacks to manual revisions. They are difficult to prepare. They have unexpected effects. They are difficult to trace. For these reasons, we suggest you keep them to a minimum.

Notice the awkward repetitions in this example. This text does not show that the items listed as drawbacks are related. Compare this with the improved version, below.

> Manual revisions have some drawbacks: They are difficult to prepare and trace, and they have unexpected effects. Therefore, keep them to a minimum.

Also avoid overly complicated or run-on sentences with too many ideas crammed into them. Complex subjects do not require complicated sentences. On the contrary, the simpler you make your description or explanation, the better for your reader. The following examples illustrate my point.

> Run-on Sentence:
> In the Super-Kludge transaction, individual and multiple transaction history records are updated, and fields in the Master File are adjusted, which does not produce errors but can produce unexpected results, especially for records with pending general ledger memo adjustments, which have their pending adjustments deleted.

-versus-

> Simple Sentences:
> The Super-Kludge transaction updates single or multiple transaction history records and adjusts fields in the Master File. Although the transaction does not produce errors, it can cause unexpected results. For example, if a Master File record has pending general ledger memo adjustments, the Super-Kludge transaction deletes the pending adjustments.

Use different sentence lengths and structures to vary the reading pace and create interest.

Compound sentences (those with several clauses) are often difficult to take in all at once. Consider using a list in place of a compound sentence, as in the following example.

> To edit a document, call the directory menu, select a document, type the document label, and press the enter key.

-versus-

> To edit a document:
> 1. Call the directory menu.
> 2. Select a document.
> 3. Type the document label.
> 4. Press the enter key.

CONCISE WRITING

Strive to be brief but not vague. Avoid needless words and phrases that clutter your sentences. Make your writing clear and concise. Compare the two versions of the following example.

> At this point in time I would say that we are ready to move ahead with our project.

-versus-

We are ready.

SENTENCE TIPS

Here are a few tips on avoiding common problems with sentences.

Double Negatives

Avoid double negatives and logical negatives. Which of the following versions is easier to understand?

> Make sure the status flag is not off.

>> -versus-

> Make sure the status flag is on.

Antecedents

When you use the pronoun "it" to replace a noun, make sure the word it replaces (the antecedent) is clearly expressed or implied. Here is an illustration.

> The system date is used by the Super Accountant system. It controls transaction dates.

>> -versus-

> The system date is used by the Super Accountant system. This date controls transaction dates.

The first version leaves you wondering "Does the system date control transaction dates, or does the Super Accountant system control transaction dates?" The second version leaves no room for doubt or confusion.

Reversed Sequences

Make sure the sequence of events in your sentences matches the sequence of events the reader experiences. The first example below is in reversed sequence; the second in parallel sequence.

> Before you quit the system, close all files and folders.

>> -versus-

> Close all files and folders before you quit the system.

PARAGRAPHS

ROLE OF PARAGRAPHS

Paragraphs are groups of related sentences. A paragraph can express a large concept or develop a complex thought, sentence by sentence. A well-written paragraph should be able to stand alone as a complete and meaningful message.

Paragraphs cue your reader to changes in subject or thought. They divide a page of text into parts and give your reader places to pause in a long discussion.

Paragraph length can vary. A one-sentence paragraph may be appropriate in certain situations. The upper limit for paragraphs is about a half-page of text. Readers habitually pause at the end of a paragraph to make sure they have understood its content. Long blocks of text provide fewer opportunities for your readers to check their comprehension.

PARAGRAPH STRUCTURES

In technical writing, paragraphs should have a clear structure. The most versatile structure is introduction, body, conclusion. Start with a central idea or topic in the introduction sentence. Move to supportive or developmental information in the body sentences. Finish by tying the paragraph together with a concluding sentence.

PARAGRAPH SEQUENCES

I will discuss the details of development or presentation sequences in Chapter 12. Any body of text should be developed in a clearly defined sequence, including paragraphs. Appropriate paragraph sequences are

- Introduction, body, conclusion
- Simple to complex
- Ordo Dei (define, explain, illustrate)
- Chronological
- Cause and effect
- Spatial
- Order of priority

TRANSITIONS AND CONNECTORS

Once you decide which sequence to use for a paragraph, link the sentences with transitional words and phrases. Here is a list of transitional words and phrases, classified by the relationships they signal.

Additional Idea	Comparison	Contrast
also	in comparison	but
and	likewise	conversely
further	similarly	however
in addition		in contrast
		nevertheless
		on the other hand
		otherwise
		still
		yet

Example	Explanation	Location
for example	in fact	beside
for instance	in other words	beyond
namely	simply stated	inside
specifically	that is	near
		opposite to
		over
		to the right

Result	Summary or Conclusion	Time
accordingly	in brief	finally
as a result	in closing	first
because of this	on the whole	in turn
consequently	to conclude	later
hence	to summarize	meanwhile
so		next
therefore		now
thus		second
		subsequently

HOW TO WRITE A PURPOSE

As I noted earlier, the largest blocks of text in system specifications are statements of purpose and descriptions, which take the form of single or multiple paragraphs. Here is a summary of how to write the purpose paragraph.

The purpose is a statement of the object for which a thing exists or is done. How you define the purpose, as you already know, depends on your audience.

The purpose paragraph can start with a sentence definition of the item. Make sure you identify the item clearly. Use the most convenient identifier for your audience, usually the English name.

For functional elements, describe or list the primary function or functions. You may need to express the function in terms of the goals the reader can accomplish by using the element. Remember to state the purpose in terms of *what* the element does, not *how* it does it.

For grouping elements, name or otherwise define the content of the element. Do not provide excessive detail. Simply name the next level of elements contained in the element you are discussing. Describe how the element is used or the major role it plays in the system.

Keep the statement of purpose to a single, short paragraph. Use a list format rather than long, complicated sentences.

HOW TO WRITE A DESCRIPTION

A description is a verbal picture or representation of an activity or object. It is a textual description or explanation of the item.

Start by forming a clear idea of the purpose and audience for your description. Keep the description short. One to three paragraphs should suffice.

Make sure you clearly identify the item you are describing. State the identifier most helpful to your reader—name, number, label, and so on. You may wish to list the aliases or synonyms for the item.

Depending on your purpose and audience, the description could include

- An explanation of the item's role or function in the system
- A portrayal of the item's appearance or features
- A discussion of the item's component parts
- An explanation of how the item works

Anticipate and answer the reader's questions about the element you are describing. What is it? What does it do? How do I use it? How does it work?

For functional elements, the description provides an overview of how the element works. This is still not enough detail to construct the element, but enough to define each important aspect of its operation. The description is the ideal place to present conceptual models for the element.

For grouping elements, name the content of the element. You can also present the classification scheme used to define the group.

A description can start with a statement of purpose and include supportive or explanatory information that expands on the purpose. Descriptions can also take the form of expanded definitions.

11

Creating Graphics

To create manuals or other system documents aside from specifications, you need to create additional text and graphics. In the last chapter we discussed the creation of text. In this chapter we'll look at the creation of graphics. The next chapter shows you how to integrate the two.

PURPOSES AND TYPES OF GRAPHICS

A graphic is any table, diagram, chart, or picture that presents information. Graphics can clarify, expand on, or even replace text; they are a condensed form of information. Graphics engage the reader's attention and increase both the level and speed of understanding information.

Text can be organized in several sequences, but it can be read in only one sequence—from start to finish. Graphics, by contrast, can be scanned in several directions. Complex or obscure relationships can be clearly shown in graphic form.

Whatever their purpose, in system documentation graphics must add to your text, not simply decorate it.

There is some confusion and ambiguity in naming the different types of graphic. Here is a structured list that shows the names I will use for each type of graphic. The list also shows how the graphic types are related.

Graphic
> Table
> Figure
>> Graph
>> Chart
>> Diagram
> Picture
> Sample

The major types of graphic are the table, figure, picture, and sample. There are several types of figure: graphs, charts, and diagrams. We'll examine the use and construction of each type.

TABLES

A table is a matrix of numerical or textual data. The information in a table is arranged in horizontal rows and vertical columns. Each row contains information on a specific item. Each column is a category of information about all items in the table. Figure 11-1 shows a simple table. The reader would use this table to determine which hard drive code to enter in a command.

Tables are simple to construct and read. They are best used for displaying numbers or attributes that are precise or discrete.

Table 2-4: Drive Labels

Drive Label	Make	Size (in Mbytes)
T	Hardco	40[1]
V	Hardco	60
R	LoSort	100
S	Signal	60
M	SpinRite	30
N	SpinRite	60
X	All Others	—

[1] Applies to 40.5 and 40.8 Mbyte versions.

FIGURE 11-1: Table of Drive Labels

Follow these guidelines when developing a table:

1. Start by defining your purpose, audience, and subject.
2. Number each table by order of appearance within the text.
3. Give the table a clear name that promises exactly what the table delivers.
4. Place the number and title at the top of the table in the format Table 9: Name of Table.
5. Begin each vertical column with a heading that identifies the information listed. (Examples from Figure 11-1: Drive Label, Make, Size.)
6. For each heading, include the specific unit of measure used (where applicable).
7. Align numeric entries in the columns by their decimal place. Align text entries either by left justification or centering in the column.
8. No vertical rules (lines) are needed. Let the white space between the columns separate them.
9. Use footnotes to explain or clarify certain headings or entries. Place them at the bottom of the table.
10. Set the table off from your text with framing rules and white space.
11. Stay within the text margins of your page.
12. Keep tables on a single page if possible. Otherwise, write "continued" at the bottom of the first page, write the full title and "continued" on the next page, and repeat the column headings. If the columns are totaled, the first row on the second page should be a subtotal from the first page.
13. Keep tables upright on the page. If they must be turned sideways, put the top at the inside text margin of the page.
14. Introduce each table in your text and discuss its content or use. Do not leave your reader to interpret raw data in tables.

GRAPHS

Graphs play a surprisingly small role in system documentation. Of the two types, bar and line, bar graphs are more useful. Graphs are made by plotting a set of points against a coordinate system. Whereas a table is a digital representation of information, a graph is analog. Entries in graphs tend to be less discrete and more continuous.

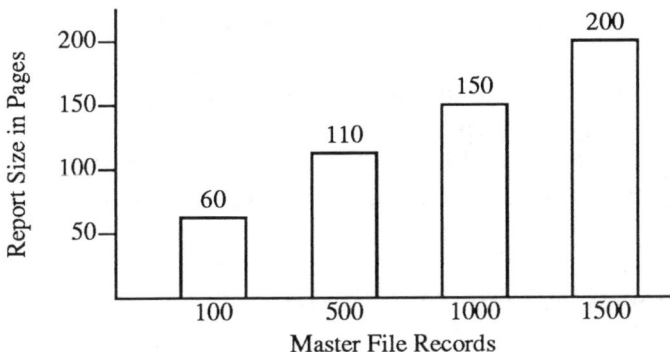

FIGURE 8-3: Report Size versus Master File Records

FIGURE 11-2: Bar Graph of Report Size

Graphs show the relationship between two variables. They can illustrate comparisons or changes over time.

In all graphs, the horizontal axis or line lists items whose value is fixed (independent variables). The vertical axis lists values which change (dependent variables). Dependent variables change according to changes in the independent variables. For example, Figure 11-2 is a bar graph that shows how the size of a report increases with the number of Master File records.

To construct a bar or line graph, follow these guides:

1. Start by defining your purpose, audience, and subject.
2. Number each graph, along with all other figures, by order of appearance within the text.
3. Give the graph a clear name. The name should include both the dependent and independent variables. (From Figure 11-2: Report Size versus Master File Records.)
4. Place the number and name at the bottom of the graph in the format Figure 9: Name of Graph.
5. Label the horizontal and vertical lines, including the units of measure.
6. Use a legend to identify items on multiple bar or line graphs. Place the legend in a clear area of the graph itself.
7. Experiment with the divisions and scaling of each axis until the graph has an effective appearance.
8. Use footnotes to explain or clarify items in the graph. Place these below the number and name.

9. Set the graph off from your text with white space above and below.
10. Stay within the text margins of your page.
11. Keep graphs upright on the page. If they must be turned sideways, put the top at the inside text margin of the page.
12. Introduce each graph in your text and discuss its content or use.

The following guides apply to bar graphs:

1. Make all bars of equal width, to avoid confusing the reader about their relative importance.
2. Begin all bars on the horizontal line.
3. Show negative values by dropping a bar below the horizontal line. Extend the vertical line below the horizontal line, keeping the same scaling and divisions, but indicating negative values.

CHARTS

Charts, like graphs, show relationships. However, they are not plotted against a coordinate grid. We will examine only a few of the numerous types of chart. Those useful in system documentation are organization chart, flowchart, Melanson chart, and Gantt chart.

Here are the construction guidelines for all charts:

1. Start by defining your purpose, audience, and subject.
2. Number each chart, along with all other figures, by order of appearance within the text.
3. Give the chart a clear name that identifies the content of the chart.
4. Place the number and title at the bottom of the figure in the format Figure 9: Name of Chart.
5. No matter how you will actually produce the final version, start by making a rough sketch of the chart on graph paper.
6. Align the symbols and lines of the chart with the lines on the graph paper. Work for a balanced, pleasing appearance that clearly illustrates the important information and relationships.
7. Use footnotes to explain or clarify items on the chart. Place them at the bottom of the chart.

8. If your audience is not familiar with the symbols or conventions used on the chart, include a legend on the first page of the chart. You can even make this a separate block of text or a table if you wish.
9. Stay within the text margins of your page.
10. Keep charts on a single page if possible. Otherwise, write "continued" at the bottom of the first page, and write the full title and "continued" on the next page. Flowcharts have their own conventions for multiple page charts.
11. Keep charts upright on the page. If they must be turned sideways, put the top at the inside text margin of the page.
12. Arrange labels and text on the chart so they can be easily read from a single viewing orientation.
13. Separate charts from text by using borders or white space.
14. Introduce each chart in your text and discuss its content or use.

ORGANIZATION CHART

Organization charts partition the functions of an organization or system. They show the rank or level of each partition and the relationships between them. Organization charts often take the form of menu maps in system documentation. Figure 11-3 shows a

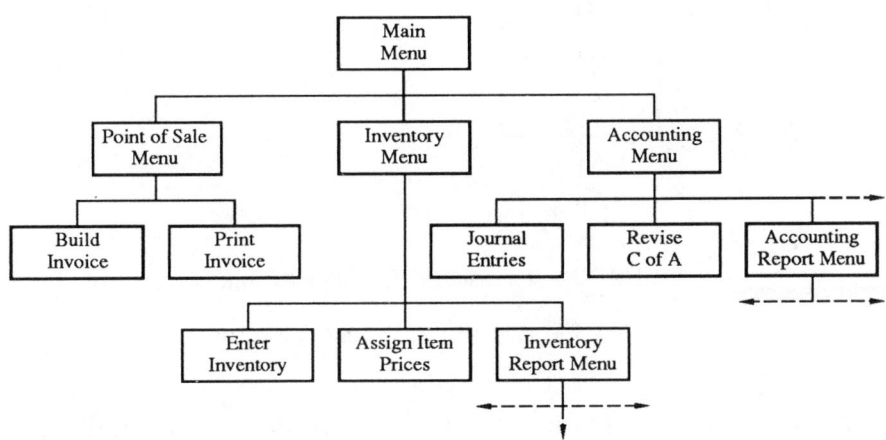

FIGURE 1-14: System Functions

FIGURE 11-3: Organization Chart of System Functions

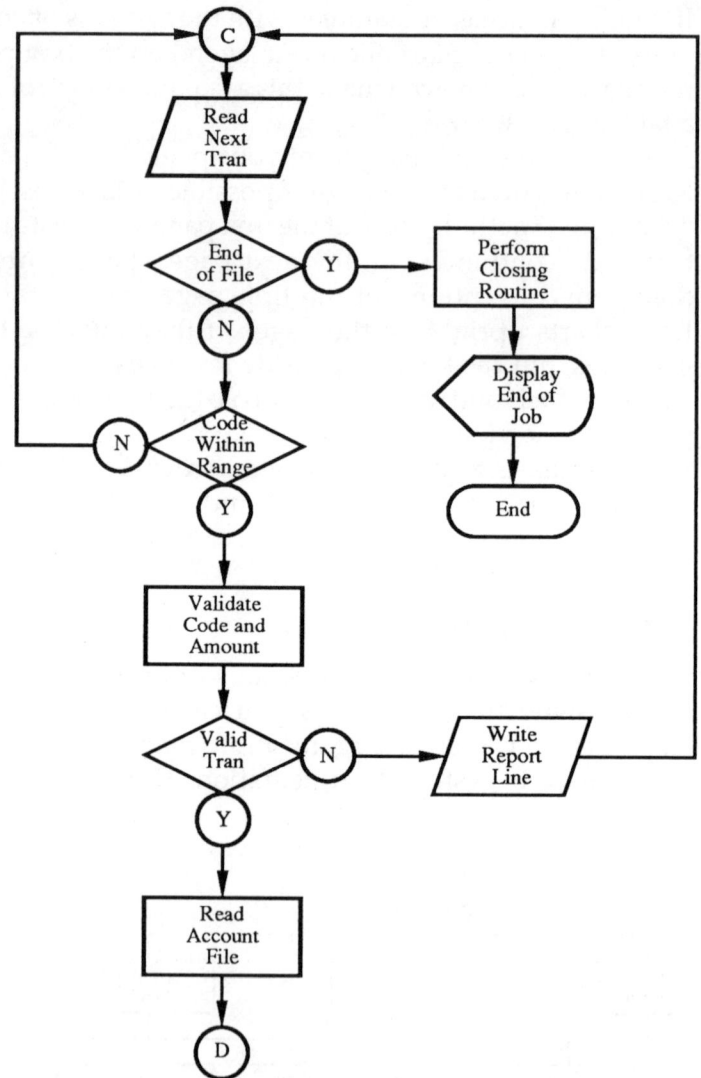

FIGURE 3-3: Transaction Validation Routine

FIGURE 11-4: Flowchart of a Program Segment

portion of the organization chart or menu map for a retail sales system.

One of the drawbacks of this chart is the space it requires. When it is not important to present the reader with a total picture of your system structure, consider using a structured list in place of an organization chart.

FLOWCHART

Flowcharts show the flow of control or sequence of steps in a process. They use specific symbols to represent the objects or events in the process. Flowcharts trace the process from beginning to end.

Figure 11-4 is a sample flowchart. It shows a small portion of the coding for a program.

As you can see, flowcharts have their own problems and limits. There is little room inside the symbols for identifying or explanatory text. Flowcharts are more concise than text, but still require a large amount of space. Your reader must be familiar with the symbols and their meanings to make use of the chart.

I suggest that you limit your use of flowcharts to specifying small portions of code. Try to keep each flowchart small enough to produce on four or fewer 8½-by-11-inch pages.

Rather than using multiple connection points to link the different pages of a flowchart, frame each area of interest on a single page, with a single entry and exit point. Show connections by picturing the related pages as boxes.

MELANSON CHART

In Chapter 4 we discussed the Melanson chart as a technique for displaying soft attributes in a manual documentation system. Figure 11-5 shows a generic Melanson chart.

The chart is similar in format to a table, but the vertical rules are

A / B	A1	A2	A3	A4	A5	A6	A7	A8
B1								
B2								
B3								
B4								
B5								

FIGURE 9-9: Melanson Chart

FIGURE 11-5: Generic Melanson Chart

a necessary visual guide. It is best to display the names of the "A" items vertically, so the chart can be read from a single orientation.

Entries in the body of the chart can be simple yes/no indicators (such as an X or a space) or can indicate multiple values (input, output, input/output). If the body entries are not familiar to your reader, include a legend at the bottom of the chart.

Melanson charts are a useful way to display soft attributes, even in automated documentation systems. They can also be used as checklists, showing components or elements needed for different versions of a system or document.

GANTT CHART

Gantt charts show the scheduling and duration of processes, as well as the relationships and dependencies among events or processes. Traditionally, Gantt charts are project planning and control tools. They can also be used to show the scheduling and relationships of system processes. Figure 11-6 shows a Gantt chart used in this fashion. The chart shows periods during each month when various subsystems of a batch system can be operated.

DIAGRAMS

Diagrams are sketches or line drawings of the parts of an item or the steps in a process. I include data flow diagrams in this section, although strictly speaking they are a form of chart.

Here are the rules for constructing diagrams of parts (mechanical

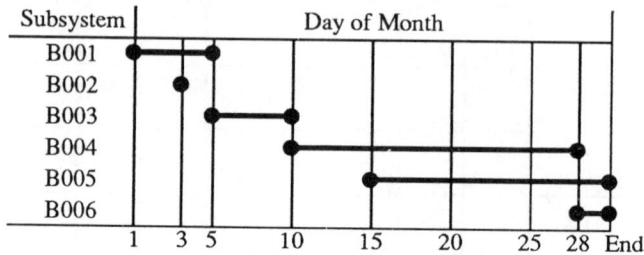

FIGURE 8-2: Subsystem Timing

FIGURE 11-6: Gantt Chart of Subsystem Timing

diagrams) and diagrams of process steps (process diagrams). Data flow diagrams have additional, special rules and conventions of their own, which I discuss later.

1. Start by defining your purpose, audience, and subject.
2. Number each diagram, along with all other figures, by order of appearance within the text.
3. Give the diagram a clear name. The name should include the perspective from which the diagram is drawn.
4. Place the number and name at the bottom of the diagram in the format Figure 9: Name of Diagram.
5. Label each item in the diagram. Place the labels inside the part where possible. Otherwise, connect the label and the part with a straight line.
6. Place labels so that they can be easily read from one orientation.
7. Set the diagram off from your text with borders or white space above and below.
8. Stay within the text margins of your page.
9. Keep diagrams upright on the page. If they must be turned sideways, put the top at the inside text margin of the page.
10. Introduce each diagram in your text and discuss its content or use.

MECHANICAL DIAGRAMS

Accompany your description of a mechanism (or any physical object) with a diagram that shows its parts or illustrates its operating principles. Diagrams can be realistic or representational. Keep shading and other ornamentation to a minimum. Let these devices serve to highlight or emphasize important information.

Figure 11-7 shows a diagram of the parts of a typical personal computer system. Notice that the figure is representational; it shows only the general shape and appearance of each part of the system.

PROCESS DIAGRAMS

Diagrams of procedures or processes are useful for clarifying instructions. They illustrate how a procedure or step should be performed.

Figure 11-8 is a familiar process diagram. It shows a computer novice how to correctly hold and insert a floppy diskette.

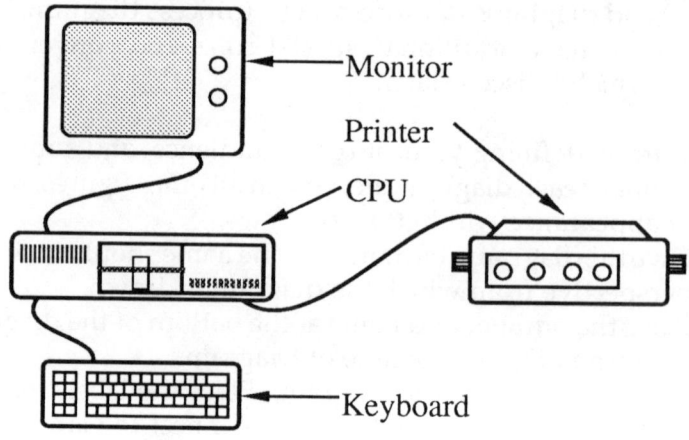

FIGURE 15: A Microcomputer System (front view)

FIGURE 11-7: Mechanical Diagram

DATA FLOW DIAGRAMS

The data flow diagram is a powerful and versatile tool. It can be used to specify the logical design of a system or process. Further, data flow diagrams are an efficient way to present conceptual models or overviews to nontechnical readers.

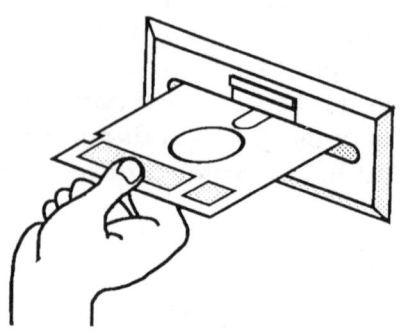

FIGURE 2-2: How to Insert a Diskette

FIGURE 11-8: Process Diagram

This charting system was designed around several useful criteria:

1. There are only four symbols: source or sink, data flow, data store, and process. The meaning of each symbol can be inferred from the context of the diagram.
2. Each portion of the diagram occupies a single 8½-by-11-inch sheet.
3. Subordinate levels of detail are represented by exploding a process box onto another single page.
4. Each symbol shows the name (or other identifiers) of the item. Each item is defined in appended text.

As a result of these design criteria, data flow diagrams are easy to create, use, and maintain. You have already encountered examples of data flow diagrams in Chapters 1 through 4 of this book (for example, Figure 1-1 or 2-10). Notice that I did not need to define the symbols used in my diagrams. You understood them intuitively.

When I first discovered this technique, I thought it was only another form of flowchart. This is not the case, but the differences will be apparent to you only if you use the technique. I encourage you to do so.

Remember to abide by the conventions. Use only four symbols. There are no conventions for the shapes of the symbols. Figure 11-9 shows the shapes I prefer. Whatever symbols you use, be consistent.

Do not show decisions or processing logic on the diagram itself. These belong in textual descriptions of the processes. The arrowed lines represent flows of data, not control or processing logic. You can think of them as pipelines that convey information between the sources, stores, and processes of the diagram.

PICTURES

Normally photographs, sketches, graphic designs, and other types of picture are classed as figures. In this discussion, I reserve the term "picture" to refer to icons, line drawings, or other computer art that is outside of the normal text-and-figure treatment.

When icons or symbols are used as visual keys to certain types of text (such as system messages or user entries), they simply appear with the text. You do not need to number or refer to pictures.

226 • System Documentation

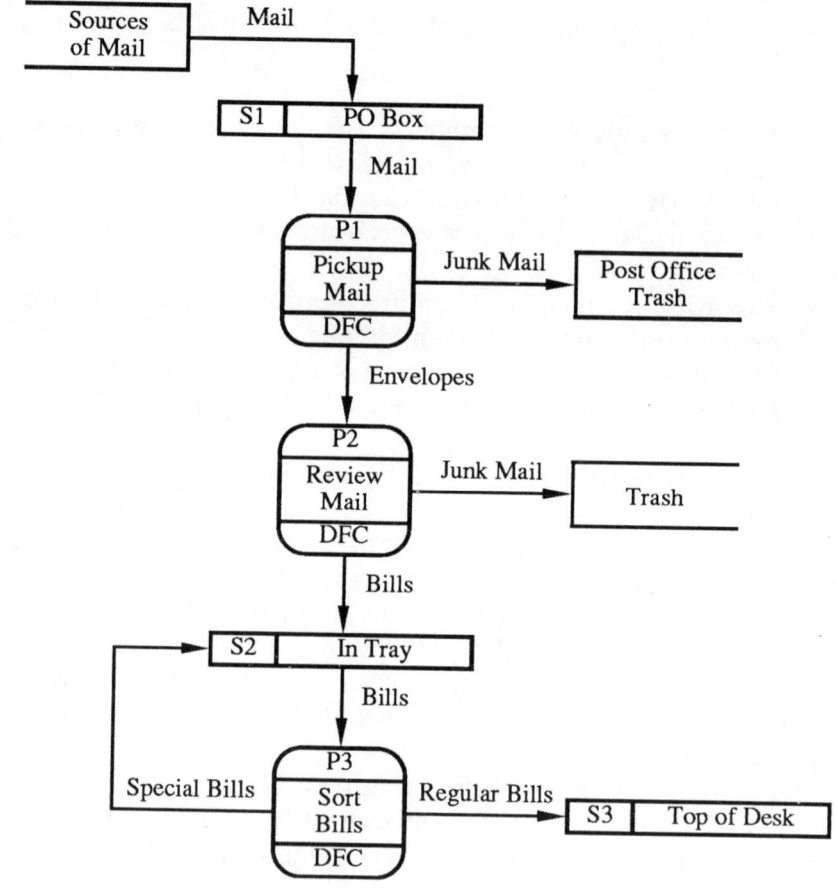

FIGURE 3.1: DFD For Month-End Process

FIGURE 11-9: Data Flow Diagram

See Figure 11-10 for an example of how icons are used as pictures in a user manual.

SAMPLES

Samples usually require special treatment, because of the nature of the subject. Often, a sample illustrates a full page, such as an input form or a report.

STEP 5: Log on to the system. The system displays the password prompt:

ENTER PASSWORD:

Enter the master password and your security code, in the format shown below.

`master.999`

Where 999 = your security code.

FIGURE 11-10: Icons Used as Pictures

Whenever you can, treat samples as you would other figures. Assign them a number and name, and refer to them in your text.

You can relax the rules about margins, orientation, and placement of samples so as to improve their effectiveness.

Samples can also be assembled into a special appendix of your document, or introduced with a cover sheet page.

12

Organization

So far, we have looked at creating independent units of text or graphics. When you create multiple-page documents or manuals, these units must be organized in some fashion. Your organization must be both expected by and obvious to the reader.

In this section I present some structures for text, graphics, and combinations of the two. Not only are these structures useful and effective ways to communicate information, they are also familiar to the readers of system documentation.

We'll also look at ways to organize various text and graphic structures into documents or manuals. This involves arranging the material in a particular sequence. We will examine the sequences that are most useful in documenting systems. As you'll find, most of these sequences can be applied to individual structures as well as to documents and manuals composed of text and graphic structures.

INSTRUCTION VERSUS DESCRIPTION

Before we look at specific structures, I must warn you about two general structures, or two different ways of structuring system information. These can be called instruction and description, or functional and structural organizations. Consider, for example, two ways of documenting a process. The instruction structure shows how you perform the process. The description structure shows how the process happens.

Description structures are excellent for designing and specifying systems. They show what each part of the system does and how the parts fit together. Description structures are not appropriate for showing users how to use a system; users need information in instruction structures.

Let me illustrate this distinction with another example. I could exhaustively define and describe a motorcycle by using a descriptive approach. I would partition the machine into its major functional groups, such as the frame, motor, drive train, suspension, and so forth. I would define the purpose and function of each part, including the controls. However, the document that I produce will not tell anyone *why* they would use a motorcycle, or *how* to use it.

It is easy to produce a user manual organized in parallel with the system's menu structure. It is simple to define and describe each menu, screen, and function of the system. However, such a manual will leave the readers to interpolate how the system can be used to accomplish their business tasks.

Be aware of which general structure you are using, and make the structure match the needs of the audience.

STRUCTURE

We will examine the following specific structures:

- List structure
- Cookbook structure
- Playscript structure
- Structured list
- Structured text
- Logic tree structure
- Decision table structure
- Text flowchart
- Foundation structure
- Feature-based structure
- Structured writing

Some of these apply only to text; some combine text and graphics. Several include a specific page format designed to provide the reader with a consistent frame of reference.

LIST STRUCTURE

Lists are an attractive alternative to a series of short sentences or a long, complicated sentence. They are ideal for displaying the functions or content of system elements. They are also an excellent way to present a sequence of steps.

Lists are a text structure. They need no number or name. If you refer to a particular list throughout a document, you can treat the list as a figure, assigning a number and name that can be used to refer to the list. Otherwise, introduce the list with a simple sentence, leave a blank line, and start the list.

Each item in the list should be identified with a number or a bullet. This shows the reader where each new item begins. Use numbers only to identify items that have a specific sequence. Otherwise, use bullets.

Align the bullets or numbers at the left margin of your text. Write the number followed by a period. Leave a single space, then write the text of the item. Place a single space after bullets.

Make all items in your list parallel in format and structure. Make them agree with the sense of the introductory sentence. For example:

The Repair Management system has

- Extensive profit margin controls
- Custom accounting reports
- It updates inventory automatically
- Seven levels of security control

The third item in the list does not parallel the structure of the others or agree with the introductory sentence. This item should read

- Automatic inventory updating

When the items in your list are single words or short phrases, they can be printed in lowercase letters. When the items are complete sentences, start each with a capital letter and end each with a period.

COOKBOOK STRUCTURE

The cookbook structure is primarily for text, but it may include graphics. It is an instructional rather than a descriptive structure,

JOB RAMJ014: Prepare and Send Report RAMO212

Step	Action
1	Decolllate the report into three separate copies.
2	Destroy the carbon papers by shredding them.
3	Trim and burst the first copy of the report.

4	Put the trimmed and burst copy into an inter-office envelope. Address the envelope to:
	    Personnel Manager
	    Main Office

5	Seal the envelope and place it in the EDP mail pickup box.
6	Bind one of the remaining copies in an 8.5 by 15 inch report binder
7	Etc.

FIGURE 12-1: Cookbook Structure

and thus suited to user manuals. It is useful for clearly structured tasks that must be performed in a prescribed sequence and is often tutorial in nature. The cookbook structure is ideal for defining tasks like data entry, editing, and report preparation. We have already used it in specifying procedural system elements, such as transactions or jobs.

Figure 12-1 illustrates how the cookbook structure could be used in an operator's manual. As you can see, this format is more effective than embedding the steps in an extended paragraph structure.

Identify the procedure by its correct name and number. The cookbook structure need not be treated as a table or figure, since it is primarily textual. Number each step, using the format shown. The step numbers can appear in a separate column, or they can begin the text of each step.

Each step is one or more concise sentences. Begin each with an action verb. In the cookbook structure the reader is always the actor. Here is a list of commonly used action verbs:

Check	Decide	End	Find	Get
Issue	List	Place	Prepare	Provide
Put	Receive	Record	Request	Send
Show	Start	Tell	Use	

When you use this structure in a user manual, you may decide to include graphics in the form of screen, message, or report figures.

Insert figures that illustrate what the readers will experience (features of the user interface) as they perform the procedure.

PLAYSCRIPT STRUCTURE

The playscript structure incorporates text and a specific page format. Originally, it was used to describe procedures with multiple actors. It has been expanded to include procedures with complex logic.

The original playscript format is a two-column page. The first column names the actor. The second column describes the action. See Figure 12-2 for a sample of this structure.

This figure illustrates the key construction points of the original playscript structure. You can treat each playscript as a table to integrate it with supporting text, or let the structure stand on its own. Identify the procedure appropriately. Column headings for the actor and action columns are optional, as are step numbers.

Raise Purchase Order

Actor	Step	Action
Purchaser	1	Fill in Sections A through C of the Purchase Order form. Make sure you enter both the quantity and the unit of measure for each item.
	2	Sign and date the form.
	3	Send the form to your Department Manager.
Manager	4	Review the Purchase Orders you have received during the day.
	5	Disapprove the purchase by signing the Disposition box and noting the reason.
	6	Return the Purchase Order to the Purchaser.
	7	If the total is $500 or less, approve the purchase order by signing the Approval box.
	8	Send the approved Purchase Order to the Purchasing Department.
	9	If the total is over $500, approve the Purchase Order by initialing the Manager box.
	10	Send the aproved Purchase Order to the Comptroller.
Comptroller	11	Etc.

FIGURE 12-2: Original Playscript Structure

The Archive Command

Destination	Archive Document	Archive Folder
To same disk.	Copies it to the disk.	Copies it and its contents to the disk.
To different disk.	Copies it to the specified disk and directory.	Copies it and its contents to the root directory of the specified disk.
To Vault.	Moves it to the current disk Vault.	Copies it and its contents to the System Vault.

FIGURE 12-3: Expanded Playscript Structure

Left-justify each entry in its column. Begin each step with an action verb.

Figure 12-3 shows how the playscript structure has been expanded to cover procedures with no fixed sequence. In expanded form, the structure resembles a table or matrix. The rows and columns contain the desired results, conditions, and actions associated with the process.

The reader uses this structure by selecting the action and condition of interest. The outcome is found in the cell at the intersection of the action and condition.

STRUCTURED LIST

The structured list is an alternative to the organization chart. As we have seen, it is a text structure that shows the content and hierarchy of a system or system element. Structured lists can be used to show the entire menu structure of a system or the code structure of a single program or module.

Technical system players will be more accepting of this structure than of the organization chart. It is useful in design and specification steps. Nontechnical readers may initially prefer the graphic approach of the organization chart but can learn to interpret structured lists in short order. Structured lists have the advantage of being much more concise than their equivalent organization charts. See Figure 12-4 for an example.

Transaction Routing Module
1   Control
2   Setup
3   Determine Transaction Type
3.1   Add Record
3.2   Change Record
3.3   Delete Record
4   Error Handler
5   Close

FIGURE 12-4: Structured List

Structured lists can be treated as figures or simply introduced within your text. Treat each item in the list as if it were a title (this is usually accurate, as the items are the names of subordinate system elements). Rely on horizontal indentation to define the different levels of the list. In addition to the indent convention, you can add decimal numbers to the list. If you do this, leave the highest level of the list unnumbered.

STRUCTURED TEXT

Structured text is a restricted and logical form of English. It resembles a high-level programming language. The most common use of structured text is to communicate program logic between the system designer and builder. It can also be used to support process definitions in data flow diagrams.

Since it is essentially English, nontechnical readers can readily grasp the information in structured text, once they have been introduced to its terms and conventions. We have already applied this structure to specifying programs. Figure 12-5 shows an example of how structured text could be used in a user manual.

Structured text uses four types of term: instruction, decision, loop, and branch. Instructions can be data processing commands or steps in a manual procedure. Write instructions as single lines of text.

Decisions define the item or condition being tested and show resulting actions for each outcome. As the result of a test, you may specify instructions or branches. Decisions can be expressed in the familiar if/then/else form, or as cases.

How to Enter a Batch of Receipts

```
01  IF System Date is correct
02     THEN continue at line 05
03     ELSE reset System Date
04  END IF
05  DO WHILE more receipts left
06     ENTER date of receipt
07     ENTER amount of check
08     IF receipt is regular
09        THEN select Add to Batch Total
10        ELSE select Skip Total
11     END IF
12  END DO
13  Print Receipt Batch Total Report
14  Attach report to receipts
15  END
```

FIGURE 12-5: Structured Text

Loops define iterative processes. The loop process is repeated until a specified condition or test is met. Counters that control the loop can be specified explicitly or may be implicit to the loop statement.

Branches are logic control commands. They transfer control to a labeled point in the structured text.

You can use structured text to guide the reader through optional paths in a document or process. To do this, you must label (address or number) each portion of the text consistently.

LOGIC TREE STRUCTURE

Compare the following paragraph of instructions with Figure 12-6.

> Complete the sale whenever the customer pays by check, unless the invoice total is $40 or more. In this case, request identification from the customer. If the identification is acceptable, write the identification type and number on the face of the check and complete the sale. Otherwise, call the manager for further instructions.

The logic tree structure combines text and graphics into an easily read chart. Treat each logic tree as a separate figure in your text. The

236 • System Documentation

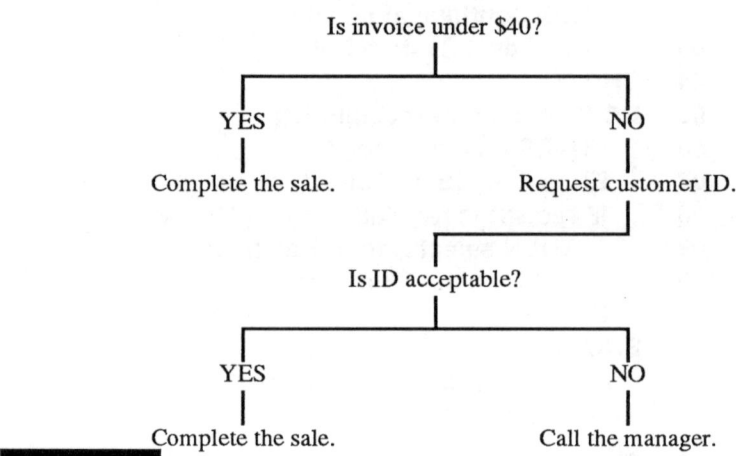

FIGURE 12-6: Logic Tree Structure

readers can work their way through complex decision logic without having to extract it from text.

DECISION TABLE STRUCTURE

We encountered the decision table structure earlier, as a technique for program logic specification. Decision tables are a concise but somewhat forbidding way to express conditions, outcomes, and actions. They are a graphic structure and should be handled like tables. See Figure 12-7.

The table is divided into four parts. The left side is called the stub, the right side the entry. The top half of the table shows the conditions that are tested. The bottom half shows processing actions taken as a result of the tests.

Construct the table by filling in the condition and action stubs. Next, sketch out all possible logical outcomes for each condition in the condition entry portion. This is a mechanical process. For each condition, repeat one set of outcomes for each outcome of the condition above it.

The vertical columns in the entry half of the table are called the rules. Once you have completed the condition entries, review each rule and record the appropriate action entries.

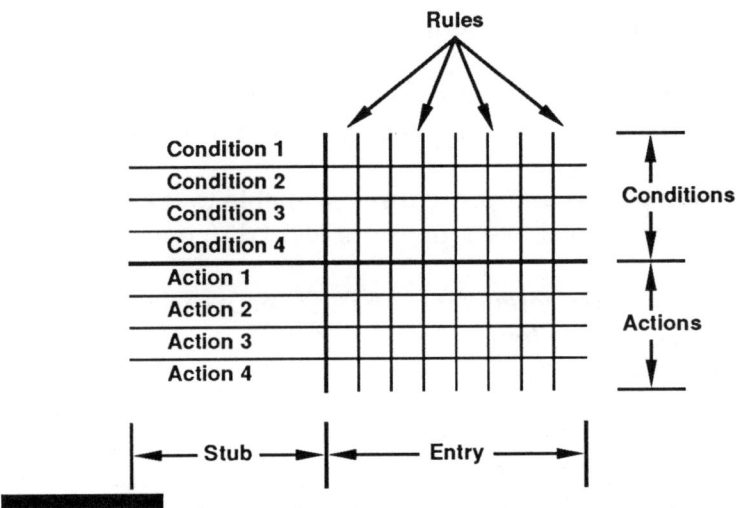

FIGURE 12-7: Decision Table Structure

After recording the actions for each rule, search the table for rules with identical action entries. Combine them to reduce the table to its simplest form.

Treat the completed table as a table, giving it an identifying number and a descriptive name.

TEXT FLOWCHART

The text flowchart combines the graphic flowchart with descriptive text. To use this structure, label each flowchart symbol with the element identifier (name, number, or label) and a paragraph number. Number the paragraphs of your supportive text as per the flowchart symbols.

Readers will use the text and the flowchart simultaneously, but do not try to print the text on the flowchart. Rather, make the pages of text continuous and separate from the flowchart. This way the readers can arrange the material to suit their needs.

The flowchart remains a figure within its supporting text.

FOUNDATION STRUCTURE

Foundation structure organizes text and graphics into a manual. It is used for procedures or systems too complex or variable to be described in a set sequence of steps.

Manuals that use the foundation structure

- Explain what the user can accomplish with the system.
- Describe the system features (screens, reports, etc.) that result from using the system.
- Describe the tools and procedures available to the user.
- Present illustrations, cases, or examples of different uses of the system.
- Contain detailed reference information about each function or operation of the system.

FEATURE-BASED STRUCTURE

The feature-based structure is primarily a graphic structure. It is similar to the cookbook structure, but the graphics predominate, representing the features of the user interface, such as forms, screens, or reports.

This structure has restricted application, being useful only when procedures center around a system feature. Figure 12-8 illustrates how the feature-based structure could be used with an input screen.

Each item on the screen (form, or report) is identified by a number. The numbers correspond to the step numbers. Each step is a description of the procedure the reader must follow or an explanation of the numbered item on the screen.

Number the items and steps according to the sequence the reader should follow. Where possible, number the items as the reader would scan the screen: from upper left to lower right.

This structure is useful for both instruction and description. It is a good way to define the content of forms, screens, and reports.

STRUCTURED WRITING

Structured writing developed from a technique called STOP. STOP is an acronym for Sequential Thematic Organization of Proposals. It is a text and graphic structure developed by the Hughes Aircraft Company.

The central concept of STOP is that the page format should structure the content so that information is easy to grasp for the reader. This idea has been expanded and developed into structured writing.

Structured writing uses a two-page grid for each topic or section

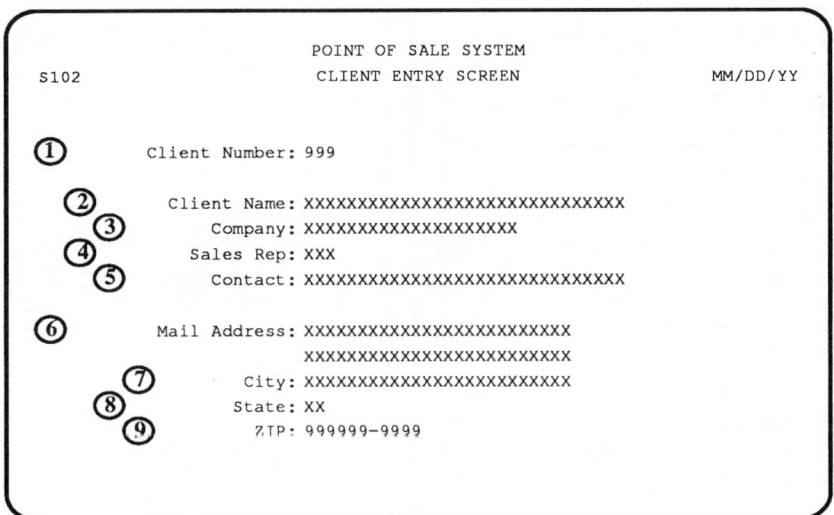

1. The system assigns Client Numbers. You cannot revise this item.

2. Enter the Client Name in First M. Last format.

3. Enter the Company Short Name as listed on your Company Directory Report.

4. Enter the initials of the sales representative who prepared the Client Sheet.

5. The system duplicates the Sales Rep initials as the Contact. If a different Contact is specified on the Client Sheet, enter the correct Contact initials. Otherwise, press <ENTER> to skip to the next field.

6. Etc.

FIGURE 12-8: Feature-based Structure

in a manual. See Figure 12-9 for the page layout and grid used in structured writing.

In addition to using the page layout, there are six simple rules to follow when using this structure.

1. All information must be organized and fitted into the double page layout of a section. A section can describe an idea, a system function, or a procedure. When the readers turn a page, they are moving on to a new topic.

2. Each page bears a title or headline that defines the section.

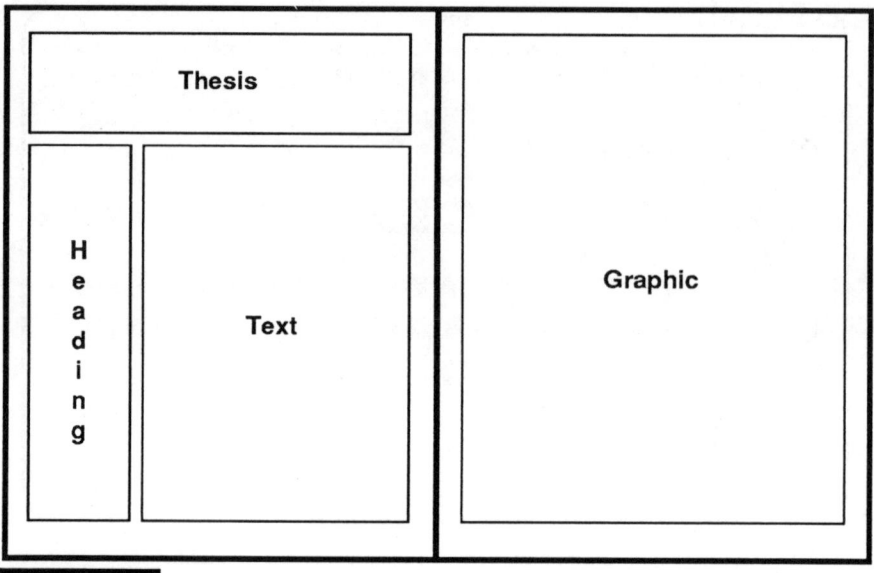

FIGURE 12-9: Structured Writing

The headline should be more than the usual noun or verb-noun combination. It should be a phrase or sentence that shows the scope and intent of the section.

3. The top block of the text page (left page) is a thesis statement, which corresponds to the statements of purpose or the descriptions we have discussed. It shows the reader the main idea expressed by the section.

4. The text page also has a block of text. The text block can be further divided into heading and text columns. The text must not exceed 500 words. This volume of text is optimal for reader comprehension.

5. The right page is the graphic page. It contains supportive graphics, whether tables, graphs, charts, or diagrams. This page may also present examples in either text or graphic form.

6. Any graphic used should have an extended name or caption. Three or four lines of text are ideal. This caption should present the important ideas in the graphic and allow the reader to gather the most important information in the section.

OUTLINE

Successful technical writers spend more time planning than writing. This may be hard for you (or your supervisor) to accept, but it is a fact. You must plan each level of your system documentation, think about each idea until it is clear, develop the idea, divide it into parts, arrange the parts in a sequence, and finally express the idea in text and graphics.

The best way to develop, partition, and sequence your ideas is by outlining them. There are two types of outline, informal and formal. We'll look at both.

INFORMAL OUTLINE

The informal outline is nothing more than an ordered list of topics. All items in the lists are at an equal level. Here is an example of an informal outline used in the development of an installation guide for an online microcomputer system.

> Outline for Installation Guide
>   Introduction
>   Select a Site
>   Unpack the Hardware
>   Assemble the Hardware
>   Install the Software
>   Wrap up

The informal outline is useful for small documents or blocks of text. It is a starting point, even for larger projects. The informal outline is easy to create and revise. It breaks the cycle, "How can I know where I'm going if I don't have a plan? How can I plan if I don't know where I'm going?"

Creating an informal outline is simple. Follow these steps:

1. State the purpose, audience, and subject of the document.
2. Brainstorm to develop a list of topics.
3 Arrange the topics into an appropriate sequence.

We'll examine alternative sequences later in this chapter. For now, it seems obvious that the best sequence for our sample installation guide is chronological. We should present the reader with the information needed at each step in the installation procedure.

An informal outline can be developed into a formal outline.

FORMAL OUTLINE

A formal outline is a detailed and systematic arrangement of topics and subtopics, using a numbering and indentation scheme. You can choose between two common numbering schemes: roman-letter-arabic, or decimal. Each scheme is illustrated below.

Roman-Letter-Arabic	Decimal
II	2
A	2.1
1	2.1.1
2	2.1.2
B	2.2
1	2.2.1
2	2.2.2
3	2.2.3
III	3
etc.	etc.

The roman-letter-arabic scheme requires indentation of the numbers as well as the text, in order to show which topics contain which subtopics. The decimal scheme internalizes this information, with the varying lengths of the numbers providing their own visual clues about topic or subtopic level.

I must caution you to limit this format of numbering and indentation to outlines. The relationships shown by indentation are lost when spread over several pages. Outline format is not useful in documents or manuals.

A good outline will have the following attributes:

- All topics are covered fully.
- Each topic has adequate partitioning.
- Each division yields two or more parts.
- Parts or subparts of equal rank are at the same level.
- Parts add up to the whole of what they divide.
- Parallel construction is used for parallel headings.

In addition to identifying outline items by numbering and indentation, you can apply a scheme of text size or case. Here is one such scheme, showing how the items in four levels of division would be distinguished.

> LEVEL ONE—ALL CAPITALS
>   Level Two—Title Capitals
>   Level three—sentence capitals
>   level four—lowercase

Whatever scheme you choose, be consistent. Create headings that are clear and explicit. Be specific. Remember, these items will remind you of your purpose when you are drafting your document.

Here is how the sample installation guide might be formally outlined.

Outline for Installation Guide

1	INTRODUCTION
1.1	Welcome
1.2	How to Get Support
2	HARDWARE
2.1	Select a Site
2.1.1	Space requirements
2.1.2	Temperature and humidity limits
2.2	Unpack the Hardware
2.2.1	Content check
2.2.2	Materials to save
2.3	Assemble the Hardware
2.3.1	Special tools
2.3.2	Configuration diagram
2.3.3	Assembly procedure
2.4	Learn to Operate the Hardware
2.4.1	Start-up procedure
2.4.2	Shutdown procedure
2.4.3	Formatting diskettes
3	SOFTWARE
3.1	Unpack the Software
3.2	Check the Content
3.3	Load the Master Diskette

3.4	Load the Module Diskettes
4	WRAP-UP
4.1	Store Backup Copies
4.2	Mail the Warranty Cards
4.3	Read the Getting Started Guide

SEQUENCE

An important part of planning your manuals, documents, structures, and even paragraphs is putting the information into the right sequence. Sequence can be determined by the order in which your reader needs information, by the subject matter itself, or by a combination of both. We will examine these sequences:

- Introduction, body, conclusion
- Simple to complex
- Ordo Dei
- Chronological
- Alphabetic
- Instruction sequence
- Cause and effect
- Problem, cause, solution
- Compare and contrast
- Spatial
- Pro and con
- Priorities

INTRODUCTION, BODY, CONCLUSION

The introduction, body, conclusion sequence is the most generally useful. It best applies to small bodies of text: paragraphs, topics, or subjects. The impact of this sequence is lost over longer documents. The introduction is a statement of the controlling idea or thesis of the work. The body contains the supporting or developmental information for the thesis. The conclusion analyzes or summarizes the work.

Of course, you must still determine a sequence for the information in the body.

SIMPLE TO COMPLEX

The simple to complex sequence is also generally applicable, but it works best for documents or programs that teach the reader. The idea here is to repeat concepts in their entirety but at increasing levels of detail or complexity. Alternately, you can use this sequence to build simple ideas into complex ones.

This sequence can be seen in systems of user documentation that start with a simple tutorial manual, progress to a more complex user manual, and culminate in a detailed reference manual.

ORDO DEI

The Ordo Dei sequence is define, explain, and illustrate. It is useful when introducing new concepts to your reader. First the term or concept is defined, using one of the techniques we discussed in Chapter 9. Next, the definition is expanded by descriptive or explanatory text or graphics. Finally, the term or concept is illustrated by text or graphic examples.

As an example of Ordo Dei, consider structured writing. The thesis block defines and introduces the subject. The text block explains the subject. The graphic page illustrates the subject by example or figure.

CHRONOLOGICAL

In chronological sequence, the subject is presented in parallel with the timing of a related process. For example, our sample Installation Guide was sequenced chronologically so as to parallel the installation process. Information was presented to the reader in the sequence needed to install the system.

Use a chronological sequence for all procedural instructions.

Other parallels are possible. You could present information in the same sequence as that in which a batch system operates.

ALPHABETIC

Alphabetic sequence arranges a group of items, topics, or subjects into an order with which you expect your reader to be familiar. When subjects are arranged in alphabetic sequence, your reader can access them randomly, just as you access the telephone numbers in a telephone directory.

Since the alphabetic sequence is designed for random access, it works best in reference manuals, long lists of items, and familiar reference aids such as a glossary or an index. For example, the commands and functions of an online system can be organized alphabetically in a reference manual. This allows your reader to access the material by scanning the pages for the name of the function in question.

There are two points to remember when you consider using an alphabetic sequence. First, the reader must know the access key, that is, the name of the item or subject you use to sequence the information. For example, in the reference manual for a payroll system, should you identify and order the function Add New Employee by its name, by the selection code NEA, or by some variation of the name such as New Employee, Add? The answer, of course, is to identify and sequence the function by the key the reader will use to access it. You can add appropriate cross-reference entries to increase usefulness of alphabetically sequenced material.

The second point to remember is that your reader must be familiar with the sequence you use. While it is safe to assume that your readers know the alphabet, it is not safe to assume that they are familiar with a simple ASCII sort sequence. You may need to use manual techniques to order the items in a more familiar sequence.

INSTRUCTION SEQUENCE

Instruction sequence is a specialized version of chronological sequence, specifically intended for procedural instructions.

Begin by identifying the procedure. State the purpose of the procedure or process in terms of its goals or outcomes. List the steps in chronological sequence. Finish by identifying the next procedure (where applicable).

CAUSE AND EFFECT

When you follow actions through to results, you are using the cause and effect sequence. This is useful in defining transaction processing or when listing possible actions and their outcomes.

PROBLEM, CAUSE, SOLUTION

The problem, cause, solution sequence follows the timing of the problem-solving process. First you define the problem in terms of its symptoms. You offer one or more causes for the problem in the form of a diagnosis. Finally, you state the actions the reader must take to solve the problem.

This sequence is ideal for the troubleshooting sections of user or reference manuals. It is also the sequence we used to specify error messages in Chapter 8.

COMPARE AND CONTRAST

When evaluating two or more items or options, use the compare and contrast sequence. List all the similarities between the items; then list all the differences. An alternate to this sequence is the pro and con sequence, explained below.

As a case in point, either the compare and contrast or the pro and con sequence could be used for an item-by-item comparison of your product with that of your competitors.

SPATIAL

The spatial sequence is used to parallel the physical arrangement of the parts of your subject. To use the spatial sequence, you work from left to right, top to bottom, or front to back.

This sequence is well suited to discussing the content of forms, screens, and reports.

PRO AND CON

The pro and con sequence emulates a discussion. It can be used to describe the advantages and disadvantages of one or more options. You can alternate pro and con points in a textual treatment or arrange the points into a two-column table.

PRIORITY

Priority sequence presents information in decreasing order of importance. You might use this sequence in compiling a list of daily procedures you want a user to observe. This sequence involves a decision: Will the topics be arranged in order of their importance to you or to the reader?

DOCUMENT STRUCTURE

There is one more structure we need to examine, that of the document itself. When your documents assume the size of a manual, the reader makes a natural and easy association between the document and a book. Readers have come to expect a certain content and organization in books, and it is to your advantage to meet their expectations. Here is a list that suggests a general content and organization for your manuals: title page; copyright notice and revision information; table of content; list of figures; list of tables; introduction; chapters; appendices; glossary; and index.

It is pointless to struggle against the reader's expectation to find your manual divided into chapters. However, you have some freedom for organizing material within chapters. I suggest that if you partition chapters, you do so to only two levels.

The division of a chapter into subjects is readily accepted by most readers. A chapter is a physical grouping of related subjects. A subject can be a group of related paragraphs or graphics, or structures that incorporate both.

13

Extracting Manuals

You have learned how to design the System File by determining which elements comprise your system and which attributes of each element need to be specified. During the design, specify, and build steps of the system development process, the System File begins to fill with this information, in the form of system specifications. The System File becomes a data base of system information.

I have suggested that you automate your documentation system as much as possible. Such automation could include an actual data base system to create and maintain the System File. However, a purely automated data base system cannot meet all the information needs of all the system players.

While a data base system and query language may be adequate for the designers and builders, you can't simply ship a data base to your users. In addition to system specifications, the System File must contain manuals.

Manuals are one way of organizing the information in the System File. If you visualize the System File as a three-dimensional block of information, manuals represent a two-dimensional slice through the information. A manual presents the reader with system information from a fixed perspective.

> PROBLEM: "The users can't figure out how to run even the simplest functions for themselves. At this rate, we'll need two customer service representatives for each client, just to handle the telephone inquiries."

SOLUTION: Provide the users with the information they need to accomplish each task. Present this in the form of an installation guide, a tutorial manual or "getting started" booklet, and a user reference manual.

In addition to these three types of manual, you may need a technical reference manual, an operator manual, or a support manual.

In Chapter 2, I presented simplified versions of two important processes, the system development process and the documentation process. System development and documentation are integrated into the in-line approach by applying the documentation process to each step of the system development process.

In this chapter, we will see how the documentation process is applied to the build step of the system development process in order to create the manuals needed by the system players. To do this, we'll follow again the plan, draft, edit, review, release, and maintain steps of the documentation process. We will focus most of our attention on the plan step. Planning is essential to successful technical writing. Expect to devote at least 30 percent of each writing project to planning.

PLAN

Questions arise whenever you write a manual. You can answer them once at the beginning, or part way through the writing process. If you defer decisions until later, prepare yourself to do a lot of extra revision work. Planning a manual means answering the questions before you start writing. It also means reducing your workload and stress level.

You will need to answer questions about the structure and format of the manual, about the type of audience and level of detail, and about production and distribution methods. Having to make too many decisions during the drafting process leads to decision overload and creates blocks.

The documentation process separates the decisions from the writing. It recognizes that planning and drafting a manual are two distinct steps and that each step should be accomplished separately.

The planning step leads you to answer questions at logical, physical, and administrative levels. At the logical level, you decide the audience, subject, and purpose of the manual. You also determine the content and organization of the manual that will best meet the reader's needs. At the physical level, you answer questions about the medium, format, layout, production, and maintenance of the manual. At the administrative level, you answer questions about the cost and timing of creating and producing the manual.

Planning streamlines the creation of manuals and reduces revision work to a minimum. It keeps your documentation costs lower. Planning is also essential for team efforts, when several writers must be coordinated.

The planning step is divided into two parts. The first part is to plan the system library. The system library is the complete collection of all system manuals. The second part is to plan the individual manuals.

Let me anticipate a question you will face when you have completed your plans: Where should I store the plans? The system library plan is part of the product design document. Planning the system library is actually a part of the design step in the system development process. The product design resides in the System File.

The individual manuals are elements of the system product. They are planned (or "specified") in the same manner as other elements, such as programs, files, or reports. Each manual plan represents an element specification and is stored as such in the System File.

PLAN THE SYSTEM LIBRARY

The system library plan is a brief, concise document. It is an overview of all the manuals in the system.

The library plan shows the purpose, audience, and subject of each manual. It shows how various kinds of information are divided into different manuals.

Planning the system manuals at this level allows you to reduce and control redundancy. The system library plan makes it possible for individual manuals to cross-reference each other.

People do not read system manuals for enjoyment, and rarely even for education. Most often, they read to find the specific information they need to do their jobs. To design the system library you must determine the role of each system player, identify specific tasks the player must perform, and provide the information needed by the player to accomplish the tasks.

Start by listing all the system players involved with your product. Your list will probably include the user, designer, builder, installer, operator, and supporter. Next, list the roles and tasks performed by each player. This list need not be detailed. At this step in planning, your objective is to create an overview of the kinds of manuals needed. For each task in your list, outline the information the reader will need. As you create these lists, common groups of tasks and information may emerge. The next step is to consolidate tasks and audiences to reduce the number of manuals needed and to eliminate redundancy.

Create a finalized list of manuals needed, reorganizing your information into brief statements of the subject, audience, and purpose for each manual.

The information needs of the designer and builder may not necessitate the creation of manuals. The System File and its specifications usually suffice.

The roles played by the installer, operator, and supporter demand specialized manuals. However, for small, online systems the user often plays these roles. Consequently, your installation, operation, and support "manuals" may take the form of chapters in a single user manual. On the other hand, you may decide that the tasks of the user should be supported by separate guides or manuals. Rather than a single user manual, you may plan an installation guide, a "getting started" or tutorial manual, and a detailed user reference manual.

Once you have created the system library plan, you are ready to expand it into individual system manual plans.

PLAN EACH SYSTEM MANUAL

Let me recapitulate the steps involved in creating an individual system manual plan. They are:

1. Define audience
2. Define purpose
3. Define subject
4. Organize content
5. Design format and layout
6. Plan release
7. Plan maintenance
8. Estimate costs and timing

These planning steps guide you to answer questions about the requirements that the manual must meet, about the content of the manual, and about its physical form. The test of a system manual plan is simple: Could any competent writer create the manual from this plan? When the answer is yes, you have completed the plan.

> **PROBLEM:** They won't use the manual; it's too technical. Or, they won't use the manual; it doesn't have enough detail.
>
> **SOLUTION:** Design each system manual by clearly defining its audience, purpose, and subject.

The first three steps in creating a system manual plan should be familiar to you by now. As always, it is essential that you start by defining the audience, purpose, and subject of the manual. The following equation illustrates how these three attributes define a unique manual:

1 Manual = 1 Audience + 1 Purpose + 1 Subject

I call this the MAPS equation. This acronym reminds me that manuals are the "maps" to the system.

DEFINE AUDIENCE

All system documentation is a form of communication. You communicate most effectively when you write to your reader. To do this, you must have an image of your reader clearly in mind. Defining your audience answers questions about the tone, style, emphasis, and language of a manual. In fact, the audience can even determine the structure and content of a manual.

There are many different kinds of potential readers for your system manuals. Your audience may include analysts, programmers, system administrators, clerical workers, business professionals, students, computer operators, technical experts, and system marketers. The list is endless. Sometimes you will have a specific reader in mind. At other times, you will be writing to members of a diverse audience that you will never meet or interact with.

Your product design document should include definitions of the system environment, divided into three areas: the hardware, the software, and the human environment. Defining the human environment means defining the system players. You can design the system's users, operators, and supporters by defining their job titles or their roles in using the system. You can also specify the general education, specific training, and application experience needed by each system player.

Designing the human environment for your system greatly simplifies all aspects of the system development process. It also simplifies the process of defining the audience for a system manual.

Even when your product design includes definitions of various system players, you must refine these definitions for documentation purposes. The best approach is to define your audience by classifying it.

We have already discussed one method of classifying readers, by their familiarity with the subject matter. You can define your audience as being novice, informed, or expert readers.

Novice readers are those that have no previous exposure to the subject of your manual. They can understand small, isolated portions of the system you are describing but have not had enough experience to form their own overviews and generalizations. You can help the novice reader by providing concrete examples and analogies, and by carefully defining each new term as it occurs.

Novice readers lack confidence. As a result, they are more likely to read large portions of a manual in sequence. Take advantage of this by presenting new concepts several times, in increasing levels of detail.

After a few months of experience, novice readers develop into informed readers. Informed readers know more than novices, but less than experts. The informed reader needs some explanation and interpretation of the information presented in your manual, but relies less on definitions of basic system terms and concepts. Informed readers understand the system from a broader perspective. They are ready to explore options that can increase their productivity and to use the system in more powerful ways.

You still need to give informed readers extensive support as they explore new system functions and capabilities. However, they can use condensed reference information to remind them of functions with which they are now familiar.

As your readers evolve from novice to expert, they rely less on sequential access and more on random access of the information in manuals. Consequently, informed readers rely increasingly on the reference aids you include in manuals. We will examine reference aids in detail in the next chapter.

Experts have enough experience to view your manual and system from the highest perspective. Information directed to experts can be abstract. You can present information to expert readers in a very direct fashion. They can use lists, tables, and diagrams with a minimum of supporting text. You will not need to spend much time defining terms for experts. Neither do they require explanations, analyses, or extensive examples. Expert readers rely heavily on reference aids to scan and skim text and to access information randomly. They need condensed reference information to remind them of those functions they use infrequently.

You can refine your audience classification scheme by rating your readers in three subject areas. These are: the application, your system, and EDP in general.

For example, the audience for an accounting system manual would probably be expert in the *application* or business of accounting. First-time users of *your system* would be classified as novices, but they could range from novice to expert on the subject of *EDP* as it applies to automated accounting systems.

As another example, support engineers are usually novice or informed readers when it comes to specific applications. They will quickly become experts in your specific systems. Their ability to rapidly learn new systems stems from their status as informed or expert users of EDP systems in general.

The method of classifying readers by three levels of expertise in three subject areas results in the audience classification matrix shown in Figure 13-1. Obviously, you could refine and extend your classification scheme indefinitely. However, the three-by-three matrix

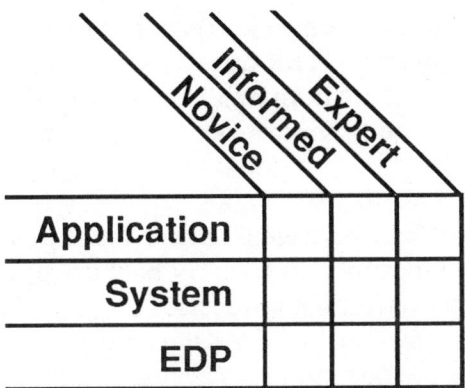

FIGURE 13-1: Audience Classification Matrix

is capable of dividing readers into twenty-seven distinct classes. This is sufficient for most system manual plans.

DEFINE PURPOSE

Purpose is the context within which you measure a manual's effectiveness. If you don't know the purpose of a manual, you can't tell if it's working well. You must define the purpose of a manual before you can draft, evaluate, or improve it.

Defining the purpose of a manual keeps you on track through all steps of the documentation process. It helps you decide what information should be included in or excluded from the manual. Including a statement of purpose in the introduction to the manual also tells the readers what they can expect to accomplish by using the manual.

Start with the purpose as defined in the system library plan. Expand on this definition of purpose by asking various questions.

Ask yourself, "What is the purpose of this manual?" The answer may be a single statement, such as, "To show the user how to install the system." It may result in a list of objectives, such as

- Present an image of professionalism and reliability to potential customers.
- Enhance the buyer's perception of value received.
- Train novice users in basic system use.
- Provide informed and expert users with detailed reference information.

Another technique is to ask, "What should result when the reader uses this manual?" This question tends to produce specific, task-oriented goals that the manual must help the reader accomplish. Task-oriented goals for an operator manual might include the following:

- Operate the daily and weekly runs for the system.
- Perform the monthly and yearly backup jobs.
- Respond to user report requests.
- Maintain the system control totals log.

Finally, you can ask yourself a related pair of questions: "What specific problems should this manual solve? What background need or problem should this manual meet?" This pair of questions is appropriate for improving or expanding an existing system library.

DEFINE SUBJECT

The sequence of defining the audience, purpose, and subject is intentional. Defining the audience and purpose first simplifies the process of defining the subject. Given a specific audience and purpose, the subject matter for an individual manual suggests itself.

You can define the subject by asking, "What information does the reader need to accomplish this goal (or list of goals)?" Express your answer as an informal outline for the manual.

Defining your subject involves you in decisions about how much detail to include. Once again, first defining your audience and purpose simplifies decisions about your subject matter. How much detail should you include? Enough to allow a specific reader to accomplish specific goals.

When it is impossible to write for a specific audience, it helps to classify and organize the subject matter for different levels of reader. Consider, for example, the ubiquitous user manual. Information needed by novices can be organized into a tutorial chapter. Here, novice users can learn basic system functions by following extensive, concrete examples. Information for intermediate readers can be presented in a reference section, organized alphabetically by system function names. Expert users can refer to the reference section and to information in appendices, or to summaries presented on quick reference pages or cards. (See Chapter 14 for more on quick reference cards.)

ORGANIZE CONTENT

Defining the audience, purpose, and subject of a system manual will result in at least an informal outline of the manual's content. The next step in the planning process is to organize the overall content of the manual.

Expand your informal outline into a formal outline that defines the content, organization, and sequence of the body of the manual. Add the standard or common elements of manuals:

- Title page
- Copyright notice and revision information

- Table of contents
- List of figures
- List of tables
- Introduction
- Chapters
- Appendices
- Glossary
- Index

In this step of the documentation process you are specifying the manual at a general level. Your focus should be on the body of the manual, the introduction, the chapters, and the appendices.

The system manual plan is analogous to a program specification. A program specification defines the structure of the program and shows what functions it performs. It does not show *how* the program performs its functions. The details are left to the programmer. Similarly, the system manual plan shows the overall structure of the manual and states the purpose or goals of the manual. Details about the structure and organization of chapters are left to the writer. These details will be determined during the draft step. Your formal outline need only define

- How information is organized into subjects
- How subjects are grouped into chapters
- How chapters are sequenced within the manual

There are good reasons for deferring detailed organization decisions to the draft step. At lower levels both organization and sequence depend on which specific techniques and structures are chosen by the writer.

DESIGN FORMAT AND LAYOUT

Before you start to draft a manual, you must accomplish one more planning step. You need to design the format and layout of the manual. This step can be divided into three smaller steps:

1. Select the medium
2. Design the page
3. Design the line

PROBLEM: They do their own documentation, and it looks like it.

SOLUTION: Hire a consultant to create general design standards for each type of system manual.

Advanced word processing and desktop publishing systems present the EDP professional with a confusing array of design choices. Unfortunately, most of us lack the training or experience needed to make sensible decisions. At this step of the documentation process, you can benefit from the experience of experts. For a low, one-time cost, a consultant can create manual design specifications that provide the basis for all your future work.

In this section I'll play the role of your design consultant. I'll give you a quick introduction to design variables and criteria for the printed page.

Medium

Defining the audience, purpose, and subject of a system manual simplifies selection of an effective medium. Traditionally, system manuals were restricted to the printed page. However, it is now possible to conceive of "manuals" in other media.

We have already seen how the product design "document" is an excellent candidate for multimedia treatment. Audio and video tapes are being used more and more as user training vehicles. System "manuals" now take the form of online help systems.

This flexibility involves more choices and decisions, but fortunately there is a strategy that simplifies the decision process: Match the medium to the audience's preferred mode of learning. You can classify your audience by the way in which they absorb information most quickly and easily: aurally, visually, or experientially.

Aural learners prefer spoken instructions. They want another human being to tell them what to do. The best medium for an aural audience is audiotape.

Visual learners like to see what they should do. They think in images and can absorb and retain visual information readily. A visual audience can benefit from paper manuals that include both text and graphic material.

Experiential learners learn by doing, by experimenting in a hands-on situation. The medium for an experiential audience is the online tutorial and help system.

We'll confine the rest of our discussion to the more traditional medium of the printed page. Even this medium requires several design decisions.

Printed manuals can take a variety of forms. Your manual can be produced in the familiar book form. It can also be a smaller guide or brochure, or even a single-page reference card. Select the form of your manual according to its purpose and content, and according to how the reader will use it. Consider the physical situation in which the reader uses the manual.

Printed pages can be bound in several ways. They can be assembled in a loose-leaf three-ring binder, or they can be coil bound, stapled, or perfect bound (stitched and glued).

You must also select a page size. The $8\frac{1}{2}$-by-11-inch page is a good choice for most system manuals. It lets you use a wide range of structures and layouts, and readers are familiar with it. Using a standard page size simplifies the production, binding, and storage of your manual.

Half-size pages have gained wide acceptance and use since their introduction as the medium for personal computer user manuals. Unfortunately, there is no standard size for half-size pages. They can range from $5\frac{1}{2}$-by-$8\frac{1}{2}$-inches to 7 by 9 inches. This can complicate the production and binding of your manual. However, half-size manuals have several offsetting advantages:

- They are less intimidating to the reader.
- They are easier to handle on a crowded desk or at a terminal.
- They decrease the column width of text, making it easier for the reader to scan lines of text.

Select the page size of your manual according to how the reader will use the manual, the text and graphics structures you plan to use, and your production capabilities.

Page

You should separate page layout decisions from the process of drafting your manual and define the page layout before you create the draft. At first, it may seem more sensible to reverse this sequence and let your text and graphics define the page layout. If you do this, you are allowing the *content* of the manual to control the *form* of the manual. Since the page layout determines how easily your reader can use the manual, *you* must retain control of it.

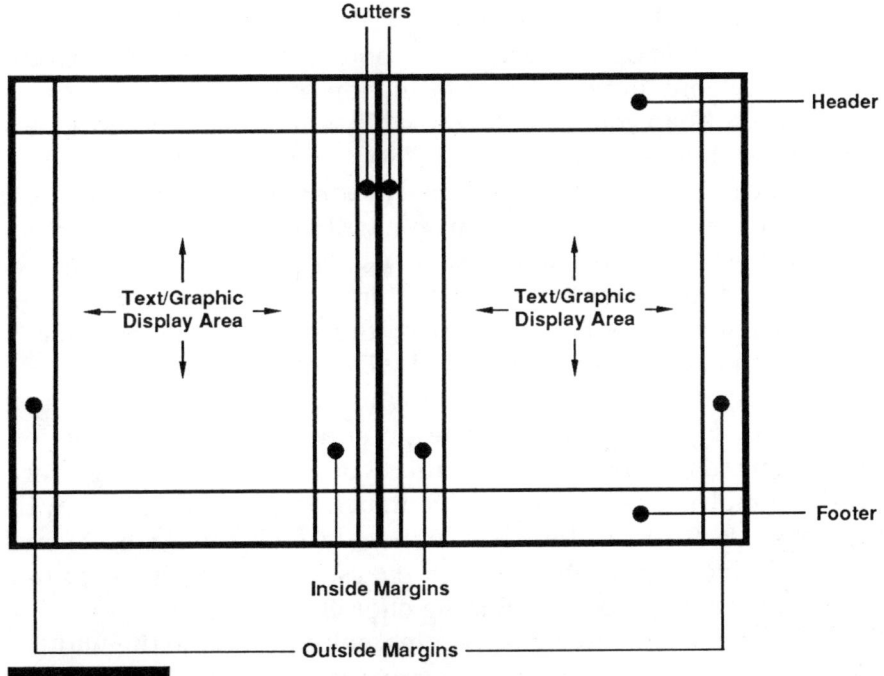

FIGURE 13-2: Common Page Elements

In practice, you will find that a predefined page layout actually helps you create text and graphics. It provides useful guidelines about paragraph and heading text and about the size and placement of graphics.

To design a page layout, you specify the size and location of the elements that comprise the page. Figure 13-2 shows the elements that are common to all pages, regardless of their content.

Margins—the white space at the sides of a page—define the left and right limits for the page content. Margins are passive space. They do not contribute to the organization or structure of the page content. However, they do contribute to the overall visual impact and usability of the manual. Ample margins are far less formidable to the reader than narrow margins.

Let your own experience and sense of proportion determine the margin widths you specify. As a starting point, I suggest inside and outside margins of 1 inch for $8\frac{1}{2}$-by-11-inch pages or $\frac{3}{4}$ inch for $5\frac{1}{2}$-by-$8\frac{1}{2}$-inch pages.

Headers and footers define the upper and lower limits of your page content. They are the white space at the top and bottom of the page. When you define header and footer sizes, remember that this space may contain reference information in the form of header or footer text. Keep your page layout simple by using either header or footer text, but not both.

Make footers slightly larger than headers, or the text will look as if it is falling off the page. Again, you will need to rely on your own experience and sense of proportion. As a rough guide, I suggest the following dimensions: for headers, 1 inch for $8\frac{1}{2}$-by-11-inch pages or $\frac{3}{4}$ inch for $5\frac{1}{2}$-by-$8\frac{1}{2}$-inch pages; for footers, $1\frac{1}{2}$ inches for $8\frac{1}{2}$-by-11-inch pages or 1 inch for $5\frac{1}{2}$-by-$8\frac{1}{2}$-inch pages.

Gutters are additional areas of white space that appear only at the inside edge of your pages. The gutter width you specify for your page depends on the binding method you use. Be sure the gutter is wide enough to prevent the page content from being obscured by the binding. Start with these guidelines: $\frac{1}{2}$ inch for $8\frac{1}{2}$-by-11-inch pages; $\frac{1}{4}$ inch for $5\frac{1}{2}$-by-$8\frac{1}{2}$-inch pages. Then adjust the gutters according to your specific binding choices.

Within the left and right margins, columns define the width of the text and graphic content of your page. Column width is determined primarily by the mechanics of reading.

People normally read by placing a page 14 to 18 inches from their eyes. Their eyes scan lines of text by sweeping through an 8 degree arc, centered on the nose. This means that the maximum column width for comfortable reading is about $4\frac{1}{2}$ inches. People have difficulty reading text set in longer lines. Their eyes cannot scan wide columns properly, and they lose their place.

Sometimes this limit to column width is expressed as $1\frac{1}{2}$ alphabets. This takes into account the additional effects of the type size. We can read wider columns of large type comfortably because the page can be placed farther from our eyes, and because the type itself provides visual place-marking cues.

An $8\frac{1}{2}$-inch-wide page with a total of $2\frac{1}{2}$ inches of margin and gutter has a 6-inch-wide space available for the content of the page. This print area can be divided according to several useful column layouts.

You can use two columns of equal width, separated by a $\frac{1}{4}$-inch column margin. This layout is easy to manage and provides the reader with a comfortable reading width.

This layout can be used for almost any type of manual. It is particularly well-suited to index pages. For text and graphics pages, however, it forces you to use cross-headings—headings that fall within the text columns. You need to use additional vertical white space to make cross-headings effective.

You can also divide the print area of your page into two columns of unequal width. Use one column for side headings and the other for text and graphics. Make the heading column roughly half the width of the text column. The heading column can also contain pictures (icons or other visual organization cues).

Half-size pages offer less flexibility in designing a column layout for your page. A 5½-inch-wide page with a total of 1¾ inches of margin and gutter has a print area only 3¾ inches wide.

This area is ideal for a single text and graphics column, but is difficult to divide into heading and text columns. A single column forces you to use either cross-headings or hanging headings, headings that start to the left of the left text margin.

Some writing structures demand a particular page or column layout. The obvious example is structured writing, which uses a specific page layout to organize textual and graphical material.

When the writing structure does not dictate the page layout, you can benefit by using a page grid. A page grid divides the print area of your page into cells. Each text or graphic element can occupy one or more of these cells. The page grid defines how writing structures (paragraphs, headings, lists, graphics) are mapped onto the page. It provides a constant but invisible format for the content of your pages. Your reader will benefit from the added organization and balance a page grid provides.

While there are many page grid schemes, I will focus on only two. These are the grids for full and half-size pages that I have found to be most generally useful for system manuals. I encourage you to experiment with page grids and develop your own favorites.

The first page grid applies to 8½-by-11-inch pages. It is shown in Figure 13-3. Each cell in this grid is 1⅞ inches wide and 1½ inches high. The columns are separated by 3/16-inch margins, while the rows have ¼-inch margins.

These cells allow you to use a side heading and text column arrangement, with heads in one column and text occupying the other two. They also let you integrate several different size graphics with your text. Graphics can be two or three cells wide, and two to five cells high. The three-by-three cell size is ideal for picturing screen layouts or samples.

The second page grid applies to half-size, or 5½-by-8½-inch

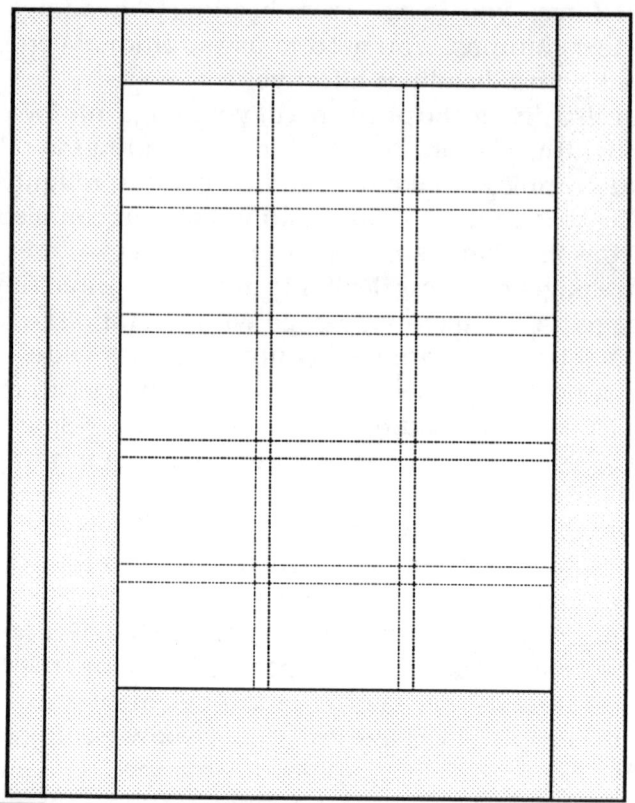

FIGURE 13-3: Page Grid for 8½-by-11-Inch Pages

pages. It uses the single column layout but divides the print area into four rows. Each cell is 3¾ inches wide and 1½ inch high. These cells let you integrate four different sizes of graphic with your text: ¼-, ½ -, or full-page. See Figure 13-4 for an illustration of the grid.

Line

Designing your text line is far simpler than designing your page layout. To design a line, you need only specify three attributes of the line: the font, the leading, and the justification.

A font is a complete collection of letters and symbols for a given typeface and size. For example, 12-point Helvetica includes capitals, small capitals, and lowercase letters, in roman (normal), italic, boldface, and boldface italic styles, all in 12-point size. See Figure 13-5 for examples of fonts.

Extracting Manuals • 265

FIGURE 13-4: Page Grid for 5½-by-8½-Inch Pages

Select an effective font for the text of your manual by matching the font to the audience. In most cases, readers expect a traditional "nuts-and-bolts" typeface for technical information. Times is an excellent choice.

Normally, the typeface should be invisible to the reader. Be careful not to distract or hamper your reader with your selection of typeface. However, there are exceptions to this rule. For example, headings should provide visual clues to the organization of your material and consequently should be readily visible and distinguishable from the text.

Typefaces in common use, such as Times, Helvetica, Letter Gothic, or Courier, are equally legible. Typefaces with serifs (the extra lines at the top and bottom of the letters) can be read more easily. The serifs give the reader's eye additional tracking guides. Serif typefaces are good for sustained reading.

Courier typeface is a good choice if you plan to produce your

<u>Times 12 Point Font</u>

ROMAN CAPITALS
BOLD ROMAN CAPITALS
ITALIC CAPITALS
BOLD ITALIC CAPITALS
ROMAN SMALL CAPITALS
BOLD ROMAN SMALL CAPITALS
ITALIC SMALL CAPITALS
BOLD ITALIC SMALL CAPITALS
roman lower case
bold roman lower case
italic lower case
bold italic lower case

<u>Helvetica 12 Point Font</u>

ROMAN CAPITALS
BOLD ROMAN CAPITALS
ITALIC CAPITALS
BOLD ITALIC CAPITALS
ROMAN SMALL CAPITALS
BOLD ROMAN SMALL CAPITALS
ITALIC SMALL CAPITALS
BOLD ITALIC SMALL CAPITALS
roman lower case
bold roman lower case
italic lower case
bold italic lower case

FIGURE 13-5: Sample Times and Helvetica Fonts

manual on a photocopy machine. The line widths of this typeface are equal. This helps prevent degradation when you photocopy text.

The italic styles of a font make for slower and more difficult reading. Save italics for emphasizing single words or phrases. Mixed typefaces also slow your reader down. Limit yourself to three typefaces in a manual. Use one for text, one for headings, and one for special displays (such as system messages or user entries).

People do not actually read the letters in a word; they recognize the shape of the entire word. Words set in upper case all have the same general shape—rectangles of various widths. You can help your reader by restricting your use of uppercase words to emphasize single words. Use upper and lower case (mixed case) in your text and headings.

Font sizes are specified in points. A point is 1/72 inch. You need not drag yourself through elaborate mathematical conversions to select a font size. Simply experiment with your equipment, study the efforts of others, and form your own preferences.

The best sizes for text fonts range from 9 through 12 point. Directories and indexes can be set in a smaller font (say 8 or 9 points), as they do not require sustained reading.

For your heading lines, select a typeface that complements, but is clearly distinguishable from, the face of your text line. Helvetica headings over Times text works well. Times headings over New Century Schoolbook text is another harmonious pairing.

Limit yourself to three or four font sizes for different levels of heading. Make sure that different heading font sizes are easily visually distinguishable.

The vertical spacing between lines is determined by their *leading*. This term, pronounced "ledding," is derived from the thin strips of lead inserted between lines of type in metal typesetting. Leading is also specified in points.

Leading affects the visual density of type. As you increase leading, the appearance of text moves from black to grey. Two point leading is standard. Thus, a type line might be specified as 9/11 ("9 on 11"). This notation indicates a font size of 9 points set on a line that is 11 points thick including the leading.

For system manuals, there are only three acceptable ways to set lines of type:

- Flush left, ragged right
- Fush left, hyphenated
- Centered

Flush left, ragged right text is aligned on the left side and has a ragged or staggered right side. The right side can vary greatly, as lines break only between words. This may not be as aesthetically pleasing as fully justified text, but it is easier to read. The ragged right side actually helps the reader's eye, providing visual clues to mark his or her place in the text.

Ragged right text can be improved by breaking lines at hyphenation points within words. Hyphenation is actually transparent to your reader. Test this yourself the next time you read any magazine or textbook. You will find that you are unaware of hyphenation unless you consciously look for it. Hyphenation limits the stagger of the ragged right margin. It improves the visual balance of text without hampering your reader. Flush left with hyphenation is your best approximation to typeset text. Take care to limit the number of sequential lines that end in a hyphen, as this too can be distracting. Hyphenation can only be limited by manual editing.

The third method, centered text, is for use only with headings. It is difficult to read blocks of centered text, but centering headings is a good visual clue to organization.

Why not use fully justified text? The reason is simple. The additional space introduced between words and letters hampers your reader. It is difficult to scan over unevenly spaced letters and words. Further, the additional space tends to create "rivers." Rivers are the bands of vertical white space that run through poorly justified text. These distract the reader and interrupt the horizontal scan of the eye.

PLAN RELEASE

During the planning stage, the production and distribution of your manual may seem remote. Still, it is to your advantage to do some basic planning for the inevitable release of the manual.

Planning the release involves decisions about the two major steps involved. First, you must decide how to produce the manual. Second, you must decide how to distribute the manual in a controlled fashion.

Production

To produce the manual you must

1. Create the text
2. Create the graphics

3. Integrate text and graphics into a duplication copy
4. Produce distribution copies

The way you decide to create text and graphics will probably depend on your publishing software and hardware. Your decisions will also be influenced by the methods available to you for integrating the two.

You should also plan which portions of the text and graphics must be created from scratch and which can be extracted from the System File.

The term "duplication copy" is probably new to you. Long ago, I gave up the attempt to identify and distinguish between versions of a manual as the original, master copy, artwork copy, camera-ready copy, and so on. I now consider all versions of a manual to be copies. I name the copy according to the primary function it performs. Thus, the duplication copy (formerly the original or artwork copy) is the version of the manual that is duplicated into multiple distribution copies. And yes, a distribution copy is one that is distributed to the reader.

Once you create the duplication copy, you must decide how to produce the distribution copies. Three printing options are available: photocopy, quick printing, and printing. Remember that after you produce the pages, you will still need to bind them into manuals. Plan the binding materials and services you will need well in advance of your distribution deadline.

The photocopy process uses xerography to produce low- to medium-quality copies of your duplication copy. It is inexpensive and adequate for small quantities of small manuals. The process does not reproduce detailed graphics well.

Quick printing uses a special type of photographic process to create disposable plates. The plates are used in an offset printing process to produce distribution copies. The quality of quick printing copies is acceptable for all types of manual. Quick printing reproduces most line art well, but is still inadequate for photographs. Most quick print shops also offer collating and binding services, so you can have the final distribution copies produced by a single vendor.

Printing is the most expensive but highest-quality process for producing your distribution copies. Printing is cost-effective only for producing large numbers of distribution copies. In this process, metal plates are produced and used in an offset printing press.

Printed manuals can be produced in the full range of paper sizes, weights, and ink colors. Rely on the printer to help you make decisions about this complex production method. Print shops offer all the collating and binding services you will need to produce and package distribution copies of your manual.

Distribution

Releasing a manual includes distributing it to your readers in a controlled fashion. They key word is *controlled*. How you record the distribution of your manuals is strongly related to how you record the distribution of your system products. The in-line approach encourages you to view all system documents as integrated components of the system product itself. This implies that distribution of software and manuals should be controlled with a common process.

Falling short of this ideal, you will need to plan a control log for each manual you release. The content of your control log depends on the nature of your shop, distribution method, and clients.

At the planning stage, your control log is a list of potential recipients. Use the control log to plan who will receive copies of the manual and to estimate how many copies you must produce.

You may also need to record individual names and addresses of manual holders so that future revisions can be sent to them. In this case, include detachable registration cards at the back of your manual.

Your control log should also show the history of revisions to the manual. This can be as simple as a list of version numbers or revision dates that identify previous and current versions of the manual.

Store the control log with the system manual plan in the System File.

PLAN MAINTENANCE

Software and systems are more susceptible to change than other products. Consequently, planning for the revision and updating of your manual is important. Planning for maintenance means reviewing your decisions about binding, title page content, page header text, and page numbering.

Make sure that the binding method you have chosen matches the frequency and method of revising your manual. The fewer the updates, the more permanent the binding should be. Use a loose-leaf binding method if you anticipate frequent revisions or if you will need to revise single pages. Use coil or staple binding when revisions are infrequent or if you plan to replace entire manuals or sections of a manual. Use perfect binding only when you intend to replace the entire manual with a revised version.

Print the system version number on the title page of your manual. If the manual is revised between system versions, identify different versions of the manual by a revision date. Also print the manual revision date on the title page. Whenever you distribute a set of revision pages, you can include a new title page that shows the current system version and document revision date.

Readers must know that they are reading the correct version of the system information you provide. When you distribute revised pages, readers need to know which manual the pages belong to and where they go in the manual. There should be no confusion about which version of a page is correct. You can anticipate and solve these problems by printing the manual title, page number, and revision date in the page header or footer.

If you plan to revise and replace the entire manual as a unit, you can number pages sequentially from front to back. Otherwise, number pages within chapters or sections to reduce the impact of insertions on page numbering. Rather than adding pages 2-36a and 2-36b after page 2-36 in Chapter Two of your manual, consider renumbering and distributing the entire chapter. This approach is more expensive in terms of paper and shipping costs, but makes it easier for your reader to keep a manual up-to-date. Replacing a block of pages is easier for your reader than searching out and replacing five or six single pages within a chapter.

Planning for maintenance also means controlling the content of the pages themselves. Apply your software maintenance experience when you plan manual maintenance. Control your use of such "embedded literals" as cross-references to page numbers. (See the discussion of cross-references in the next chapter.)

When your readers receive a package of revision pages, they naturally want to know, "What's changed? Why? How will this affect me?" Bar marking schemes are not adequate. They show changes to existing pages, but do not answer all of the reader's questions. I suggest you plan a revision package that includes a cover sheet or a revision notes bulletin. The revision notes summarize the changes, describe their impact on the reader, and tell the reader how to update the manual.

In the previous step, plan release, you designed a control log for your manual. This log is stored with the system manual plan in the System File. It shows the history of revision and distribution for the manual.

Treat each revision to the manual as a project, just as you would for program maintenance. Keep the control log brief, and use project numbers to point to detailed revision project information in the Project File.

So far we have planned for two different versions or copies of the manual. The duplication copy is used to produce distribution copies. Distribution copies are issued to your readers. I suggest that you plan a third copy of your manual, called the revision copy. Use the revision copy to mark pending changes to the manual. This is analogous to maintaining production and development versions of your software. The revision copy is the development version of your manual.

ESTIMATE COSTS AND TIMING

The cost of system documentation cannot be avoided; however, it can be hidden in the cost of other activities. For example, your users may be creating their own reference guides. The cost of an adequate user manual may be hidden in training and support costs.

Your first estimate for a system manual always seems high, but realize that you are simply isolating the hidden costs of communicating system information from the remainder of the system development process. Yes, creating an effective system manual *seems* expensive, but by restricting your communication costs to the production of a manual, you can control and reduce them.

Let's pause for a moment to take our bearings. We are working in the build step of the system development process. We are building a system manual. Strictly speaking, estimating the cost and timing of this effort is part of project planning for the entire system. After all, the manual is simply another system element. In practice, you will integrate the planning and estimating steps for each manual into the overall project planning and control process for the system.

There are published standards and guidelines for estimating the cost of creating a manual. However, the best approach is to develop your own estimating methods and factors from experience. Start with the steps I present here, but revise them to suit your specific situation.

1. Estimate the page count of the finished manual. Use this to determine both labor and material costs.

2. Express the labor cost in terms of person hours. Each page of the manual will take 4 to 8 hours to create, depending on the complexity of the subject and on how much information is available in the System File. This estimate includes the hours for all project members: writers, editors, and reviewers.

3. Calculate the material cost according to the production method and the number of manuals you have planned. Add the cost of binding materials and labor.

4. Divide the total person hours among the steps in the documentation process, according to the following percentages:

30% Plan
30% Draft
10% Edit
15% Review
15% Release

5. Schedule the project by scheduling each step in the documentation process. Use a simple scheduling technique. Gantt charts work well.

DRAFT

Chapters 10 through 12 were devoted to the details of the draft step. We examined techniques, structures, organizations, and sequences that you can use to draft manuals. In this chapter we will focus on how existing information in the System File can be extracted for inclusion in manuals. You'll discover that very little new text and graphics need to be drafted for the creation of an in-line system manual.

I deliberately named this chapter "Extracting Manuals" rather than "Creating Manuals." The in-line approach lets you extract manuals from the System File, rather than creating them from scratch.

The System File is an essential component of the in-line approach. It is a data base of system information, expressed in the form of system specifications. By adopting the in-line approach, you eliminate the need to add on system manuals. System manuals represent "snapshots" of information already in the System File. Manuals are simply one way of presenting System File information in a format that is useful for a specific audience.

Drafting an in-line manual involves two simple steps:

1. Create any additional text and graphics needed.
2. Extract and format existing System File information.

CREATE ADDITIONAL TEXT AND GRAPHICS

When you draft additional text and graphics for your manual, your strategy should be to revise what exists in the System File, rather than to add new and isolated information. Treat the System File and system specifications as control points for the information in your manual. Revisions that originate in the system specifications will automatically radiate out into your derived manuals.

In many cases you can simply edit and revise what has already been written. When the information in a system specification cannot be revised to match two diverse audiences, consider adding the new version to the system specification itself. For example, function specifications for online systems have two statements of purpose: a technical purpose written for the builders who implement the function, and a user purpose for those who use the function.

Similarly, when you decide to use structures like playscript or structured writing in your manual, explore the possibility of applying the structure to the system specifications that contain the original information.

Most of the new material you draft for your manual will be demanded by the format, organization, and structure of the manual itself. These additional blocks of text can be stored in the System File as text elements. Storing fragments of text in the System File (rather than permanently assembling them into a manual) makes it possible to compile manuals automatically from elements in the System File.

Your manual will probably require overviews or introductions to subjects and chapters. These play the same role as the statements of purpose for programs, functions, or reports. They tell the reader whether or not the information sought has been found. Your introductory text should also give the reader the gist of the subject at hand, show how different readers can use the information, and point to supportive or related information.

Installation guides and user tutorial manuals present special problems. You will probably need to create most of the text for these two types of manual. However, environment requirements for batch and online systems are recorded in the system specification. You can make good use of form, screen, and report samples when drafting tutorials, especially if you convert these samples to cases (series of related examples).

EXTRACT SYSTEM FILE INFORMATION

Let's review the information already in the System File to see how it can be extracted for use in manuals. You may want to skip ahead to the section entitled Four Model Libraries at the end of this chapter to see some concrete examples.

System overviews should appear in most user, operator, and support manuals. Both batch and online system specifications contain text and graphics that you can incorporate into a system overview chapter. For example, specifications contain information about system conventions and options, as well as models of the control and information structure of your system.

A statement of purpose or a description has already been written for each system element. These require little revision, as they were written with a specific audience in mind. These are useful as introductory text to all forms of reference material.

Samples of forms, screens, and reports are the most generally useful graphics in the System File. You can use them in all types of manual.

Here is a wonderful aspect of the in-line approach to system documentation. Many system element specifications can be compiled into reference chapters or manuals without any revision or reformatting whatsoever.

For batch systems, subsystem and transaction specifications can comprise user reference manuals. Run specifications can be assembled into operator manuals. Job specifications can be incorporated into user and operator manuals or can form a complete data entry manual.

For online systems, you can create large portions of user reference manuals by assembling menu and function specifications in an appropriate sequence.

You can use data item specifications to create useful directories or manual appendices for either batch or online systems. The same is true for report, screen, and message specifications. You need only decide which attributes are suitable for a given audience.

EDIT

The purpose of the edit step is to convert the draft version of your manual into a finalized version, ready for review. Editing corrects deficiencies that the writer cannot see in the draft. In practice, editing and drafting are often iterative. Editors can make suggestions that result in moderate or heavy reworking of a draft before it is even reviewed.

Who should edit the draft? First of all, it should be a person. Computers have neither the wit nor the perspective to perform editing functions. Second, the editor should be someone other than the writer. Editing requires that you be detached from the writing effort.

I suggest that you divide the edit step into three major levels of edit: a management edit, a mechanical edit, and a content edit. The job of editing at each level should be assigned to the person best qualified to make the decisions required.

The management editor checks and corrects the draft so that it reflects the current operating and financial policies of your company. This editor also ensures that such legal issues as copyrights and protection for proprietary information are handled correctly in the manual. Finally, the management editor ensures that your manual reflects the correct image of your department or firm.

The mechanical editor is responsible for your manual's integrity. The editor ensures that cross-references, references to figures and tables, tables of content, and the index are correct. The mechanical editor ensures that your manual uses consistent formats, structures, spellings, and abbreviations. During the mechanical edit, the editor pays close attention to the definition and use of special terms and notations.

The content editor works to improve the text of your draft. This editor makes sure that the language matches the specified audience and that the information is complete and accurate. The content editor removes abstractions, complexity, nonessential preliminaries, dense or obscure writing, and jargon.

No matter who edits, or at which level, the manual must be edited in a form that is as close to its final version as possible. This means that paper manuals must be edited in printed form, not on a CRT screen. The organization, layout, and visual cues of a printed manual cannot be edited on a screen-by-screen basis.

When all editors' corrections have been made to the draft, it is ready for review.

REVIEW

Reviewing the edited draft of your manual is the last step before production. Alas, few reviews are actually final. Like editing, the review step is part of an iterative loop that can take you back to the drafting and editing steps several times before you produce and release your manual.

Like editing, reviews involve reading and correcting a draft of the manual at several levels and from several perspectives. Assign the work to the people best suited for the specific tasks.

I suggest that you conduct a plan review, a technical review, and an editorial review. In addition, you will need to conduct a reader review. A more accurate name for this last review is "testing."

In the plan review, you compare the draft to the system manual plan. This ensures that the manual will serve its specified purpose for the defined audience.

The technical review ensures that the manual is technically accurate and complete. This review may involve exercising the system and comparing its performance to the information presented in the manual.

The editorial review is a final check of the format, layout, typesetting, and overall style of the manual. The objective is to weed out any remaining inconsistencies or mechanical flaws.

The reader review is the first actual test of the manual. You should select readers who are representative of the manual's intended audience and provide them with a version of the manual that is an accurate reflection of the final product.

For all but the simplest manuals you will need to create a test plan. Set up actual tasks that the reader must accomplish by using the manual and system. Plan how you will record and evaluate the results. Check your plan by doing an in-house controlled test before you send your manual off for external tests.

You may need to show your reviewers how to review. Few people have education or experience in reviewing manuals, so be prepared to train your reviewers. Use a cover letter to accomplish reviewer training. Tell the reviewers the purpose of the review and give a rough estimate of how long the review should take. Tell them what to look for. Provide a checklist or a list of questions that will keep them on track. Finally, show them how to mark problems or additions to the manual and how to return the manual to you.

It is also important to give your reviewers feedback. Show them how their efforts affect the final version of the manual. Show the changes that will and won't be made. You can do this by adding notations to the review copy. Providing feedback acknowledges your reviewers' contributions and encourages them to participate in future reviews.

RELEASE

The review step results in a final version of your manual, ready for production and distribution. Now you must implement your release plan. If you have not already done so, divide production into manageable tasks, schedule the tasks, and execute them.

Your first objective is the creation of a duplication copy from which the distribution copies will be produced. Follow your plan for creating and integrating the text and graphics into a duplication copy. Produce the distribution copies by the photocopy, quick printing, or printing process you have chosen. Bind or otherwise package the distribution copies.

The next step is to distribute copies of your manual to the readers. Use your control log to distribute the manual. Convert each recipient from "potential" to "actual" status.

In addition to the primary readers, your manual will probably have secondary readers; remember to distribute copies to them. For example, a user manual should go not only to your users, but also to your support staff.

Your manual has now graduated from a development version to a production version. Place a distribution copy in the production section of the System File. Destroy all draft, edit, and review copies of the manual, or relegate them to the history section of the Project File.

Finally, reserve a distribution copy for yourself. This becomes your revision copy, ready to be marked up for future revisions and releases.

MAINTAIN

PROBLEM: "We used to have an operator's manual around here somewhere. But it hasn't been updated in four years. We just keep it all in our heads."

SOLUTION: Use a project team approach to all system maintenance projects. Assign one or more team members the responsibility of producing and distributing revisions to system manuals.

This is the sort of problem that disappears when you adopt the in-line approach to system documentation. When you view system documentation and the human environment as part of the system itself, revisions to manuals are no more troublesome than revisions to software.

The maintain step of the documentation process is actually identical to that of the system development process. It does not exist as a separate process step but rather represents a repeat of the entire process from front to back.

For large-scale revisions, the maintenance step may carry you back to the initial planning steps. For smaller revisions, it may be enough to return to draft, edit, and review iterations.

No matter how small or large the revisions, you must repeat the release step for each revision to your manual. Decide whether your revision will be distributed as separate pages, as an entire section or chapter, or as an entire manual. Use 30 percent as a revision threshold. If 30 percent or more of the pages in a chapter will be revised, distribute the entire chapter. If 30 percent or more of the pages in a manual will be revised, distribute the entire manual.

Work through the plan, draft, edit, and review steps with the objective of producing the duplication copy of a revision package. Use the revision copy of the manual for this work, and remember to incorporate the miscellaneous revisions you have recorded there.

To minimize your confusion about the duplication, distribution, and revision copies, I have illustrated their use and relationships in Figure 13-6.

The duplication copy is produced from information in the System File. It is used to produce, by duplication, the distribution copies of the manual. Distribution copies are distributed to the readers of your manual. One of the distribution copies is placed in the System File as part of each release. A second distribution copy becomes your revision copy. You mark the revision copy with pending revisions, and incorporate the revisions into the next release of the manual.

Be sure to change the revision date on each page you revise. Check the table of contents, index, and other reference aids whenever page numbers change. Produce a new title page, showing the revised system version and overall manual revision date.

The revision package should include a revision bulletin that shows the reader

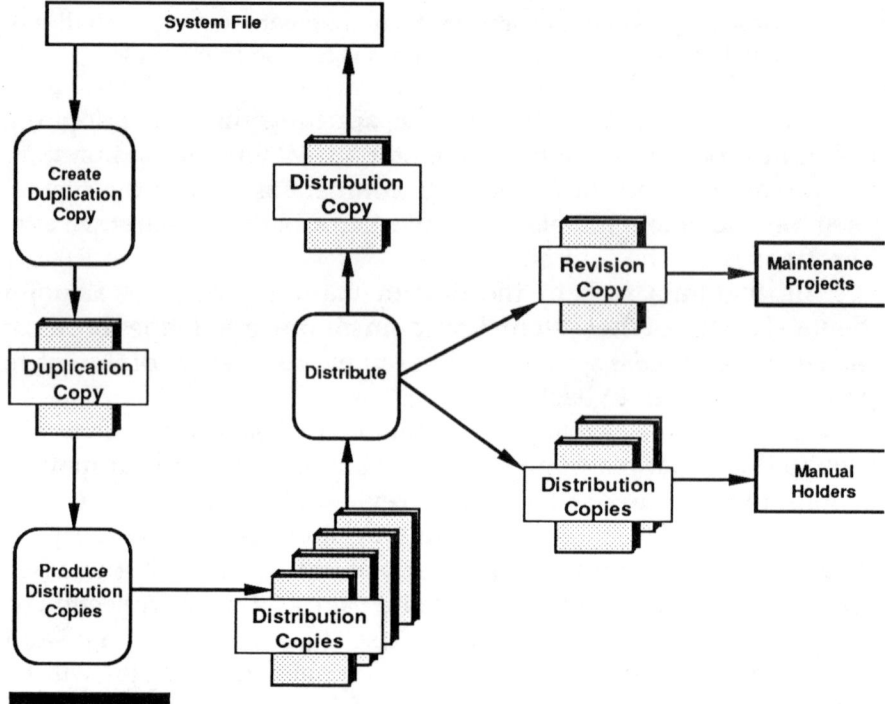

FIGURE 13-6: Duplication, Distribution, and Revision Copies

- A summary of what changes have been made
- The impact of these changes
- How to update the manual
- Whether to destroy or return obsolete versions

Use the finalized version of the duplication copy to produce distribution copies of the revision package. Your control log will show you who should receive the revisions. Update the log to reflect the actual distributions you make.

You will also need to update the control log to show the changes you have made. Keep the control log brief. You need only record the system version or manual revision date. Use the project number to point to detailed information in the Project File.

Update the System File as part of the release. Update or replace the distribution copy of the manual stored in the System File, just as your readers will update or replace their copies of the manual. Destroy outdated versions of the manual, or store them in the Project File.

FOUR MODEL LIBRARIES

Here are four model system manual libraries. I do not offer them as paradigms to be imitated. They are models only in the sense of generalized examples. The libraries and manuals you plan must be tailored to your specific situation. However, these models will give you a more concrete experience of the power of the in-line approach. I have outlined the content of the manuals by showing the System File information that belongs in each.

You will notice that none of the libraries contain a technical reference or programming manual. The reason for this is simple; the System File itself serves this purpose. Though I have tried, I have not been able to create a reference manual that serves the needs of system designers and builders better than the System File.

For brevity I have also omitted the reference aids we will discuss in the next chapter. These belong in every manual but the smallest, and you should not omit them from your planning.

LARGE BATCH SYSTEM

The first library is for a large batch system. It would apply to the system products of an internal EDP department. Here, installation of the system takes the form of a conversion project. There is no separate support function in the department, support services being provided by all the staff members. User training is conducted in-house. The library consists of the following manuals:

- System Administrator Manual
- User Manual
- Operator Manual
- Data Entry Manual
- Data Dictionary
- Form Directory
- Report Directory
- Message Directory

The content of each manual is outlined below.

System Administrator Manual
    System Overview (from batch system specification)
        Purpose
        Control Methods
        Information Structure
        System Conventions

                Requests
                Errors
            Options
            System Chart
        Subsystems (from subsystem specification)
            Purpose
            Cycle
            Trigger
            Transactions
            Subsystem Chart
        Security (from file, record, data item specifications)

User Manual
    System Overview (from batch system specification)
        Purpose
        System Conventions
            Requests
            Errors
    Transactions (from transaction specification)
        Purpose
        Method
        Results
    Additional Procedures (from job specification)
        Purpose
        Cycle
        Input
        Steps
        Output

Operator Manual
    System Overview (from batch system specification)
        Control Methods
        System Conventions
            Labeling
            Errors
    Runs (from run specification)
        Purpose
        Trigger
        Cycle

Operating Job
　　　Control
　　　File Allocation
　　　Run Chart
　　Files (from file specification)
　　　Description
　　　Organization
　　　Medium
　　　Backup
　　Additional Procedures (from job specification)
　　　Purpose
　　　Cycle
　　　Input
　　　Steps
　　　Output

Data Entry Manual
　　Data Entry Jobs (from job specification)
　　　Purpose
　　　Cycle
　　　Input
　　　Steps
　　　Output

Data Dictionary
　　Data Items (from data item specification)
　　　Description
　　　Used In
　　　Values
　　　Code List or Calculation
　　　Validation
　　　Security
　　　Display Heading

Form Directory
　　Forms (from form specification)
　　　Purpose
　　　Preparation Job
　　　Sample

Report Directory
    Reports (from report specification)
        Purpose
        Sequence and Breaks
        Print Specification
        Distribution Job
        Source
        Sample

Message Directory
    Messages (from message specification)
        Text
        Meaning
        Action

LARGE ONLINE SYSTEM

The second library might apply to the large, online systems produced by an independent software developer. The systems are large enough to warrant a system administrator. In this situation, installation teams deliver and install the system. The software developer provides ongoing support services and maintains a staff of support technicians. The library consists of the following manuals:

- Installation Guide
- System Administrator Manual
- User Tutorial Manual
- User Reference Manual
- Support Manual
- Data Dictionary
- Message Directory

The content of each manual is outlined below.

Installation Guide
    Requirements (from batch system specification)
    Installation Steps
    Options

System Administrator Manual
    System Overview (from online system specification)

Purpose
Control Structure
Information Structure
Menus (from menu specification)
Description
Route or Command
Functions
Screens (from screen specification)
Purpose
Source
Sample
Reports (from report specification)
Purpose
Sequence and Breaks
Print Specification
Source
Sample
Security (from file, record, data item specifications)

User Tutorial Manual
Main Functions Used
Reference to More Information

User Reference Manual
System Overview (from online system specification)
Purpose
Control Structure
Information Structure
Menus (from menu specification)
Description
Route or Command
Functions
Sample
Functions (from function specification)
Purpose
Route or Command
Steps
Messages (from message specification)
Text
Meaning
Action

Support Manual
- System Overview (from online system specification)
  - Purpose
  - Control Structure
  - Information Structure
  - Requirements
  - System Conventions
- Menus (from menu specification)
  - Description
  - Route or Command
  - Functions
- Functions (from function specification)
  - Technical Purpose
  - User Purpose
  - Route or Command
  - Steps
  - Processing
  - Elements Used
- Programs (from program specification)
  - Purpose
  - Files
  - Control
  - Structure
  - Modules
- Files (from file specification)
  - Description
  - Organization
  - Medium
  - Sequence/Access Key
  - Content
  - Backup
  - Size
  - Security
- Screens (from screen specification)
  - Purpose
  - Type
  - Content
  - Source
  - Sample
- Reports (from report specification)

Purpose
Sequence and Breaks
Print Specification
Volume
Source
Sample
Messages (from message specification)
Type
Text
Meaning
Action
Source

Data Dictionary
Data Items (from data item specification)
Description
Used In
Values
Code List or Calculation
Validation
Security
Display Heading

Message Directory
Messages (from message specification)
Text
Meaning
Action

SMALL BATCH SYSTEM

The third library is part of a small batch system. The scenario for this library involves either an internal or external EDP department. The users' EDP department or operator installs the system. Neither the developer nor the user has support staff. The library contains these manuals:

- User Manual
- Data Entry Guide
- Operator Manual

288 • System Documentation

Here are outlines of each manual.

User Manual
   System Overview (from batch system specification)
      Purpose
      Control Methods
      Information Structure
      System Conventions
         Requests
         Errors
      Options
      System Chart
   Tutorial Section
      Main Subsystems and Transactions Used to Do Job
      Reference to More Information
   Reference Section
      Subsystems (from subsystem specification)
         Purpose
         Cycle
         Transactions
         Subsystem Chart
      Transactions (from transaction specification)
         Purpose
         Method
         Results
      Additional Procedures (from job specification)
         Purpose
         Cycle
         Input
         Steps
         Output
   Reports (from report specification)
      Purpose
      Sequence and Breaks
      Source
      Sample
   Messages (from message specification)
      Text
      Meaning
      Action
   Data Items (from data item specification)

　　　　Description
　　　　Used In
　　　　Values
　　　　Code List or Calculation
　　　　Validation
　　　　Security
　　　　Display Heading
Data Entry Guide
　　Data Entry Jobs (from job specification)
　　　　Purpose
　　　　Cycle
　　　　Input
　　　　Steps
　　　　Output
Operator Manual
　　System Overview (from batch system specification)
　　　　Purpose
　　　　Control Methods
　　　　Information Structure
　　　　System Conventions
　　　　Options
　　　　System Chart
　　Installation Section
　　　　Requirements (from batch system specification)
　　　　Installation Steps
　　　　Options
　　Operation Section
　　　　Runs (from run specification)
　　　　　　Purpose
　　　　　　Cycle
　　　　　　Operating Job
　　　　　　Control
　　　　　　File Allocation
　　　　　　Run Chart
　　　　Additional Procedures (from job specification)
　　　　　　Purpose
　　　　　　Cycle
　　　　　　Input
　　　　　　Steps
　　　　　　Output

Files (from file specification)
    Description
    Organization
    Medium
    Sequence/Access Key
    Content
    Backup
    Size
    Security
Records (from record specification)
    Description
    Size
    Type
    Layout
    Security
Messages (from message specification)
    Type
    Text
    Meaning
    Action
    Source

SMALL ONLINE SYSTEM

The last library is for a small, online system, such as those produced by independent software shops or individual programmers. The user installs and operates the system. The developer does not provide support. The library consists of a single manual, the User Manual. Its content is outlined below.

User Manual
    Installation Section
        Requirements (from online system specification)
        Installation Steps
        Options
    System Overview (from online system specification)
        Purpose
        Control Structure
        Information Structure
        Requirements
        System Conventions

Tutorial Section
   Main Functions Used to Do Job
   Reference to More Information
Reference Section
   Menus (from menu specification)
      Description
      Route or Command
      Functions
   Functions (from function specification)
      Purpose
      Route or Command
      Steps
Screens (from screen specification)
   Purpose
   Source
   Sample
Reports (from report specification)
   Purpose
   Sequence and Breaks
   Print Specification
   Source
   Sample
Messages (from message specification)
   Text
   Meaning
   Action
Data Items (from data item specification)
   Description
   Values
   Code List or Calculation
   Validation
   Display Heading

14

Reference Aids

With few exceptions, the material in system manuals is read in a "random access" fashion. Your readers will not read your manuals sequentially to find the information they want. Rather, they will use the reference aids you provide. Because of the "random access" use of manuals, reference aids are as important to your manual as record keys and directories are to indexed files and data bases.

Here is a list of the reference aids you may decide to include in your manual. We'll examine each one in this chapter.

- Manual table of contents
- List of figures and tables
- Introductory text
- Tabs
- Chapter table of contents
- Headers and footers
- Pagination
- Headings
- Figure captions
- Cross-references
- Appendix
- Glossary
- Index
- Reference card

MANUAL TABLE OF CONTENTS

The table of contents for your manual is not actually a table (as defined in Chapter 11). Rather, it is a structured list of the content of the entire manual. Format and layout are as important for the table of contents as for a body of text.

In your table of contents include all the items that follow it. Normally, this will be the list of figures through the index. Use the same format for all items in the table of contents.

Here are some rules to follow when you create a table of contents.

1. Title the table of contents clearly and simply. The word "Contents" is sufficient. Center the title at the top of the first page. Set the title in a large font size or in upper case, bold, and underlined. Repeat the title on all remaining pages of the table, either as a running head or in the upper left corner of the page. Use a small font size and mixed case for the continued title.

2. Use narrow columns that make it easy for the reader to scan each line. Do not base column width on the longest item. If an item is wider than the column, use two or more lines.

3. Each item in the table of contents shows the name of a part, chapter, or subject plus the page number on which it begins. Use exactly the same text in the table as you use for the headings in the body of the manual.

4. Show only two or three levels of heading. More levels will confuse the reader. Showing all levels in the table of contents will reduce its effectiveness as a reference aid. One reason is that as chapter entries stretch over more pages the visual cues to subordination (white space and indentation) are lost. If your manual has more than three levels of heading, show these in chapter tables of contents, not in the manual table of contents.

5. Stay within one font family throughout the table of contents. Use different font sizes, boldface, upper and lower case, and white space to show the structure of your manual. Here is one scheme to use if you are restricted to a single font size:

- Chapter: Three space lines before; boldface; upper case
- Subject: One space line before; indent two spaces; upper case
- Topic: Indent four spaces; Mixed upper and lower case

LIST OF FIGURES AND TABLES

Lists of figures and tables are optional reference aids. They are most useful when you have used figures and tables to help segment the information in your manual. When this is not the case, they are more of a convenience than a necessity for the reader.

When you include these lists, place them immediately after the table of contents. Use separate lists for the figures (graphs, charts, and diagrams) and tables. Appendices that contain samples are shown in the table of contents, not here. Some guidelines for creating the lists follow.

1. Title the lists clearly and simply. "List of Figures" and "List of Tables" are fine. Treat these titles as described for the table of contents, above.

2. Use narrow columns that make it easy for the reader to scan each line. Do not base column width on the longest item. If an item is wider than the column, use two or more lines.

3. Each item in these lists is the name of a figure or table in the manual. Usually, the name of the figure or table is given in its caption. You need not repeat the caption exactly, but make sure that each name in your list clearly and uniquely identifies the figure or table.

4. Show the number, name, and page number of each figure or table in the manual. Use three columns, formatted as shown below:

Figure 9-99   Name of Figure   9

The first column is the figure or table number. The second column is the name or caption. The third column is the page number. These columns need not be titled.

INTRODUCTORY TEXT

Include an introduction to your manual. In large manuals this can be a separate section, equivalent to a chapter. The introduction shows what is in the manual, whether it contains the kind of information the reader is looking for, and how to use the manual. This is an ideal place to state the subject, audience, and purpose of the manual.

You can simplify the reader's task by explaining how to use the manual to best effect. If the manual is designed for different audiences, show each audience how to use the manual. For example, you could include a graphic representation of different paths or tracks through the manual. There might be a different track for novice, informed, and expert readers.

An introduction has the best chance of being read sequentially. Keep it short and concise to encourage the reader to read it.

Present information that applies globally to the manual. Show the reader any special terms or notations used throughout the manual so that you will not have to explain your conventions at each use. I always include definitions of the terms *type*, *press*, and *enter* in the introduction to user manuals. By defining *enter* to include pressing the enter key at the end of a line, I avoid having to remind the reader to do so each time I describe a response.

Remember to define your use of special typefaces, icons, or other visual aids in the introduction.

TABS

Tabbed dividers let your reader access a group of information without having to read the pages of your manual. They serve the same function as thumb cutouts in a dictionary. Use tabs only where they are needed—that is, for large groups of pages (20 or more) within a multiple-chapter manual.

Make it possible for your reader to access both subjects and page numbers by printing subject titles and numbers on the tabs. You will probably need to use a condensed version of the subject title, but avoid abbreviations. Print the same information on both sides of the tab.

How many tabbed dividers should you put in a manual? The answer has less to do with the content of the manual than with the number and arrangement of the tabs themselves. Use between four and ten tabs, depending on the number of pages in the manual. Use no more than five tab positions from the top to the bottom of a page. This provides tabs wide enough to be useful and makes it easy for the reader to scan them. Use multiple sets of tabs (repeating the same tab positions) for manuals with more than five tabs. This is a compromise between the visibility of the back tabs and the width of each tab, which determines how much text you can print on the tab.

CHAPTER TABLE OF CONTENTS

I recommended that you show only two or three levels of heading in your table of contents. The table might thus contain the chapter titles, subject titles, and perhaps topic titles. What if your chapters are divided into three or four levels? The answer is to show additional heading levels in a chapter table of contents.

A chapter table of contents appears at the beginning of a chapter. It is identical in form and function to the overall table of contents, but it applies to a single chapter.

To create a chapter table of contents, use the same rules as for the overall table of contents. Again, limit yourself to showing two or three levels of detail. Remember, the chapter table of contents is a summary and guide to the chapter organization. More detail will simply confuse the reader.

HEADERS AND FOOTERS

Headers and footers are the blank spaces at the top and bottom of a printed page. This space is commonly used to present reference information, called running heads or feet. It is also becoming common to confuse these terms and call both the space and the information a header or footer.

You can use headers and footers to show page numbers, document and chapter titles, and revision dates. Headers and footers often consist of a single line, but they can contain two lines rather than a single dense line.

When your manual is produced in loose-leaf form, it is helpful to include both the manual and chapter titles in a header or footer. The manual title will help the reader put revised pages in the right manual.

The reader unconsciously learns to ignore running heads and feet while reading a manual. Help the reader by visually identifying and isolating them from your text. Use thin rules and white space to isolate them. You can also use a distinctive font for this information, but be careful not to distract the reader. Use a small type font or other techniques that make the headers and footers visually subordinate to the text.

PAGINATION

Page numbers serve two purposes. They uniquely identify each page in a manual, and they show the correct sequence of pages within the manual. As reference aids, page numbers are analogous to memory addresses. They are the location of various blocks of information in a manual.

Readers use page numbers to flip to the correct page once they have found a subject of interest in the table of contents or index. Remembering this purpose will help you make decisions about page numbering and displaying page numbers.

You can number pages either within a chapter or other major division, or sequentially throughout the entire manual.

Which method you choose depends on how the manual is bound and on how frequently it is revised. When manuals are revised frequently, you can limit the impact of revisions by numbering pages within chapters.

Pages numbered within chapters must contain the chapter number. Two formats for the chapter number are C.PP (for example, 4.23) and C-PP (for example, 5-18).

Avoid using more than two levels of page subdivision. True, you could gain the revision and maintenance benefits by numbering pages within a subject (for example, 12.4.18), but this slows your reader's access time.

When your manual is seldom revised, or if it is perfect-bound, number the pages sequentially from front to back. Sequential page numbers provide the easiest reader access. They allow readers to estimate their position in the manual and adjust "flipping speed" accordingly.

As a third alternative, you can incorporate header and page number information into a "composite" page number. Composite page numbers can contain a key word that identifies the chapter, rather than a chapter number. Here is an example of how three page numbers from a manual using this scheme might look:

INTRO.11
KEYBOARD.4
FUNCTIONS.102

Display page numbers in the header or footer of each page. Do not use the word "page" to identify the page number. The position and behavior of page numbers identify them as such.

Place the page numbers in the same place on each page, either in the center of the page or at the outer edges of facing pages. This helps your reader use the page numbers as a reference and access aid. For the same reason, do not "bury" page numbers at the inside margin of a page. In this position the reader cannot see the page number when flipping pages.

HEADINGS

Headings serve two important purposes. They support the reader's understanding of how the information is organized, and they provide visual clues for locating specific information.

Headings are hierarchical in nature, as shown in the following structured list:

> Document Title
>   Chapter Title
>   Subject Title
>   Topic Title
>   Sub-Topic Title
>   etc.

In a large or complex manual you could extend this hierarchy almost indefinitely, but don't. Remember the purpose that headings serve, and make them useful within the context of that purpose. Use no more than three levels of subject heading within a chapter. Readers do not retain more than three levels, and many become confused beyond two levels.

Military and technical manuals traditionally use numbering schemes (similar to those used for outlines) to show the hierarchy of headings. This approach places a needless burden on your reader. It forces him or her to make logical comparisons to extract the organization of the headings. It is kinder (and more effective) to use such visual clues as white space, location, rules, font size, and boldface to show the hierarchy of headings. (See the exception to this rule under Cross-References, below.)

When you have the capability to do so, use different fonts for text and headings. Whether or not you use different fonts or sizes, it helps to set all headings in boldface type. Here is a commonly used scheme for headings.

Manual Title
- Separate page
- Centered horizontally and vertically
- Large font size
- Upper case
- Bold

Chapter Title
- New page
- ¼ to ⅓ page of white space before heading
- Centered on text line
- Font size text plus 12 points
- Upper and lower case
- Bold

Level 1 Heading
- Two lines of space before
- Flush left on text line
- Font size text plus 8 points
- Upper and lower case
- Bold

Level 2 and 3 Headings
- Same as Level 1 heading, but...
- Level 2 font size text plus 4 points
- Level 3 font size same as text

Headings act as signposts for your reader. They allow skimming and scanning of the text. The reader can use headings to gain an overview of the text or to rapidly locate specific portions of the text. Make your headings useful by wording heading text carefully.

Start with the heading text you developed in your outline of the manual, but be prepared to improve on it. Here are some guidelines for creating effective heading text.

1. Keep headings brief. Try to keep them shorter than a line of body text.
2. Use parallel syntax for each related series of headings.
3. Make headings understandable outside of the context of the text itself. Avoid cryptic headings.
4. Remember the audience you are writing for. Make headings meaningful to that audience.

5. Write headings as phrases, clauses, or complete sentences. Avoid single nouns or verbs. Avoid long strings of nouns and adjectives.

6. Make sure the reader will not confuse nouns and verbs. This rule is best explained by an example.

Confusing:
Enter Command Syntax

Clear:
Syntax of the Enter Command

7. Be specific. Make the heading text describe exactly what information it identifies.

FIGURE CAPTIONS

Each figure and table within a manual must have an identifying title or caption. Figure captions can serve two distinct purposes for your reader. Decide which purpose they are serving and create the caption text accordingly.

First, a caption can serve as a cross-reference between the text and the figure. In this case, strive for short, concise caption text. Identify the figure clearly and uniquely, but do not burden the reader's short-term memory.

Alternately, a caption can be explanatory or descriptive, as in structured writing. Such captions let the reader skim only the graphics in a manual yet absorb the important information or gain an accurate overview. Follow the guidelines for writing a description when you create expanded caption text.

CROSS-REFERENCES

Cross-references in a manual are as difficult to handle as embedded literals in a program. If you are not careful about how you cite cross-references, you are faced with reviewing the entire manual each time you make a revision that changes its page numbering. Simplify your maintenance work by restricting both the frequency and format of cross-references.

Cross-references have a limited number of valid uses. They can be used to reduce redundancy, to compare ideas, or to link text and graphics within a manual. Never use cross-referencing to correct poor organization.

When you make a valid cross-reference, do not cite page numbers. These are the "physical addresses" of information. Page numbers are only loosely related to the information they identify; they are subject to frequent revision.

Rather than page numbers, use the "logical addresses" of the information you cross-reference. Cite chapter, subject, or topic headings.

To cross-reference between text and graphics, use the figure or table numbers. Do not refer to the text or illustration on a specific page, either by page number or by the terms *previous* or *next* page. Rather, use the terms *above* and *below* to refer to material that immediately precedes or follows the reader's current location. The above/below convention is readily accepted by most readers. Asking your reader to adopt this convention is far less damaging than exposing him or her to invalid specific references.

Earlier, I discouraged you from using numbering schemes to show the hierarchy of your headings. There is, however, one situation that warrants their use. When the nature of your manual demands heavy cross-referencing, it can help both you and your reader to number headings, or even paragraphs. Paragraph numbers are another form of "logical address" for the information you are cross-referencing. They are a stable way to identify units of information in a manual.

APPENDIX

Appendices are not for afterthoughts. Only certain types of information should reside in appendices. Appendices can contain detailed, supportive information that would hinder the reader's comprehension if placed in the body of the text. They can also contain specialized information that is of interest to only a small portion of your audience. Beyond this, keep your appendices vacant.

Here are some example topics that illustrate the kind of material suitable for inclusion as appendices:

- File conversion
- Configuration or installation options

- Peripheral device setup
- System recovery procedures
- Error messages
- Data dictionary
- Character sets
- Reserved words
- Advanced features or options

Use an appendix for information that is essential to the purpose of your manual but that would decrease the manual's effectiveness if placed in the text proper. Your reader should be able to understand the manual without having to refer to the appendix.

Appendices are roughly equivalent to chapters in a manual and should be treated accordingly. Include the appendices in your table of contents. Cross-reference them by citing the appendix number. Here are some additional points to bear in mind.

1. Title the appendix clearly. Treat appendices as you treat your chapters. That is, use the same format and layout for the title page and any headings.

2. Number the appendix for reference purposes. The format is Appendix 9: Appendix Title.

3. Put each major topic or item in a separate appendix.

4. Limit the appendix to two or three pages, unless the subject dictates greater length.

5. Start the appendix with an introductory or descriptive paragraph. This should show the purpose and content of the appendix for readers who read it out of context.

6. Describe the appendices in the introduction to the manual. Refer to each appendix at appropriate points in the body of the manual, just as you would refer to a figure or table. For example: Refer to Appendix C for a list of supported printers.

GLOSSARY

A glossary is an alphabetic list of sentence definitions for important or unusual terms used in your manual. You may suspect that this is redundant information. After all, you have determined your audience and written your manual accordingly, defining each key term carefully. Why should you have to repeat such definitions?

A glossary *is* redundant, but there are excellent justifications for including it as a reference aid. First, remember that the readers will use your manual in a random access mode. They will not read the manual sequentially. Thus, an excellent definition of a term in Chapter 4 is of no use to a reader who starts at Chapter 6.

Further, novice or even informed readers are tackling a large body of unfamiliar information. They are loading their short-term memories with new concepts and relationships. They may be reading sequentially and may have read the definition in Chapter 4 but forgotten it by the time they reach Chapter 6. You can help them by providing an easily accessed summary of unfamiliar terms.

Treat a glossary as you would treat a chapter in your manual, but place it after the appendices and before the index. This is where the reader will expect to find it. Include the glossary in your table of contents.

If you use very few unfamiliar or specialized terms, you may choose to define these terms in the introduction to the manual, rather than in a glossary. There is no harm (and little maintenance overhead) in placing definitions in both places.

Select terms for inclusion in a glossary according to the purpose and audience of the manual. Define each term with at least a sentence definition. Add expanded definitions and examples to clarify terms where needed. Do not use the glossary to define procedures or otherwise expand on the text of the manual.

Arrange the terms in alphabetic order. Format the list to make it easy for the reader to find specific terms. Use hanging headings for the terms. You need only hang the headings four or five characters to the left of the text, just enough for the reader to scan alphabetically.

Set each heading in boldface, using upper and lower case. End the heading with a colon, and start the definition on the same line as the heading.

INDEX

An index is the most valuable reference aid you can include in a manual. An index (or its absence) is a good indicator of how much consideration your manual shows for your reader.

Informed and expert readers rely heavily on the index. They use it to access rapidly specific information in the body of the manual. An index makes it possible for readers to use a manual in a random access fashion. In addition, the index resolves those problems created by synonyms and aliases.

Compiling an index manually is drudge work. Even automated indexing systems must be supplemented by a healthy amount of brute labor before they will produce a useful index. However, for all but the shortest manuals, the value added warrants the work needed to create an index.

As a rough guide, expect your index to contain three or four entries per manual page. To compile an index, work with a draft of the manual that has the finalized page numbers. Follow these steps:

1. Read the manual and highlight terms that should appear as entries in the index. Mark any substantive term that is significant or meaningful to the reader in context. Make rough notes on potential topics, terms, and synonyms as you go.

2. Scan the manual. Transfer each highlighted term to a single 3-by-5 index card. Record the page numbers on the cards.

3. Analyze the terms to make sure they are meaningful out of context. You may want to revise the terms at this point, or compile lists of alternatives and synonyms.

4. Arrange the cards into topics and terms. A topic is a group of related terms. Topics and terms will become the entries in your index. Bear in mind your definitions of the manual's audience and purpose. How will the reader name a topic or term? What specific task names should the reader find in the index? Be specific when you analyze and create topics or terms for inclusion in the index. Compare the following two organizations:

Date, 1.22, 2.14, 2.57, 4.06

Date
    default format, 2.14
    entry, 1.22
    optional formats, 4.06
    report header, 2.57

5. As a result of your analysis, you may need to add cards or repeat previous steps, working with the manual.

6. Alphabetize the cards by term within topic, then by topic. Revise the text of the entries so that articles and pronouns do not interfere with alphabetic sequencing.

7. Convert the index cards into a rough draft of the index. Do not format the draft yet.

8. Add synonyms, aliases, and generic terms for specific entries. Add these as "see" entries. A "see" entry is a one-way arrow,

pointing the reader to another entry in the index. In place of a page number, it shows an already existing entry, where more information is listed.

9. Show important relationships between the terms by adding "see also" entries. A "see also" entry is a two-way arrow. It is added to an existing entry, after the page numbers. Each entry in a list of related entries should have a "see also" entry added to it.

10. Format the draft into a finished index. In most cases a two-column format is best. Single-space the entries, but use white space to mark the beginning of each new letter. Capitalize the first letter of primary entries. Set subordinate terms in lower case. Here are a few examples of index entries, showing the formats and techniques we've discussed.

> Starting the system, *see* Booting
> Station
>   clerical, 9.99
>   system administrator, 9.99
>   *see also* Terminal
>
> Terminal
>   log on, 9.99
>   log off, 9.99, 9.99
>   types supported, 9.99
>   *see also* Station
> Trapping errors, 9.99

11. Verify the index by testing each entry against the manual.

I have described these steps as if you were compiling your index manually. No doubt you can think of ways to automate almost each step of the process. However, do not rely on automation to perform those steps that *must* be done by a human being:

- Creating terms that are meaningful to your reader
- Adding generic, synonym, and alias terms
- Indicating important relationships between terms
- Checking the index against the manual

REFERENCE CARD

Quick reference cards are a type of reference aid. While they are usually packaged with a manual, they are not actually a part of it.

One of the important features of reference cards is that they can be used independently of other documentation.

A reference card can be a single page, several separate sheets, a small (four to eight page) booklet, or a keyboard overlay. Reference cards can be printed on the same paper as the manual that contains them, or on special card stock. How the card is produced depends on its purpose and on how it will be used.

Reference cards provide your reader, usually the expert system user, with a small amount of key information in an easy-to-use format. Most cards are intended for permanent display or handy access at a work station. Familiar examples are cards that show the key commands or data codes used by a system.

Reference cards and sheets seem to have a life of their own. If you fail to create them, your users will create them on their own initiative. More than half of the reference cards I've added on to existing system manual libraries were already drafted by system users. I simply formatted, released, and assumed responsibility for maintaining the cards. There is a message here. Reference cards are a valuable form of user documentation.

When you design a reference card, treat it as a miniature document. Define the purpose, audience, and subject of the card. Make use of other design techniques, too. Use adequate, active white space and effective headings. Organize the information in an obvious, expected fashion.

Remember to plan for maintenance of your reference cards. Include a prominent date or version number so that your readers can easily distinguish between current and outdated versions.

15

Online Documentation

What do messages, menus, help screens, and online tutorials have in common? Obviously, they are part of a system's human interface. Less obviously, they are also forms of system documentation.

The human interface contains two types of communication. One type is communication between system players, the other is communication between the system players and the software. Online systems reduce or remove the distinction between these two kinds of communication.

You can easily distinguish between player-player and player-software communication in a batch system. Player-player communication takes the form of the printed page, organized into various manuals. Batch system documentation is separate from the software it describes. It is accessed in traditional ways, just as any printed training or reference material is accessed.

With online systems and online media, the distinction between the software and the system documentation becomes blurred. You find it increasingly difficult to distinguish player-player communication from player-system communication. The human interface and the system documentation merge.

System players use the same medium to interact with online documentation and online software—the CRT screen. System users enter commands and receive messages through the screen; they also participate in tutorials and refer to support information through the screen.

There are several possible access methods for online system documentation. The documentation can take the form of an independent online manual, can be incorporated as a function of the system, or can be completely integrated into the behavior of the software itself.

For online systems, the distinction between player-player and player-software communication tends to vanish. This is not a problem, but a natural and welcome evolution of information systems. Online documentation, when fully integrated with the software it describes, is in-line documentation. In-line perspectives and techniques that seem awkward or artificial for batch systems become natural, even essential, for effective online documentation.

Abandoning the distinction between system documentation and the human interface can help system developers. You will find it easier to create and maintain effective system documentation, easier to control and improve the design of your human interface, and thus easier to produce higher-quality system products.

Viewing system documentation and the human interface as one and the same also helps your users. Online documentation reduces the number of components in the human interface. It gives the user a single, common work method. This single method can be used to learn how to use the system, actually use the system, and access supportive information about the system.

In this chapter we'll examine general and specific problems inherent in the online medium. We'll also look at some techniques for overcoming these problems, both at the general level and for several specific types of online documentation. Let's establish a working definition for our subject.

> **Online Documentation:** system documentation in the online medium. Online documentation is system information you create, store, organize, and access using online software. Online documentation is displayed via the screen (CRT) medium. Online documentation is identical with the human interface. It includes both player-player communication and player-software communication—that is, online manuals, tutorials, help screens or systems, menus and commands, and messages.

Why should you be concerned with online documentation, rather than sticking to the more traditional and familiar medium of paper? There are several good reasons for voluntarily creating systems with online documentation.

Online is the ideal medium for system documentation. It simplifies the production and integration of text and graphics. Online documentation gives you fast, flexible access to all information stored in the System File.

Online is a fluid medium with few limits on its format or content. Unlike paper manuals, the content of online documents can adapt to the specific needs of specific readers.

Online documentation can be more than a different medium: It can provide the system players with an access window to the software itself. The online medium transforms system documentation into the human interface.

There are also unavoidable forces that will eventually compel you to move to this new medium. Most obvious is the lower cost of distributing and maintaining online documentation. It is faster to create, to use, and to revise than paper. Online documentation reduces your development costs by letting you automate system documentation.

Paper documentation has several inherent problems. First, it is static. A manual presents System File information from a fixed perspective for a specific audience. Paper manuals can't be all things to all readers. Second, paper documentation has a physical presence that can intimidate your readers. The sheer bulk of manuals makes them difficult to handle and uninviting to read. Third, paper documentation is difficult to produce and package. Do you create your own system documentation and manuals? If so, you will find that you actually have two separate production facilities in your shop: one for software and one for manuals.

Online documentation has benefits and drawbacks. On the plus side, it can help your users get started fast. Most people find it more fun and exciting to learn from a computer than from a book. In addition, online tutorials can teach novice users the basic techniques and conventions they will use to operate the system itself. People find even limited interaction more stimulating and encouraging than none at all.

On the minus side, you need additional software to create and to use online documentation. You may need to purchase a software package to create your online manuals or help systems. You may need to spend additional programming time to integrate your documentation and software into a cohesive human interface. And, of course, online documentation is only available when the user's system is operating. In some cases, such as installation or troubleshooting guides, paper documentation is the only reasonable alternative.

PROBLEMS WITH THE ONLINE MEDIUM

Online documentation has its own inherent limitations and problems. Creating online documentation isn't a simple matter of converting your manuals from one medium to another. There are problems in creating online documentation, in formatting screens, and in organizing and using online documentation. However, these problems have solutions. Once you have a handle on the problems it will be easier to understand and apply the general and specific solutions presented in this chapter.

PROBLEMS IN CREATING ONLINE DOCUMENTATION

The greatest strength of online documentation is also the biggest problem: The online medium is flexible. Flexibility gives online documentation the potential to be tremendously effective. But it also presents you with the certainty that online documentation will be difficult to create.

You are faced with choices and decisions. How strongly should you integrate the software and the documentation? How can you effect the integration? Should the documentation adapt to the reader, the situation, or to both? And if so, how?

The medium of the printed page imposes physical and logical restrictions on your documentation, but these restrictions also provide you with a framework. Paper manuals require structures, overall organization, sequence, and reference aids. The online medium removes the restrictions but also removes the framework for planning and creating documentation.

PROBLEMS WITH SCREEN FORMATS

Obviously, the standard 80-character-by-24-line screen has a smaller display area than an $8\frac{1}{2}$-by-11-inch page. Even with luxurious margins, headers, and footers, the printed page can still accommodate $1\frac{1}{2}$ times as much text as a screen.

Text density is the percentage of a page or screen that is occupied by text. Not only do screens have a smaller display area, but they also have a lower tolerable text density. The density of printed pages can range from 30 to 50 percent, but the useful range for screens is 15 to 25 percent.

This restriction arises from two other problems with screens. First, screens have low resolution. While a typeset character is created from 800 dots, and a laser printed character from 300 dots, the equivalent character displayed on a screen is composed of only 63 dots.

Second, type quality is poor. People read screens more slowly than they read printed pages. Perhaps the motor skills of scanning the displayed screen differ from those we have all acquired for the printed page. However, it is certain that screen displays of text are less legible than printed versions.

For one thing, shortened or "squashed" descenders (the parts of a letter that extend below the text line) distort the shape of letters and words. Recall that readers recognize the shape of a whole word. Squashed descenders can destroy the shape of a word as effectively as printing it in all upper case.

Inadequate leading (space between lines) and monopitch text also reduce the legibility of text displayed on screens.

Finally, most CRTs reverse letter and background colors from those we are used to for printed pages. Screen letters are white or light colors, displayed on a dark or black background. Does this have an adverse effect? Imagine reading a page of white letters printed on black paper.

PROBLEMS IN ORGANIZING AND USING ONLINE DOCUMENTATION

The online medium involves you in larger problems than screen design. There are also difficulties in organizing online material according to how the reader uses it. For one thing, your readers have an abundance of experience and skill with printed information. This is not the case with online information.

The physical structure of printed manuals matches their organization. Printed information is organized into subjects and chapters. These map onto the pages of the manual in a direct fashion.

Online documentation has no physical structure at all. The only structure it has is the logical structure you create. Unless you pay close attention to the logical structure of online documentation, your readers will easily become confused and lost.

To compound this problem, online manuals have fewer traditional reader access or reference aids than paper manuals. Readers can't compare a series of related headings for clues about the level of the topic they are reading. Readers can't memorize the location of information by its position in a book or on a page.

In poorly designed systems, online documentation completely replaces the reader's work screen. This is distracting and makes it difficult for the reader to maintain a sense of continuity in either working or learning tasks. By contrast, paper manuals can be used in parallel with the software. Readers can easily flip from page to page in a paper manual, or even lay out several pages at once for simultaneous access to the information.

All too often the screen is treated as a tiny window through which online documentation is scrolled. It feels rather like trying to drive a car with a frosted windshield by peering through a hand-sized area you have scraped clear. The reader loses the overall perspective and sense of organization because the screen focuses attention on the details. This is why you must edit printed manuals in printed form. Editing online, you focus on the details presented in individual screens, and lose your overview of the entire page, subject, chapter, or manual.

There are practical limits to the kinds of system documentation you can present in the online medium. Since online documentation is available only when your system is running, you can't present installation or recovery information online.

GENERAL TECHNIQUES FOR ONLINE DOCUMENTATION

Now that we've surveyed the problems of online documentation, let's turn to the solutions. First, we'll look at some general techniques. These apply to all forms of online documentation.

TECHNIQUES FOR CREATING ONLINE DOCUMENTATION

The documentation process presented in this text applies to all media, including online documentation. You can (and should) go through the same steps whether you are creating paper or online system documents. The first step is to define your audience, purpose, and subject. You still need to choose or create techniques, structures, sequences, and organizations that will help your reader perform specific tasks. The online medium results in more flexible products, but the planning and drafting steps are still solid. You still need to edit and review the online documents you create. You still need to release and maintain them.

Planning

When you plan an online manual, add two new attributes to your medium specification: integration and adaptability.

You can integrate online documentation with your software at three levels.

The lowest level is the online manual. Online manuals are actually free-standing systems in their own right. They are displayed by software that is separate from your system's software. To use an online manual the reader must exit from (or suspend) your system and invoke the online manual system.

The next level of integration is the system function. Here, online documentation is one of the functions of your system. It is displayed by software that is an integral part of your system. Online documentation is accessed by selecting a tutorial, help, or debugging function from a menu. Alternately, a function key or key combination (such as control-h or control-?) can be used to invoke the online documentation software.

The third level of integration is the system feature. Online documentation can be integrated so thoroughly with your software that it appears as an aspect or feature of all system functions. Examples of this include interactive command prompts, displays of data item formats or codes, and even entire menu structures.

Your online documentation can adapt in two ways: to the specific user and to the specific task.

System users evolve from novices to experts as they gain experience with your system. We handled this problem by organizing paper manuals into tutorial and reference sections, and by providing quick-reference cards. Online documentation is flexible enough to identify different audiences and (in effect) rewrite itself to match their individual needs. For example, a user could request one of three different levels of help from an online help system and receive an appropriate level of detail. Your online documentation can match itself to novice, informed, and expert readers.

Online documentation can also adapt itself to the specific task at hand. Help systems that adapt to tasks are often called "context sensitive." The idea is simple. Your system keeps track of where the user is, determines what function is being used, and automatically provides supportive information about that specific function or task.

Drafting

To organize and draft online documentation, use the storyboard technique. This technique helps you manage the increased flexibility of the online medium and provides the missing framework for planning.

The storyboard technique involves three main steps:

1. Design a limited number of structures that the reader can experience when using the online documentation. Here is a sample set of structures:

- A full-screen window of text and graphics, one to four pages long
- A half-screen box of condensed reference information, codes, or command formats
- A single-line prompt or message

2. Draft the content of the structures to match the needs of each audience for each task.

3. Design the interconnecting paths or reference logic that links the structures.

The storyboard technique lets you define and impose arbitrary limitations on online documents. It gives you a degree of control over the variability of screen formats and content. It preserves your sanity.

TECHNIQUES FOR DESIGNING SCREEN FORMATS

There are a few basic rules that govern effective screen design. These apply whether the screen is part of an online manual, a menu, or a data entry screen.

1. Do not display large blocks of text. A good screen has at most 70 to 80 words. The rest is white space. (I call blank screen areas white space, even though they are usually black.) Do not clutter

screens in an attempt to shrink printed pages to fit them. You must work in exactly the opposite direction to compensate for the legibility shortcomings of screens.

2. Use short lines. Observe the $1\frac{1}{2}$ alphabet rule whenever possible: Limit your lines to between 30 and 50 characters.

3. Use short paragraphs. Restrict paragraphs to three or four lines. Separate paragraphs with a space line.

4. Display text flush left and ragged right. Display numbers flush right or decimal aligned.

5. Limit yourself to a single level of heading within each set of screen pages.

6. Use simple structures and white space to display the organization of a screen. Tables, block diagrams, and icons are effective screen graphics. Paragraphs, lists, and playscripts are effective text structures. Structured lists are also useful, provided the entire list can be displayed on a single screen.

7. Use screen emphasis devices (such as blinking, color, and reverse video) sparingly and consistently.

8. Screens usually display two types of information. In addition to their content (text and graphics), they show control or reference aids. Examples of reference aids are paging, menu selection, and entry or exit points. Use position, color, and shape to visually distinguish between these two types of information.

In addition to following these rules, design screens as simply, consistently, and logically as possible. Put key information in a prominent location. Group logically related information. Compose screens from common elements, and place the elements in consistent locations. Common elements might include screen title, instruction line, text or body, message line, menu bar, and command line. Design screens so that your reader need learn only one template for scanning the information on all screens.

You may find it helpful to use a screen grid, analogous to the page grid we discussed earlier. It is difficult to suggest a generally applicable screen grid for all systems. You should match screen design to the application and the needs of the users. Screens for independent online documentation systems should match those of the application system. However, Figure 15-1 shows a screen grid that can act as a design starting point.

The header area contains the screen number and name. It may also contain the date and time, and perhaps navigating information (route) or operating conditions (mode).

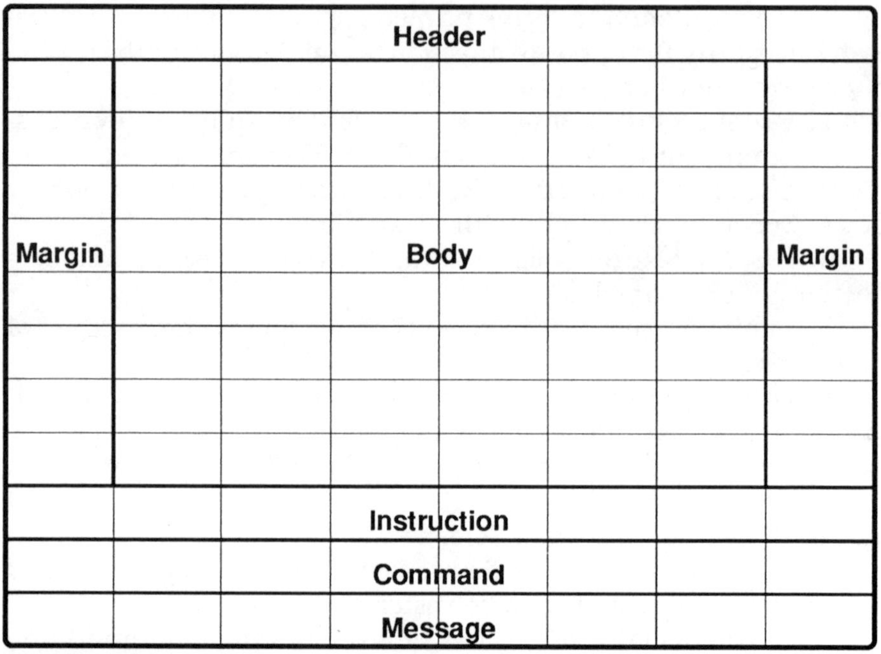

				Header			
Margin				Body			Margin
				Instruction			
				Command			
				Message			

FIGURE 15-1: Screen Grid

The body area contains text and graphics, data items, or menu selections, depending on the type and use of the screen.

The instruction line shows the reader how to manipulate the information in the body, how to navigate to other screens, or how to exit from the screen. It presents the reader with options for player-software communication.

The command line accepts the reader's instructions.

System messages and prompts appear in the message area. This area is normally blank. Messages appear only when the system must communicate with the reader, or when the reader requests additional prompting.

The margins are partly passive and partly active white space. They help to distinguish the body from other screen lines. They can also contain pointers or flags that advise the reader of progress through the screen body, signal the operating mode of the screen, or alert the reader to error conditions or messages.

TECHNIQUES FOR ORGANIZING ONLINE DOCUMENTATION

Organization and Control

To be effective, online documentation must be organized differently from printed documentation. Remember that readers come to a printed manual with a lifetime of experience at using printed material. Online documentation gives readers no physical structure and only that portion of the logical structure you deliberately present.

Expect readers of your online documentation to know little when they start, and to remember little as they continue. Show the reader exactly what to do at every step. Do not expect the reader to remember instructions or options from screen to screen. If the instructions are not displayed, they do not exist for the reader.

Online documentation carries a double burden of instruction. Not only must it show the reader how to use the system, it must also show how to use the documentation. Always show your reader how to proceed to the next screen, how to change access methods, how to exercise display options, and how to exit from the online documentation.

Wherever possible, use windows or split screens to display supportive or reference information. Do not replace the reader's work environment with the documentation environment. Allow readers to use online documentation in parallel with the system software, just as they would use a printed manual. Give your readers the same control over the online documentation as they have over printed documentation. Let them control entering, paging through, and exiting from the documentation.

Organize online documentation for effective access and use by designing the methods you use to connect or relate multiple screens of information.

Use the storyboard approach. Don't force your reader to scroll through text blocks. Break the information into discrete screens or screen pages (single, full screens). This limits the flexibility of online documentation in a way that is useful to both you and the reader. Limiting your flexibility lets you design and use effective structures. This simplifies the writing task for you and the reading task for your reader.

Access Methods

You need to organize online documentation at higher levels than single or multiple screens. Here, flexibility is more of a benefit than a burden. Adaptable online documentation can effectively rewrite itself for specific readers. It can also reorganize itself, allowing multiple access methods. Online documentation can be organized for alphabetic, logical, hierarchical, or relational access.

Alphabetic access behaves like an automated index. Create an index for your online document just as you would for a paper document. Give the reader access to the index at all points in the system and documentation. Restrict the index to four or fewer screens, or provide the reader with an option to scan the index for a specified topic. When the reader selects a topic, the documentation software automatically "flips the pages" and presents the selected information.

Logical access refers to program logic. With this method, information is automatically accessed and presented to the reader, according to the logical path followed through the software while using the system. Context-sensitive help systems use logical access.

You are already familiar with hierarchical organization and access. Here, you group topics into related menus, and menus into higher-level menus. This is the same organization and access method used for menu-driven online systems, but applied to online documentation. If alphabetic access is an automated index, hierarchical access is an automated table of contents.

Relational access is the free-form random access possible with data base management software. Relational access lets the reader specify multiple forms of search and multiple search arguments. When I gave up trying to create reference manuals for programmers and allowed them to access the System File through its data base management system, I was actually organizing an online reference manual for relational access.

If you choose (or are forced) to limit your online documentation to a single organization and access method, match the method to the subject and audience. Alphabetic access is best suited to reference material for novice or informed readers. Logical access is the primary choice for help systems that adapt to task and for online tutorials. Hierarchical access works well for complex reference material addressed to expert readers. Reserve relational access for expert readers, since the access method itself is complex.

Software Techniques

Use additional software techniques to match organization and access to the reader's needs. For example, the bookmarking technique lets readers leave a tutorial session and later return to the place where they left off. This technique can be extended to provide individual readers with multiple bookmarks so that they can bookmark the screens they refer to most often. Bookmarks can be implemented as reader-defined tags or as reader-edited indexes.

Adaptability

Adaptability is another way to organize online documentation. Online documentation can adapt to the reader, the task, or both.

You can organize for predefined levels of reader expertise or monitor the readers on an individual basis. To adapt to specific individuals, your online documentation software must keep a record of each reader. The reader profile record must contain

- Reader identity
- Hours of system experience
- Functions performed
- Success rates
- Time last used
- Current settings for help and prompt levels

To adapt for specific tasks, your documentation software must keep a session log for the individual reader. The session log shows

- Reader identity
- Route taken
- Current position in system
- Functions or tasks available at this point
- Relevant online documentation available

Do not let automatic adaptability take control of your reader. Always give the reader the option to select another level of detail for the current topic or to select another topic or access method.

SPECIFIC TECHNIQUES FOR ONLINE DOCUMENTATION

We've looked at general techniques that apply to all forms of online documentation. Now we'll look at some specific techniques for specific types of document. The online documents we'll consider are manuals, tutorials, help, menus and commands, and messages.

ONLINE MANUALS

Online is a new medium for manuals. There are no concrete rules and few guidelines. Most of the advice I can offer you is prohibitive rather than instructive.

Let me make a clear distinction between online manuals and magnetic manuals. By "magnetic manual" I mean a paper manual that has undergone a simple conversion of medium. Magnetic manuals have their place in system documentation, but they play a small and tightly restricted role.

You are probably familiar with magnetic manuals in the form of "Read Me" files that accompany online software or updates. This is one valid use of a magnetic manual. Here are some guidelines for creating effective magnetic manuals.

1. Format the manual so that it can be displayed by any software. Let the reader decide whether to display the manual with the operating system, a word processor, or your system's software.

2. Divide the content into separate screens so that the reader can page through the manual. Strive to make each screen a complete subject. Wherever possible, allow the reader to page forward and backward through the material.

3. Keep the manual short. Ten screens is the upper limit for most readers. Beyond this you need additional organization and access methods.

4. Use a simple organization. Display the manual name and the pagination (Screen 3 of 6) as a header on each screen. Use only one heading level to organize the content.

By contrast, an online manual is one for which the format, content, structure, and organization have been specifically designed for the online medium. All of the format, organization, and access techniques we explored earlier can be applied to online manuals.

Ideally, the organization you use should be expected by the reader and visible to the reader. Few readers have had experience with online manuals, so you may not be able to provide the organization your reader expects. Sometimes you will need to invent and display a purely logical organization, such as a menu scheme. However, you can reduce your reader's burden by observing the following rules.

1. Make the format, organization, and behavior of the online manual parallel those of your system as far as is practical. This reduces the number of new features a reader/user must learn.

2. Use access methods that are analogous to those of paper manuals. Alphabetic access is analogous to an index; hierarchical to a table of contents. Alternately, use organization and access techniques that draw on the reader's experience of other online software. If your system operates within a host data base management system, you can draw on your reader's experience and use a relational access method.

3. Provide multiple access methods. A paper manual has a table of contents, tabs, and an index. Give your readers hierarchical, bookmark, and alphabetic access alternatives. You can even consider letting the reader highlight or modify text, or fine-tune the access method by modifying or adding index entries.

4. Display a header on each screen. Include the manual title and visual organization cues (such as route, subject heading, or pagination). This provides the reader with a logical address for the information presented.

5. Leave the reader in control of the manual. Display control options on every screen (for example, how to page up or down, select another topic, or exit).

TUTORIALS

An online tutorial is a stand-alone training program. If you think I am describing software, you can appreciate the dangers of jargon. By "training program," I mean a series of related lessons. By "stand-alone," I mean that the tutorial provides the reader with all the reference material and instructions needed.

Tutorials teach the reader the basics of using your system. To do this, they must engage and instruct the reader (in that order). Here are some guidelines for creating effective online tutorials.

1. Divide the program into a series of lessons. Limit each lesson to a 20 to 30 minute session.

2. Begin each lesson with a clear statement of the intended

audience and the purpose. This tells the reader what knowledge or experience he or she will need to complete the lesson successfully. It also tells the reader what skills or information the lesson will impart.

3. Use clear, simple language. Define new terms or concepts clearly and repeatedly.

4. Simulate reality. Be specific and concrete, even if you have to invent an entire task or scenario. Use cases rather than isolated examples.

5. Give the reader feedback on his or her progress through the lesson and through the entire program. Use bookmarking, or display a checklist of completed lessons.

6. Make sure the reader stays in control of the tutorial. Allow the "students" to start and stop each session at will. Let them step forward or backward through each session at a comfortable pace.

The first rule warrants further discussion. Short-term memory is just that—short-term. We can load our short-term memory effortlessly and voluntarily, but retaining what we load requires effort. Learning something means loading it into our long-term memory. We can do this only by repetition.

Design your tutorial program to accommodate these features of human learning. Divide the program into short, repeatable learning sessions. Give the readers a readily attainable objective that does not burden their short-term memory. Focus on a few basic skills in each lesson, but repeat and reinforce the skills through all lessons. Start with simple tasks, increasing the level of detail with each repetition.

Follow the steps of the documentation process to create online tutorials, but pay particular attention to the review step. You must include reader testing in this step in order to evaluate and improve the tutorial.

Online tutorials should add to (or replace) existing paper manuals. There is no point in duplicating the information in different media. Use your system manual library plan to prevent duplication.

ONLINE HELP

Online help comes in many forms and variations. We can classify help by the degree to which it is integrated with the system it supports. The levels of integration are online manual, system function, and system feature.

A help manual is actually an independent online document system. It is composed of both help information and display software. Help manuals are a fast, inexpensive way to implement online help. You can purchase or build display software that will work with all of your system products. All you need do is create the help information that applies to a specific system.

Help manuals provide a degree of consistency. However, unless you control the operation and formatting of the display software, you can't be sure of a good match with your system. Since the display software is isolated from your system's software, it is difficult to make help manuals adaptable.

A help function is one that is integrated with your system's software. To the user, help is simply another function of your system. At this level of integration, the display software is part of your system. This means you can control the format of your help screens. You can also control the operating characteristics of the help function, including adaptability and access methods.

At the last level of integration, help no longer exists as a separate function of your system. Rather, supportive information is a design feature of each system function. Prompts, lists of job steps, and interactive command construction are all examples of help features.

For the rest of this discussion, I'll restrict myself to help functions and help features. I'll assume you have control over the software and that the help function can be performed without leaving your system.

There is seldom an either-or choice between help functions and features. Most systems use both. You can view help functions as voluntary help and help features as involuntary help.

Adaptability applies to both help functions and features. Not only can your help screens adapt but also your prompts and messages. Help can adapt to both the reader and the task.

The easiest way to adapt to the reader is to let the reader specify the level of help desired. If you automate reader adaptability, remember to leave control in the reader's hands. Provide and display manual options for selecting the level of help at all times.

Similarly, let the reader control the way help is accessed. If your help automatically adapts to task (is context sensitive), provide the reader with manual alternatives. Let your reader access the help information from a menu or index of topics.

Help can also adapt to the task manually. The reader can invoke the help function and then specify the task by navigating through a menu or entering a command.

Here are some guidelines for creating help functions.

1. Use the storyboard technique. Divide help information into topics by system functions or user tasks. Draft or assemble different versions of each topic to match different levels of reader (novice, informed, expert). Map the topics onto a limited number of display structures (screens, windows, messages).

2. Define one method of invoking the help function that works in every situation. Supplement this with additional invocation methods according to the adaptability you have chosen, and according to the alternative access methods you plan to offer the reader.

3. Use screen, window, and message grids for consistency.

4. Always display the reader's options and controls. Visually distinguish between help information (instructions for using your system) and control information (instructions for using the help function).

MENUS AND COMMANDS

Menus are an excellent example of how the online medium blurs the distinction between system documentation and the human interface. After all, menus are simply a hierarchical access method—a textual or graphic representation of categories of system functions. They are more of a reference aid than they are processing software. They are closer to system documentation than to software.

When you design a menu structure, start with the screen layout and then design the reader-software interaction. Here are some guidelines for designing menu layouts.

1. Use wide rather than deep menus. Limit yourself to a menu structure that has four or fewer levels. Three levels is the comfort limit for most people. You need to balance text density and menu complexity. For example, putting twenty items on a single menu may burden your reader, but so will an additional level of menus.

2. Use a screen grid for consistency. Place common screen elements (name, number, date, message line, and so on) in the same location on all menu screens.

3. Assign each menu screen a name and number, just as you would for a data item or dialog screen. Be perfectly consistent with cross-references. That is, when one of the items in a menu is another menu, the text for the item must be identical with the name of the lower-level menu.

4. Display the menu items (system functions) as unstructured

lists. Arrange the items alphabetically or in functional groups. Do not simply add new functions to the bottom of the list.

5. Follow the guidelines for creating lists. The lists do not need headings or titles. Screen headers can appear in upper case, but display the items in mixed case (upper and lower) case.

6. Do not number or letter the items unless the reader selects them by number or letter. Start numbering from 1 and lettering from A, and leave no gaps. Bullet unnumbered lists to give the reader a visual cue to separate items.

After you have designed the header and body of the menu screens, design the reader-software interactions, the menu controls. Finish designing the screens according to the selection and control method you design.

There are several efficient selection methods. You need not limit your system to only one. Here is a list of selection methods, arranged in decreasing reader preference.

1. Point to the item (with cursor, highlight bar, or mouse).
2. Type the item letter or number.
3. Type a function code or acronym.
4. Type the text of the item.

Commands provide the user with direct access to your system's functions. Design command text and syntax carefully. Be simple, logical, and above all consistent.

Name your commands with common English words. Consider your users' backgrounds and create commands that are analogs for their everyday experience. The classic example is the pseudodeleted file. Say you want to let your users change their minds about deleting files. You could introduce two unfamiliar commands to produce the set delete, undelete, erase. Alternately, you could create commands that are analogs for your users' experience with wastebaskets, creating the set put into wastebasket, take out of wastebasket, empty wastebasket.

Use consistent syntax for your commands. For example, you could choose either a Noun Verb format (Master File Reindex) or a Verb Noun format (Reindex Master File). But not both.

As I said earlier, menus are a hierarchical access method. They allow your users to access the system's functions. Why limit your users or readers to a single access method? Many online systems offer two access methods: hierarchical (menu) and direct (command). Why not more? Consider providing alphabetic and logical access methods for your software.

MESSAGES

We have defined three types of message: dialogs, displays, and prompts. All of these can be viewed as help features of your system. You can also think of messages as miniature tutorials. They help the reader with a small task or guide the reader through a decision-making process. Here are the guidelines for creating and displaying this form of online documentation.

1. Create a global design for system messages. Use a message template or grid for consistency.

2. Be consistent about the location and presence of messages. Display messages in the same location on all screens. Have a prompt or help message available for all system functions and user tasks, or display a null message such as "No help is available."

3. Don't let messages overlay or replace the reader's work.

4. Whenever your software issues a message, have it expect and wait for a response or acknowledgment. Use a standard, global acknowledgment (such as pressing the enter key), or display the reader's options.

5. Display message text in mixed case.

6. Keep messages brief and clear. Limit them to one or two lines of 30 to 50 characters each. Write message text in plain English. Do not use contractions, short forms, jargon, abbreviations, or pseudo-English (also known as "telegraphese").

7. Be specific. Display the message number at the beginning of the message line when it serves as a cross-reference to paper manuals. Otherwise, let your help function provide additional details on request. Display the signature (number or label) of the software element that issues the message at the end of the message text for troubleshooting or support purposes.

8. Avoid negative words such as illegal, invalid, and error. Be constructive and suggest appropriate action to the reader.

9. Avoid humanizing your software. Do not give software a personality, sense of humor, or condescending attitude. Do not use the first person in message text.

THE DEVELOPMENT OF TECHNICAL WRITING

PROBLEM: "I got this message "EOF ENCOUNTERED FOR LFN 0122...WAIT STATUS 20" and the system just stopped. What should I do?"

SOLUTION: A technical writer revised the text of the message to: There are no checks in the Payables File. Press ENTER to cancel your print request.

No matter what the medium, you use the same techniques to create system documentation. They are not so much documentation techniques as communication techniques. Remember, a basic premise of the in-line approach is that system documentation is communication between the system players. Perhaps it is time to expand this definition to include communication between the software and the players too.

What is the human interface? Who should design it? No doubt you can anticipate my position. More and more the human interface and the system documentation are merging into a single entity. The human interface is the arena for interaction and communication between people and software. The physical design of the human interface may be the domain of hardware and software specialists, but its logical design belongs to communication specialists.

Prepare for the future of information systems. If you are an independent programmer, improve your human interfaces by improving your writing skills. If you run a small shop, consider hiring a writing consultant to "edit" your human interfaces. If your shop includes technical writing staff, involve them early and thoroughly in the design of your human interfaces.

Index

Abbreviations, 164, 204, 203
Above and below convention, 301
Absolute input, 103, 109, 122
Absolute output, 103, 109, 123
Access key, 152, 246
Access methods, 318
Acronyms, 131, 203–04
Action attribute, 187
Action verbs, 231
Actions, decision table, 236
Active portion of test plan, 53
Active and passive documentation, 22
Active voice, 197, 206
Adaptability of online documentation, 313, 319, 323
Add-on documentation, 20–22, 49
Alias attribute, 165
Aliases, 21, 212, 303
Alignment, 267
Alphabetic access, 318
Alphabetic sequence, 245, 303
Analogy, 194, 194, 195
Analysis and design, 30
Analyst, 12
Antecedents, 209
Appendices, 301–02
Application system, 8
Apply step in engineering process, 23
Attitude in writing, 205
Attributes, 66, 83–85, 88
Audience, 13, 37, 253–55, 257
Audio tape, 11, 259

Aural learners, 259
Automobile vs. software building, 16
Automobile owner's manual, 197

Backup, 153
Bar graph, 216–17
Bar marking, 271
Batch function group, 69, 78, 99
Batch system, 70, 99
Batch system chart, 103
Batch system model, 76
Batch system specification: control methods, 102; description, 99; format, 100; information structure, 102; label, 102; name, 100; number, 100; options, 103; purpose, 102; subsystem list, 103; system conventions, 102;
Binding, 42, 260, 269–70, 297
Block diagrams, 35, 103, 129
Blocks, 39, 199, 250
Body area of screen grid, 316
Body of manual 258
Body sentences, 210
Boldface, 205, 298
Bookmarking, 319
Branch in structured text, 128, 235
Breaks, 180
Brevity in writing, 208
Build step in engineering process, 23
Build process in documentation system, 59

Build step in system development process, 32, 48
Builder, 11–12: information needs of, 59, 82, 90, 102–03, 107, 112, 119, 125, 127, 138, 148, 158, 161, 182, 249, 252; role in documentation, 14, 46, 48, 58–59; role in system development, 12, 13, 24, 30, 32–33, 42, 45, 48, 51
Bullet, 230

Calculations, specifying, 162
Capitalization, 204, 230, 267
Captions, 240, 300
Cases, 196
Cause and effect sequence, 246
Centered alignment, 216, 267–68
Chapter, definition of, 248
Chapter table of contents, 296
Charts, 218
Check protect, 164
Chronological sequence, 245
Classification, 64–65, 192–93
Client file, 8–9
Code list on data item specification, 162
Coder. *See* Builder
Collating and binding services, 269
Column headings for tables, 216
Column width, 262, 293–94
Command, 141, 145
Command line in screen grid, 316
Command syntax notation, 145, 205
Commands, guidelines for creating, 325
Common attributes, 88
Communication, documentation as, 10, 13, 45–46, 52–53, 123, 190, 253, 327
Compare and contrast sequence, 247
Compound sentences, 208
Comprehension, role of paragraph in, 210
Concise writing, 197, 208
Concluding sentence, 210
Conclusion, 244
Concrete elements, capitalization for, 204
Concrete examples, 196, 254
Concrete words, 197, 202
Conditions, decision table, 236
Consistency: abbreviation, 204; aliases, 197; data item headings, 164; form name, 168; in menu name, 139; phrasing, 198; report name, 179; screen name, 172; synonyms, 197; table of contents entries, 293; technical writing, 197; terms, 197
Contains and part of relationship, 85
Contains attribute, 165
Content attribute: file specification, 153; form specification, 170; report specification, 181; screen specification, 176
Content editing, 276
Context sensitive help systems, 314
Control attribute: module specification, 133; program specification, 127; run specification, 119
Control log, 41, 54–56, 59, 270, 278
Control methods attribute, 102
Control number, on forms, 168
Control size attribute, 154
Control structure attribute, 137, 142
Control totals, 182, 184
Conversational style, 194
Cookbook structure, 230–31
Crafting approach to system development, 16–18, 22, 24
Creates and created by relationship, 87
Creation date on specification, 93
Cross-headings, 263
Cross-reference chart. *See* Melanson chart
Cross-references: alphabetic sequence, 246; captions, 300; controlling, 271; in docu-mentation system, 60; "see" entries, 164
Cycle, 107, 115, 118, 153

Data base system, 74, 88, 249
Data dictionary, 158, 164, 165, 283, 287
Data entry guide or manual, 283, 289
Data entry job, 170
Data flow, 58, 225
Data flow diagrams, 103, 109, 224–25, 234
Data item, definition, 75, 158
Data item specification: alias, 165; code list or calculation, 162; contains attribute, 165; default values, 162; description, 160; display heading, 163; edit mask, 164; label, 160; name, 158; number, 160; picture, 161; security, 163; source, 162; unit of measure, 161; used in, 161; validation, 163
Data screens, 175–76
Data store, 225
Dates on specifications, 93

Decimal numbering scheme, 242
Decimal alignment, 216
Decision in structured text, 128
Decision overload, 199, 250
Decision table, 129–30, 133, 186, 236–37
Decisions in structured text, 234
Default value, 162
Defining purpose, 256
Defining subject, 257
Definitions, 64, 67, 88, 160, 192, 213, 245
Demonstrations in product design, 44
Density of type, 267
Derived documentation, 63
Descenders, 311
Description attribute, 141, 150, 156, 160
Description column, 121
Description structure, 228–29
Descriptions, 91–92, 212–13
Design process in documentation system, 17, 43, 58
Design step in engineering process, 23
Design step in system development process, 30, 42, 166, 233
Designer, 11–12: information needs of, 59, 131, 133, 138, 161, 249, 252; role in documentation, 11, 14, 45–46, 48, 58, 59; role in system development, 12–13, 30, 32–33, 42, 45, 48, 51
Designing lines, 264
Designing manual format and layout, 258
Designing screens, 314
Desktop publishing 41, 259
Diagrams, 222
Dialog, 146, 186
Dictionary, use of 204
Diskettes, 18
Display, 186–87
Display headings, 160, 163, 170
Distribution, 41, 53, 182
Distribution copy, 269, 278–79
Distribution job, 182
Distribution planning, 270
Document control, 41
Document control attributes, 93
Document control page, 42
Document plan, 37, 40, 42
Document structure, 248
Documentation: introduction to 8–22; de-velopment and maintenance tool, 25; feature of system, 17; in human inter-face, 35; motivation for, 13, 15, 82; part of system product, 18; part of user inter-face, 17; primary and derived, 63; problems with, 12; purpose of, 10; subject of, 10–11; as system, 24–25; technical and user, 63; what should be of system, 19
Documentation process: draft step, 39; edit step, 40; integration with system development process, 21–22, 45, 48, 51, 54, 56; maintain step, 41; overview, 36; plan step, 37; review step, 40; release step, 41; steps in, 202, 250
Documentation system, 27–28, 57–62, 83, 87–89, 249
Double negatives, 209
Draft step in documentation process, 39
Drafting manuals, 273, 274
Drafting online documentation, 314
Driver, 115
Dummy draft, 200
Duplication copy, 269, 278–79

Edit mask, 164
Edit step in documentation process, 40, 276
Editing manuals, 276
Editing online, 312
Editorial review, 277
Effective documentation, 197
Element: defining, 67; identifiers 89; notes attribute, 92; purpose and description of, 91
Element groups, 76
Elements comprising a page, 261
Elements used attribute, 107, 146
Emphasis, 205–07, 265
Engineering approach, 16–17, 22–24, 30, 33, 42
Engineering process, 23
Engineering vs. crafting, 16
Entry, decision table, 236
Environment, 12, 31, 55, 84, 138, 253
Estimating cost and timing, 272–73
Examples, 39, 195–97
Exchange group, 68–69, 75, 80, 166
Expanded definitions, 193, 213
Expectations of readers, 248
Experiential learners, 259
Expert reader, 37–38, 254–55, 303
Extended caption, 240
External block, 200
Extracting system file information, 275

Feature-based structure, 238, 239
Features, 17
Feedback, 41, 62, 199, 277
Field, 157, 160
Figure numbers in cross-references, 301
File, 74, 126, 148
File allocation, 119, 122, 126, 146
File media code, 151
File organization, 151
File specification: access key, 152; backup, 153; content, 153; description, 148; description, 150; label, 150; medium, 151; name, 149; number, 150; organization, 150; security, 154; sequence/access key, 152; size, 154
Flow column on run chart, 122
Flowchart, 129–30, 133, 186, 220–21
Flush left, 267
Font, 264–65: size, 267, 298; for table of contents, 293
Footer, 261–62, 271, 296
Footnotes, 216–18
Form, 75: caption, 163; design, 170–71; directory, 283; feature-based, 238; identifiers, 89; medium, 170; purpose, 168
Form size, 181
Form specification: content, 170; data entry job, 170; description, 167; job, 169–70; label, 168; layout, 171; medium, 170; name, 168; number, 168; preparation job, 169; purpose, 168; sample, 172; source, 169; volume, 169
Formal outline, 242–43, 257–58
Format, 39: for manual, 258–60; product design document, 16; reference cards, 306; table of contents, 293. *See also* Page grid
Format attribute, 157
Foundation structure, 237
Function, 66, 73, 133, 139, 142
Function group, 68–69
Function specification, command, 145; description, 142; elements used, 146; label, 143; name, 143; number, 143; processing, 146; purpose, 143; route or command, 145; steps, 145
Functional elements, 212
Functional specification. *See* Specification

Gantt chart, description, 222, 273

General design. *See* Product design
Generic layouts as system conventions, 139
Getting started manual, 252
Glossary, 165, 246, 302
Grammar, 191, 205
Graphic, 38, 197, 214–15. *See also* Structures
Graphics page, 262
Graphs, 216–18
Grid in structured writing, 238. *See also* Page grid, Screen grid
Grouping elements, 212–13
Gutter, 262

Half-size pages, 260–63
Hanging headings, 263, 303
Hard attributes, 90
Hardware attribute, 127
Hash totals, 184
Header, 261, 270, 296
Header in screen grid, 315
Header content, 262, 271
Heading line for reports, 183
Headings, 38, 182, 197, 268, 298–99, 301
Help functions, 323
Hierarchical access, 318
Human interface, 18, 35, 166, 307, 327. *See also* User interface
Hyphenation, 268

Icons, 225, 263
Identifiers for elements, 89
Impersonal style, 194
In-line approach, 42, 57, 65, 200, 270, 273
In-line documentation, 20–22, 25–27, 308
Index, 165, 246, 303–04
Index cards, 37
Index pages columns, 262
Informal outline, 241, 257
Information group, 68, 74, 80, 148
Information structure, 102, 138
Informed reader, definition, 37–38, 254, 303
Input attribute, 115, 122, 133
Installation guide, 55, 63, 252, 284
Installer, 11–12
Instruction in structured text, 128, 234
Instruction line in screen grid, 316
Instruction sequence, 246
Instruction structure, 228–29
Integration: design and specification with system development process,

16; documentation system with shop operation, 60; of online manuals, 313; system development process with documentation process, 21–22, 28, 42, 58
Integration testing, 33
Internal blocks, description, 199
Interviews, 200
Introduction-body-conclusion, 210, 244
Introductions, 200, 244, 294, 302
Italics, 205, 265
Iteration, 32–33
Iterative logic, 130

Jargon, definition, 203
Job, 67, 71: file backup, 153; form specification, 169–70; report specification, 182; run specification, 118
Job specification: cookbook structure, 231; cycle, 115; description, 112; driver, 115; input, 115; label, 114; name, 114; number, 114; output, 116; purpose attribute, 114; steps, 116; time, 115; trigger, 114
Justification of text, 264, 268

Label, 89: batch system, 102; on charts or diagrams, 219, 223; data item, 160; file, 150; form, 168; function, 143; job, 114; menu, 140; message, 186; module, 132; in multiple system environments, 102, 125; online system, 136; program, 125; record, 156; report, 180; run chart, 120; run, 117; screen, 174; subsystem, 105; transaction, 111
Language attribute, 127
Layout: for cases, 196; form specification, 171; for organization, 38; record specification, 157; report specification, 182; screen specification, 176; as system conventions, 139
Leading, 264, 267, 311
Learning modes, 259
Left flush, 216, 267
Legend, 217, 219, 222
Level of detail, 257
Levels of edit, 276
Levels of heading, 293
Levels of review, 277
Line design, 258, 264
Line graph, 216
List 208, 230. *See also* Structured list
List of figures tables, 294

List structure, 230
Listing, 119, 131
Logic tree, 235–36
Logical access, 318
Logical design. *See* Product design
Logical testing, 16
Logical negatives, 209
Logical vs. physical, 16
Loop in structured text, 128, 235
Loose-leaf binding, 42, 296

Magnetic manual, 320
Maintain step in documentation process, 41, 278–79
Maintenance: pagination and binding impact 42, 270; planning, 270; system 10, 12, 27, 35
Maintenance programmer, 12. *See also* Builder
Management editing, 276
Management support, 14
Manual plan, 251
Manual: common elements of, 257; creation and maintenance, 49–55; in documentation system, 59; drafting, 273–275; editing, 276; maintaining, 278–80; model libraries of, 281–91; planning, 249–272; releasing, 278; reviewing, 277; as system element, 90; title of, 41
Maps equation, 253
Margins, 39, 261, 316
Master copy, 42
Maximum file size, 154
Meaning attribute, 187
Mechanical diagrams, 222
Mechanical editing, 276
Mechanics of reading, 262
Medium: documentation, 11, 44–46; files, 148, 152; forms, 167, 170; manuals, 258; specifications, 96; system file, 60; problems with paper, 309
Medium attribute, 151, 170
Melanson chart, 87, 221
Menu, 73, 139, 324
Menu-driven, 137, 141, 145
Menu map, 138, 195, 219
Menu screen, 174–76
Menu specification: command, 141; description, 139, 141; functions, 142; label, 140; name, 139; number, 139; route or command, 141
Message, 18, 31, 76, 175, 186, 325
Message area in screen grid, 316

Message directory, 284, 287
Message specification: action attribute, 187; description, 184; label, 186; as manual, 184; meaning attribute, 187; message type, 186; name, 184; number, 184; source, 188; text attribute, 187
Message type, 186
Metaphor, 194. *See also* Tropes
Method attribute, 111
Model libraries, 281, 284, 287, 290
Modeling a system, 66
Models: batch function group, 69; customizing, 78; data flow diagram for, 224; documentation process, 36; documentation system, 57–59; exchange group, 75; information group, 74; online function group, 72; system, 76
Modem, example of definition, 67
Module, 72–73
Module specification: control, 133; description, 131; functions, 133; input, 133; label, 132; name, 131; number, 131; for online system, 146; output, 133; purpose attribute, 133; use attribute, 133
Modules, on program specification, 128
Motivation, 15, 60, 201
Multiple projects, 30
Multiple statements of purpose, 274
Multiple system environments: aliases, 165; data item numbers, 160; file organization, 151; labels, 102, 125, 136, 150; message numbers, 185

Name: batch system, 100; charts, 218; common attribute, 88; consistency, 139; data item, 158; diagrams, 223; element, 88; figures, 214, 216–18, 223; file, 149; form, 168; function, 143; job, 114; list, 230; message, 184; menu, 139; module, 131; online system, 136; program, 123; record, 156; report, 178; run, 116; run chart, 120; screen, 172; specifications, 93; subsystem, 105; transaction, 110
Narratives, 130
Nominal file size, 154
Notations, used in manuals, 205
Notes attribute, 92
Notice, 187
Novice reader, 37–38, 49, 254

Number: appendix, 302; batch system, 100; common attribute, 89–90; data item, 160; figures, 216–18, 223; file, 150; form, 168; function, 143; job, 114; list, 230; menu, 139; message, 184; module, 131; online system, 136; prefix of, 101; program, 124; record, 156; report, 180; run, 116; run chart, 120; screen, 174; segmenting, 111, 125, 150; subsystem, 105; transaction, 111
Numbered headings, 298
Numbered lists, 230
Numbering, for formal outline, 242

Objective words, 202
Objectives, to define purpose of manual, 256
Offset printing, 269
One-and-a-half-alphabet rule, 15, 262
Online documentation, 308–27
Online documents, planning, 313
Online function group, 72, 79, 135
Online help, 11, 322–23
Online manual, 312–13, 320–21
Online medium, 259, 310–12
Online menus and commands, 324
Online messages, 325
Online support system, 55
Online system, 72, 76
Online system specification: control structure, 137; description, 135; information structure, 138; label, 136; name, 136; number, 136; purpose, 136; requirements, 138; system conventions, 139
Online tutorials, 321
Operating job, 118
Operating system, 127
Operating system manual, 143
Operator: information needs of, 55, 59, 107, 118–19, 169, 182; role in documentation, 11–12; role in system development, 35
Operator manual, 55, 57, 63, 231, 282, 289
Option attribute, 103
Ordo Dei sequence, 245
Organization, 38–39, 197, 265, 298
Organization attribute, 150
Organization chart, 138, 219, 233
Organizing material, 38, 257
Outline, 241–44
Output attribute, 116, 133

Output column, 123
Overviews, 200, 224, 275

Packaging, 41
Page binding. *See* Binding
Page breaks, 180
Page design, 258, 260
Page elements, 261
Page format, 15, 238
Page grid, 263
Page header. *See* Header
Page layout, 197, 261
Page number, 42, 94, 120, 183, 270–71, 297–98, 300–01
Page size, 260
Pagination, 42, 94, 297
Paper code, 181
Paragraphs, 210, 244, 301
Parallel construction, 209, 230, 242
Parallel timing, 245
Parenthetical definition, 193, 204
Partitioning, 64–65, 192, 242
Passive, 13, 22, 53
Passive space, 261
Passive voice, 206
Perfect binding, 271
Peripheral setup. *See* File allocation
Photocopy, 269
Physical design. *See* Specify step
Picture attribute, 161
Pictures, 225
Plan review, 277
Plan step in documentation process, 37, 250
Planning: binding, 269; control log, 270; distribution, 270; maintenance, 270; online documents, 313; production, 268; release, 268; specifications, 95; system library, 251; time needed, 199, 250
Plans, 251
Playscript structure, 232, 274
Preparation job, 169
Prepared by, 93
Present tense, 206
Primary documentation, 63, 82
Print parameters, 181
Print specification, 181
Printing documentation, 269
Priority sequence, 247
Pro and con sequence, 247
Problem, what is vs. what should be, 18

Problem-cause-solution sequence, 247, 259
Problem/solution examples: cost of revisions, 29; curtail learning curves, 29; design of human interface, 327; detail in specification, 46; distribution of writing tasks, 62; document before coding, 82; document release method, 41; documentation system aids support, 25; documentation system with used-in lists, 60; error message audience, 31; level of detail in manuals, 253; library of manuals, 249; making the system file real, 15; marketing importance of user manual, 190; product design document, 17; project team approach to maintenance, 278; specifications as what should be, 19; specify critical elements, 32; text column reduction, 15
Process, 225
Process diagram, 223
Processing attribute, 146
Processing logic, 130
Processing path, 112
Product design, 13–17, 23, 33–35, 42–45, 49–51, 58–63, 100, 136, 251–53, 259
Production planning, 268
Program, 71, 73, 86–87
Program control, 127
Program listings, 14, 20
Program specification: as communication vehicle, 123; control, 127; decision table, 236; description, 123; files, 126; hardware, 127; label, 125; language, 127; listing, 131; modules, 128; name, 123; number, 124; for online system, 146; operating system, 127; purpose attribute, 125; structure, 127
Programmer. *See* Builder
Project, 8, 26, 30, 62
Project control, 26
Project file, 8, 43, 93, 190, 272
Project number, 93
Project planning, 222, 272
Prompt, 18, 31, 175, 186–87
Prototype systems, 17
Purpose: common attribute, 91; control log, 55; defining, 37, 92, 211, 256; documentation, 9, 198; multiple

statements of, 92, 143, 174; product design, 16; specification, 46; test plan, 52; user manual, 50
Purpose attribute: batch system, 102; form, 168; function, 143; job, 114; module, 133; online system, 136; program, 125; report, 180; run, 118; screen, 174; subsystem, 105; transaction, 111
Purpose statement, 212

Quick printing, 269

Random access of manuals, 246, 292, 303
Read-me files, 320
Readable text, 198
Reader-edited indexes, 319
Reader evolution, 49
Reader expectations, 38, 248
Reader profile, 319
Reader review, 277
Reader testing, 322
Reading, mechanics of, 262, 267
Record, 74, 85
Record counts, 184
Record layout. *See* Layout
Record maximum size, 154
Record size, 156
Record specification: description, 154; label, 156; name, 156; number, 156; record size, 156; record type, 156; size, 156; type, 156; layout, 157; security, 158
Record type, 156
Redundant information, 85–86, 251, 302
Reference aids: appendix, 301; captions, 300; chapter table of contents, 296; cross-references, 300; glossary, 302; headers and footers, 296; headings, 298; index, 303; introductory text, 294; list of, 292; list of figures and tables, 294; need for, 292; pagination, 297; reference card, 305; table of contents, 293; tabs, 295
Reference card, 305
Reference information, 255
Reference number or item, 171, 183–84
Reference manual, 24, 245–47
Registration card, 270
Relational access, 318
Relationships: between elements, 88; contains and part of, 85; creates and created by, 87; uses and used by, 86. *See also* Melanson chart
Relative input and output, 122
Release: definition, 34; planning, 268; purpose, 34; responsibility for, 54; via software publisher, 55
Release process in documentation system, 59
Release step: in documentation process, 34, 41; integration with documentation process, 54; in system development process, 34
Releasing manuals, 278
Report: definition of, 76; design, 183; in feature-based structure, 238; name on, 178–80; as program output files, 126; in user interface, 18
Report column title, 163
Report directory, 284
Report heading line, 180–83
Report key, 180
Report parts, 183
Report specification: breaks, 180; content, 181; description, 177; distribution job, 182; label, 180; layout, 182; number, 180; print specification, 181; purpose attribute, 180; sample, 184; sequence and breaks, 180; source, 182; volume, 182
Requirements attribute, 138
Results attribute, 112
Retention, 153
Reverse engineering, 23
Reversed sequences, 209
Review step in documentation process, 40–41, 277
Revisions, 35, 41–42, 93
Revision copy, 272, 278–79
Revision date, 93, 271, 279
Revision package, 271, 279
Revision threshold, 279
Rivers, 268
Roman-letter-arabic, 242
Route, 141–42
Route or command attribute, 141, 145
Rules, 298
Run, 71
Run chart, 119–23
Run specification: control, 119; cycle, 118; description, 116; file allocation, 119; job, 118; label, 117; listing, 119; name, 116; number, 116; operating

job, 118; purpose attribute, 118; time, 118; trigger, 118
Run-on sentence, 207–08
Run time options, 119
Run time variables, 127, 133, 147, 169, 184

Samples, 172, 177, 184, 226
Screen: classification, 175; definition, 75, 172; design, 177, 314; with feature-based structure, 238; format problems, 310; as program attribute, 87; in user interface, 18
Screen grid, 315
Screen heading line, 174
Screen item header, 163
Screen specification: content attribute, 176; description, 172; label, 174; layout, 176; name, 172; number, 174; purpose attribute, 174; sample, 177; screen type, 174; source, 176; type, 174
Screen type, 174
Secondary readers, 278
Security, 154, 158, 163
"See" and "See also" entries, 304
Sentences, 193, 205–09, 212
Sentence definition, 212
Sequence, 210, 244
Sequence, file, 152
Sequence and breaks, 180
Sequence mode, 152, 180
Sequence/access key, 152
Serifs, 265
Session log, 319
Side headings, 263
Signature, 176, 184, 187–88
Simile, 194. *See also* Trope
Simple sentences, 208
Simple to complex sequence, 245
Simple words, 202
Simple writing, 197
Sink, 225
Size attribute, 154, 156–57
Skimming and scanning, 299
Soft attributes, 86–87, 90, 222
Software file, 48, 55, 59
Software publisher, 55
Software techniques for online documentation, 319
Sorts, 71
Source, 225
Source attribute, 162, 169, 176, 182, 188
Spatial sequence, 247

Specifications: creation of, 45–47, 62, 84, 88–89, 91–97; detail in, 46, 61, 123; in documentation process, 49–51, 58–63, 82, 275; in system development process, 32–33, 45–46, 48, 61; in system engineering, 24–25, 32–33, 46
Specify step in system development process, 32, 45, 233
Specifying a system, 66
Staff flexibility, 27
Stagger, 268
Steps attribute, 116, 145
STOP. *See* Structured writing
Store, 225
Storyboard technique, 314
Structure, of paragraphs, 210; attribute, 127
Structured list, 69, 127, 138, 220, 233–34, 293
Structured programming, 127
Structured text, 128–29, 133, 186, 234–35
Structured writing, 238–40, 245, 263, 274, 300
Structures, 228–29
Stub, decision table, 236
Study step in engineering process, 23
Styles, 39, 205
Subject, 10–11, 16, 37–38, 44, 50, 53, 248
Subject definition, 257
Subjective words, 202
Subsystem, 70, 139
Subsystem chart, 108
Subsystem list, 103
Subsystem specification: cycle, 107; description, 105; elements used, 107; label, 105; name, 105; number, 105; purpose attribute, 105; transactions, 107; trigger, 107
Support manual, 55, 57, 63, 286
Supporter: information needs of, 25, 55, 59, 103, 107, 112, 161, 182; role in documentation, 11, 59; role in system development, 35
Symbols, 205, 219, 221, 225, 225
Synonyms, 212, 303
System, application 8
System administrator manual, 281, 284
System analyst. *See* Designer
System architecture. *See* Product design
System control methods, 102
System conventions, 102–03, 139

System development process: benefits of, 29–30; build step, 32, 48; designing, 35; design step, 30, 42; designing your own, 35; introduction, 29; iterative nature of, 32; release step, 34, 54; specify step, 32, 45; test step, 33, 51; use step, 35, 56
System document. *See* Document
System element. *See* Element
System engineering process, 24
System feature, 313
System file: content, 9, 42–43, 45, 49, 82, 119, 189, 249, 251, 275; definition, 9, 15, 24; queries on, 125, 133, 145, 161, 163, 171, 174; structure, 47, 55, 60, 97, 125; use of, 56, 58–60, 77, 93, 200, 273–75, 309
System function, 313
System library, 251, 281
System manual. *See* Manual
System model, 63–65, 95
System number, 136
System options, 103
System players, 11, 18, 63, 83–84, 96, 114–15, 136, 251–53
System product, 51, 55
System specification. *See* Specification
System version, 42

Table numbers in cross-references, 301
Tables, 215–16, 236. *See also* Decision table
Table of contents, 293
Tabs, 295
Talk screen, 175–76
Tasks, 252, 256
Teaching, 245
Technical documentation, 63
Technical review, 40, 277
Technical writing, 13, 189–201
Techniques, writing: classification, 64–65, 192–93; cases, 196; conversational style, 194; definitions, 64, 67, 88, 160, 192, 213, 245; examples, 39, 195–97; list of, 191; partitioning, 64–65, 192, 242; tropes, 194–95, 254; for writing better, 197
Template, for specifications, 94
Tense, 206–07
Terms, 192, 205, 234, 303
Test element, 90–91
Test information, 196
Test plan, 33, 51–54, 59, 277

Test process in documentation system, 59
Test step in engineering process, 23
Test step in system development process, 33, 51
Testing, 16, 19, 33, 40, 51–52
Text: creating, 202–13; for in-line manuals, 274
Text attribute, 187
Text column, 15, 262. *See also* Columns
Text density, 310
Text element, 90
Text flowchart, 237
Throwaway code, 17
Time attribute, 115, 118
Title, 293–94, 302
Title page, 56, 270–71
Total break, 180
Training reviewers, 41
Transaction, 70, 107
Transaction numbers, 111
Transaction specification: cause and effect sequence, 246; cookbook structure, 231; description, 109; label, 111; method, 111; name, 110; number, 111; processing path, 112; purpose attribute, 111; results, 112
Transitional words, 211
Trigger, 107, 114–15, 118, 153
Tropes, 194–95, 254
Tutorial manual, 252, 245
Tutorials, 18, 321, 325
Type attribute, 156, 174, 186
Type size, 262
Typeface, 39, 264–67, 296

Underlining, 205
Unit of measure, 161, 216–17
Usage attribute, 126, 157, 204
Usage codes, 126
Use attribute, 133
Use process in documentation system, 59
Use step in system development process, 35, 56
Used in attribute, 161
User: information needs of, 43, 45, 49, 102–07, 111, 138–39, 143–44, 148, 158, 161–62, 169, 177, 184, 229; role in documentation, 11, 18, 59, 88; role in system development, 12–13, 17, 24, 30, 33, 35, 42–43, 51, 55, 252
User documentation, 13, 18, 63

User interface, 17–18, 26, 44, 146, 163–66, 171–72, 176–78, 183, 202, 232, 238
User manual: creation, 49–50; from model libraries, 282, 288, 290; purpose, 24, 26, 33, 63; structure and sequence, 231, 234, 245, 247; types, 252
User needs, sources of, 43
User reference manual, 252, 285
User tutorial manual, 285
Uses and used by relationship, 86
Utilities, 71

Validation attribute, 163
Validation logic, 130
Validation tests, 163
Verbs, list of action, 231
Version, 42

Video tape, 11, 259
Visual learners, 259
Vocabulary, 202
Voice, 206
Volume attribute, 169, 182

Warnings, 187
What vs. how, 118, 125, 133, 212
White space, 171, 216, 218–19, 223, 261–63, 296, 298
Window, 172, 175
Word choice, 202
Word shapes, 267
Working copy, 42
Working methods for writing, 198
Writer, 49, 59, 63
Writing better, 197
Writing objectives, 201
Writing skills, 191, 197